DISASTER AND RESISTANCE
Comics and Landscapes for the 21st Century

by Seth Tobocman

AK PRESS
EDINBURGH • OAKLAND • WEST VIRGINIA

Disaster and Resistance: Comics and Landscapes for the 21st Century
© 2008 Seth Tobocman
This edition © 2008 AK Press (Oakland, Edinburgh, West Virginia)

ISBN 9781904859765
Library of Congress Control Number: 2007939196

AK Press	AK Press
674-A 23rd Street	PO Box 12766
Oakland, CA 94612	Edinburgh EH8 9YE
USA	Scotland
www.akpress.org	www.akuk.com
akpress@akpress.org	ak@akedin.demon.co.uk

AK Press is a worker-run collective that publishes and distributes radical books, audio/visual media, and other material. We're small: ten individuals who work long hours for short money, because we believe in what we do. We're anarchists, which is reflected both in the books we publish and in the way we organize our business: without bosses.

AK Press publishes the finest books, CDs, and DVDs from the anarchist and radical traditions—currently about eighteen to twenty per year. Joining THE FRIENDS OF AK PRESS is a way that you can directly help us to keep the wheels rolling and these important projects coming. As ever, money is tight as we do not rely on outside funding. We need your help to make and keep these crucial materials available. Friends pay a minimum (of course we have no objection to larger sums!) of £15 / $25 (or $30 for those outside the US) per month, for a minimum three month period. Money received goes directly into our publishing funds. In return, Friends automatically receive (for the duration of their membership), as they appear, one FREE copy of EVERY new AK Press title. Secondly, they are also entitled to a 10% discount on EVERYTHING featured in the AK Press distribution catalog—or on our website—on ANY and EVERY order. We also have a program where individuals or groups can sponsor a whole book.

The above addresses would be delighted to provide you with more information about the Friends of AK Press. You can also request the latest AK Press distribution catalog, which features the several thousand books, pamphlets, zines, audio and video products, and stylish apparel published and/or distributed by AK Press. Alternatively, visit our web site for the complete catalog, latest news, and secure ordering.

Printed in Canada on acid free, recycled paper.
Inkers: Laird Ogden, Jessica Wehrle
Design Assistant: Jessica Wehrle
Thanks to ABC No Rio for scanning services (ABC No Rio, 156 Rivington St. New York, NY 10009).
SPECIAL THANKS TO: Melissa Jamesson, Steven Englander, Zach Blue, Micha Maxer, Anthony Cardinale, Missy Galore, Bork, Steve Wishnia, Eric Blitz, Zef Noise, Dennis Kucinnich, Lovebug, Suncere, Malik Rahim, Grace Keller, Katya, Harvey Pekar, Mumia Abu Jamal, Frances Goldin, Peter Kuper, Fly, Josh Macphee, Louisa Krupp, Anton Van Dalen, Michelle D'Alessio, Grainne O'Niel, Soleil Rodrigue, everyone at the House of Excellence, Kevin Pyle, Paul Buhle, Bodi and Louisa, Barbara Lee, my Mom, my Dad, my Sister, my students, and everyone who helped me get this book out or kept me sane while I did it.

For Katya, Jacob, Rebecca, and their generation.

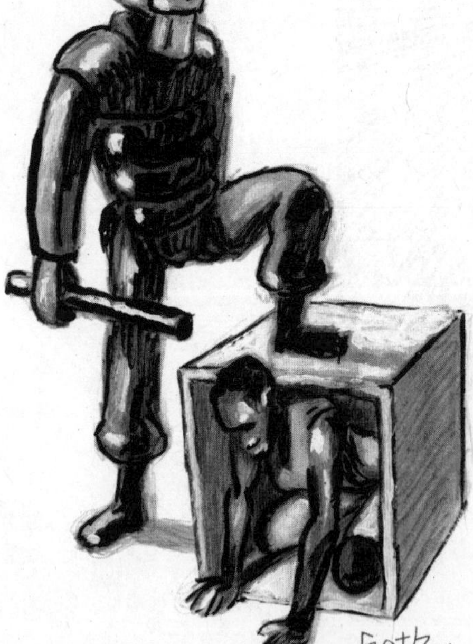
Setz

CONTENTS

PART ONE: THE NEW SIXTIES

PART TWO: 9-11 ARMAGEDDON

PART THREE: NO BLOOD FOR OIL!

PART FOUR: THE NOT SO HOLY LAND

PART FIVE: AFTER THE FLOOD

Introduction: Joy Amidst "Disaster..."
By Mumia Abu-Jamal

To "read" Seth Tobocman's extraordinary *Disaster and Resistance* is to experience joy.

Joy? while "reading" something called "Disaster...?"

Yes, joy, as in the root word of enjoyment. For the art and, equally, the sensibility of the artist, informs and enriches every panel with shadowed clarity, starkness of line, and (as the title suggests) the spirit of resistance.

For, while Tobocman uses his art to tell the harrowing tale of loss, suffering, and yes, disas-

ter, he also shows how people have resisted those societal slings and arrows. With rage and righteousness, he shows us the faces that are rarely seen, drawn with an intensity that will not allow you to avert your gaze.

In a time of virtually global repression, how can one not feel joy at these expressions of resistance?

And, more often than not, those resistors are the poorest of the poor—people who have no material worth, but who are worthy because of the life that flows through them in their various struggles for social justice.

Tobocman has a long and illustrious history of such work. From his riveting comics of the struggle for Tompkins Square Park, to his recurring series of his (and others') work in *World War III* comics. Seth Tobocman has lent his artistic genius to the struggle of the underdog.

Here, he has created a frontal response (as opposed to attack—for the state attacked the people) to the massive social, class, and racial crime that may be encapsulated in the term "Hurricane Katrina." He has crafted a clever and engaging work on the evils of the Iraq War. And he has attacked the silences around the Israeli occupation and the apartheid wall now surrounding Palestinian lands.

"Joy?"—amidst such disaster? Yet there is joy where there is resistance, and there is resistance aplenty in these pages.

All I can offer is an invitation for you to join this joy.

If you love art, and especially the popular art of political comics, *Disaster and Resistance* is right up your alley. For here, Tobocman gives us a plethora of styles. Among them, clayboards, which give a similar effect to block prints, with the grainy textures and dark shadows of drama. In "Yom Kippur 5761" (the piece on the Israeli-Arab struggle), Tobocman paints miniatures on coarse paper and enlarges them digitally, which lends the pieces a richness and depth of color that sets them apart from virtually every comic that has preceded it. While these pieces retain Tobocman's penchant for shadow work, the colors add another dimension to the work, and they are thus enjoyable even without considering their potent geopolitical messages.

Several pieces are devoted to Tobocman's posters, which are evocative of the great Black muralist Jacob A. Lawrence.

Yet, art doesn't exist for art's sake.

It tells us truths about our age and ourselves. It holds up a mirror to the society in which we dwell.

It is a form of x-ray, which shows things with a clarity one rarely sees on the front pages of newspapers.

It is a fitting record of the dismal first decade of the 21st century.

That said, enjoy.
—Mumia Abu-Jamal 1/28/08

HOW THIS BOOK CAME ABOUT

By Seth Tobocman

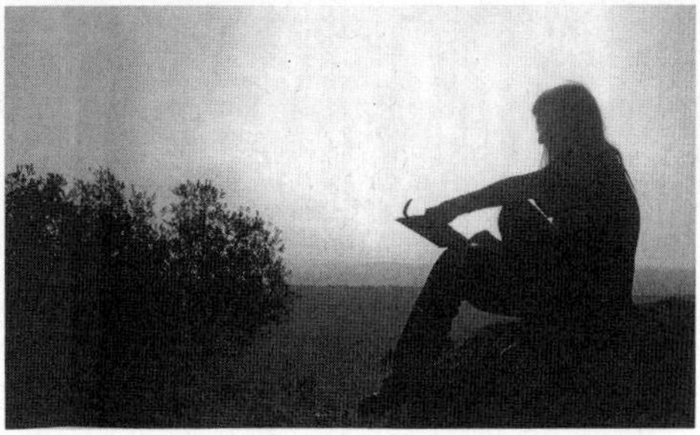

For Americans at least, the first decade of the 21st century has been the most traumatic since the 1970s. Starting with a stolen election, then a terrorist attack that killed thousands of people. Wars in Iraq and Afghanistan. Hurricanes, floods, and tornadoes caused by global warming. And now we are looking at something my parents told me was not possible: a war and an economic recession at the same time.

They say that when America has a cold, the rest of the world catches a flu. Obscenely, our government is still debating with humanitarian agencies as to how many civilians have been killed in Iraq.

There is the feeling that those in power are either criminally negligent or deliberately fucking things up for the rest of us.

But this has also been a period of incredible resistance. Massive protests against the W.T.O. in Seattle and Cancun, against World Bank meetings in Washington, against the Republican Conventions in Philadelphia and New York, and the largest global antiwar movement in history. Even more inspiring are the hundreds of nonviolent activists who risked their lives to prevent human rights abuses in Iraq and Palestine, and the thousands of volunteers who have given their labor to rebuild the Gulf Coast after Hurricane Katrina.

In 1999, having just finished ten years of writing and drawing *War in the Neighborhood*—a three-hundred page graphic novel about housing conflicts on the lower east side of Manhattan—I wanted the chance to check out what was happening in other places and to draw some comics about global issues. I was open to seeing what else was going on, eager to travel, and prepared to work with a lot of different people.

Over the course of this decade, I have had the honor of supplying posters, illustrations, and comicstrips to some of the movements that address the current crisis. This book is a collection of art works done in support of, and often in collaboration with, activists from many different parts of the globe. Some of the pieces are actual agit-prop handed out at protests or distributed over the internet. Other pieces are inspired by what I learned. The writing owes much to other people. The voice is not always my own voice but rather a collective voice. My intention is that, taken together, these stories and images form a landscape of the new century.

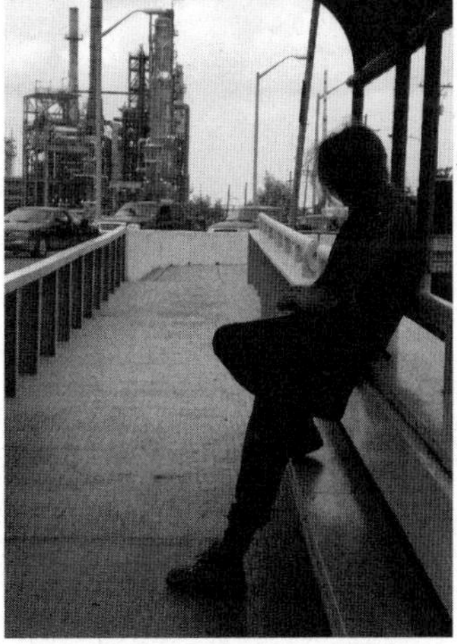

Above: Drawing in the Occupied Territories. Photo by Uri.
Right: Drawing an oil processing plant in Louisiana. Photo by Bork.

Foreword:

A Policy of Disaster

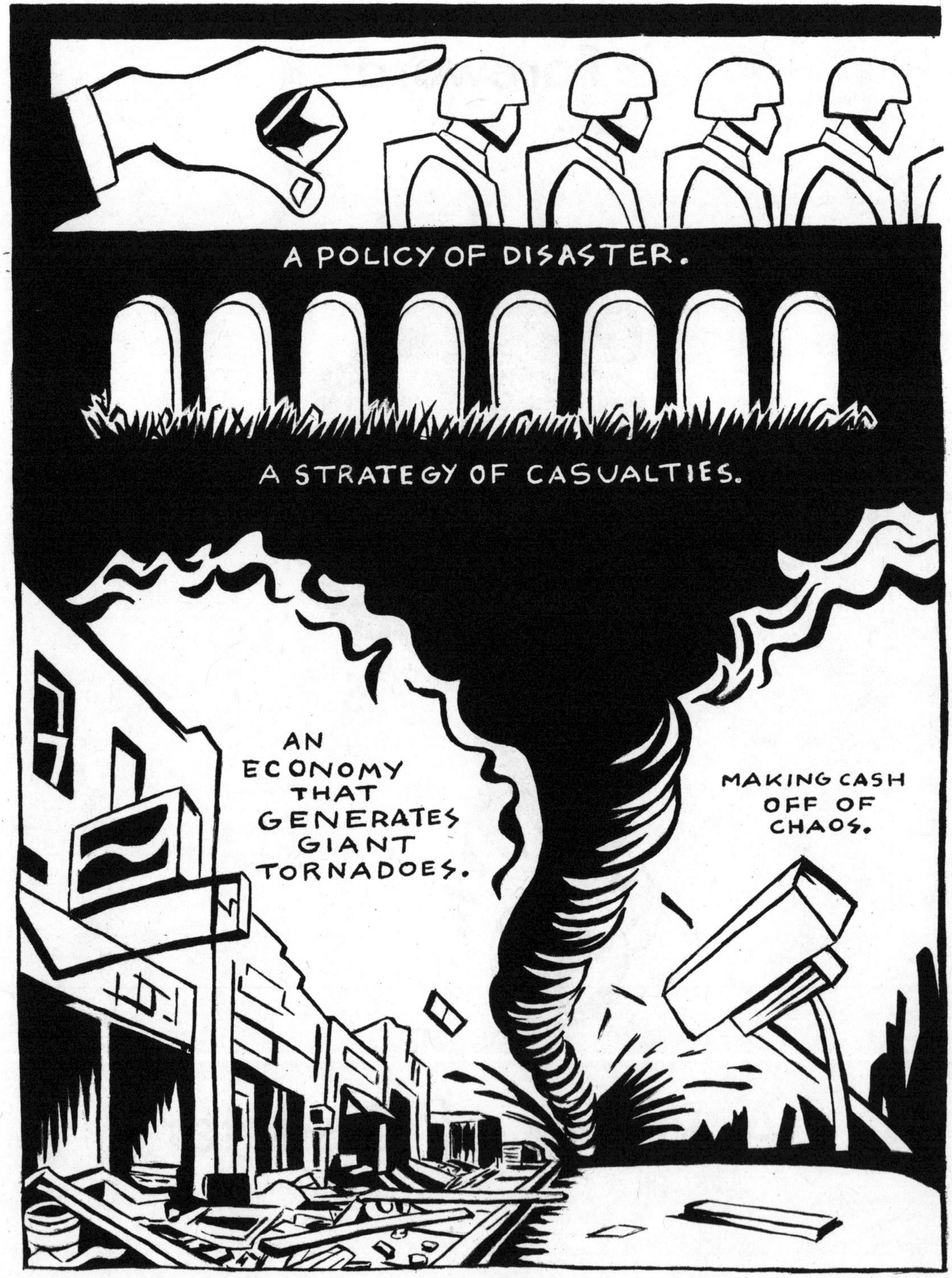
A POLICY OF DISASTER.
A STRATEGY OF CASUALTIES.
AN ECONOMY THAT GENERATES GIANT TORNADOES.
MAKING CASH OFF OF CHAOS.

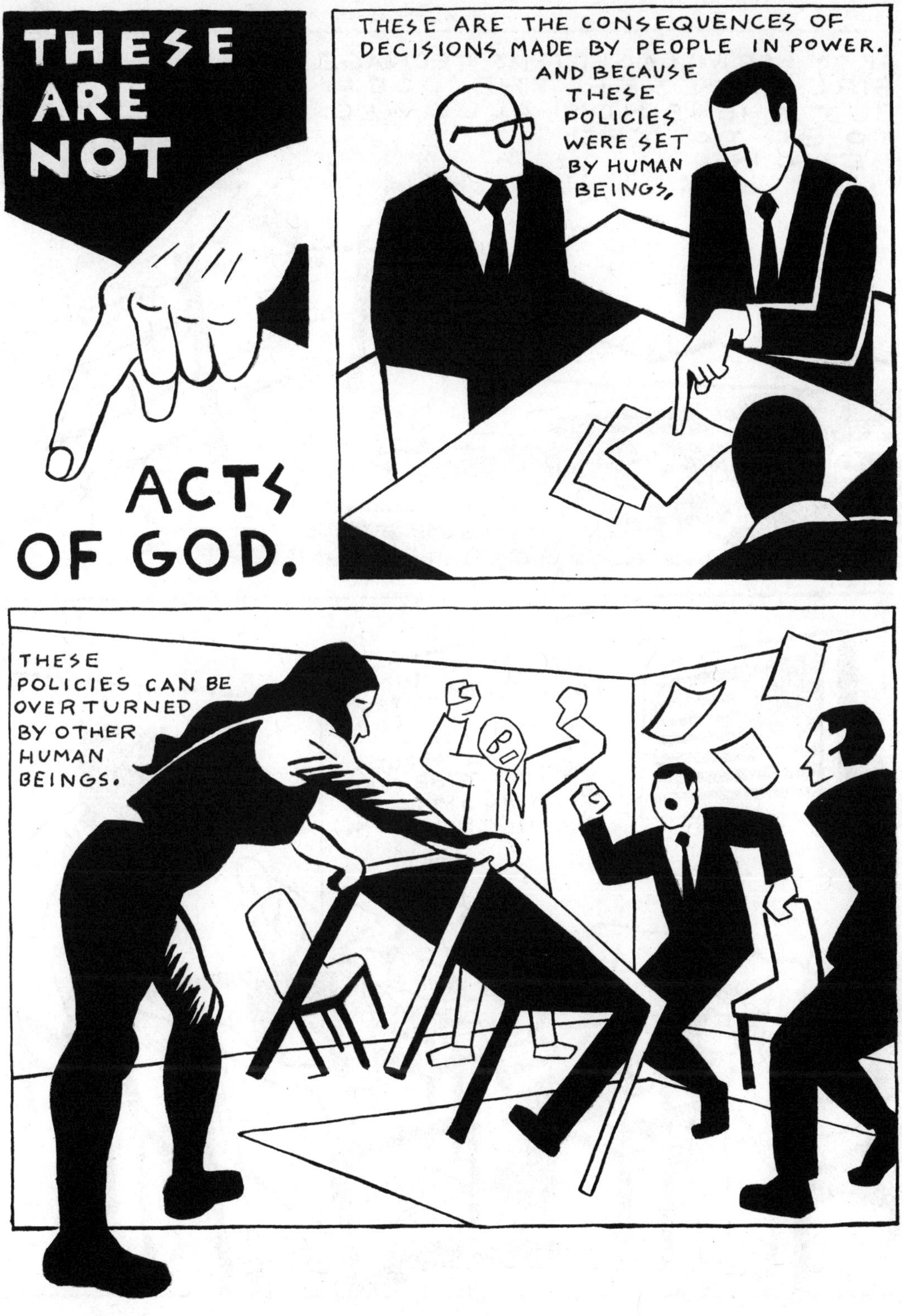
THESE ARE NOT
ACTS OF GOD.
THESE ARE THE CONSEQUENCES OF DECISIONS MADE BY PEOPLE IN POWER.
AND BECAUSE THESE POLICIES WERE SET BY HUMAN BEINGS,
THESE POLICIES CAN BE OVERTURNED BY OTHER HUMAN BEINGS.

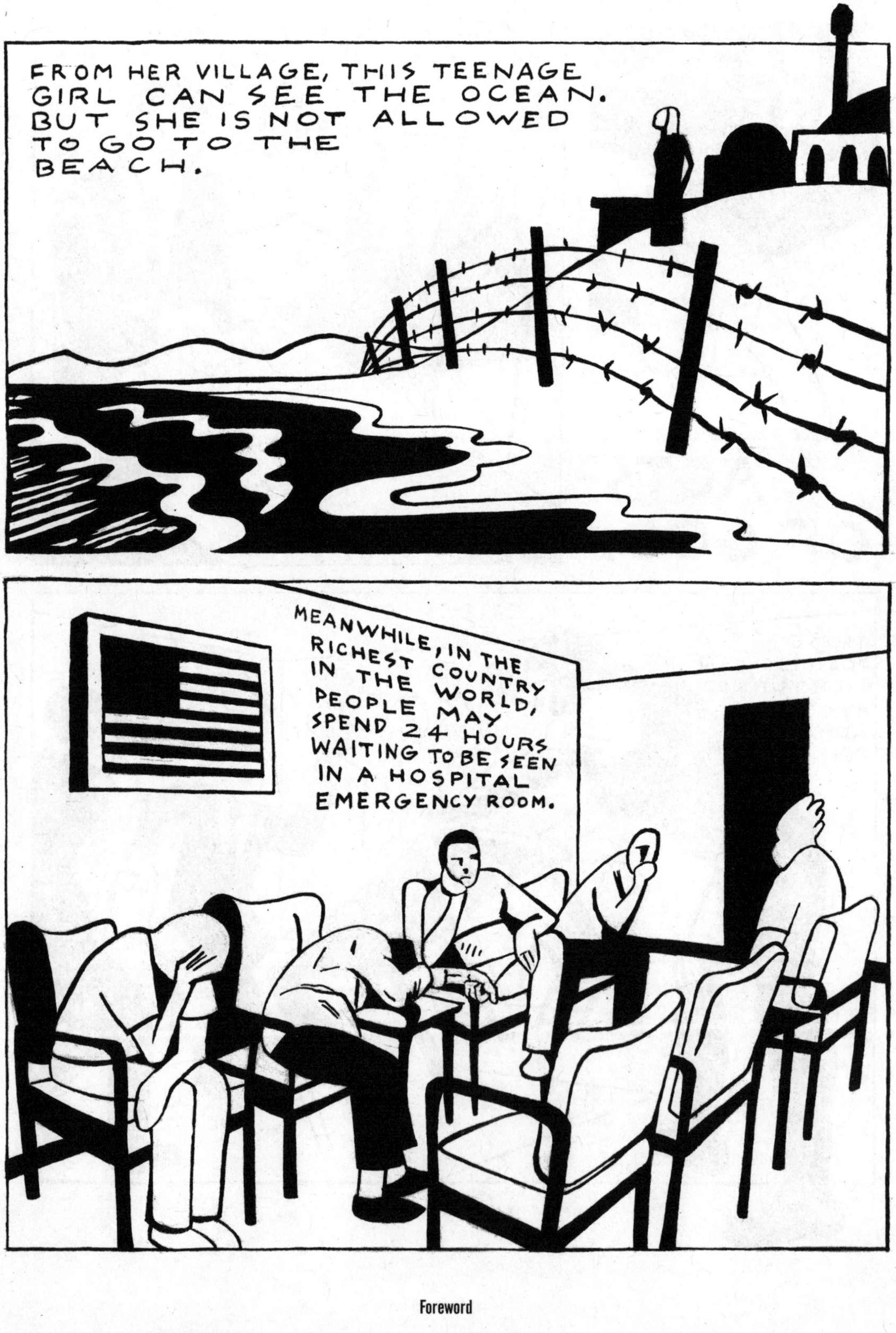
FROM HER VILLAGE, THIS TEENAGE GIRL CAN SEE THE OCEAN. BUT SHE IS NOT ALLOWED TO GO TO THE BEACH.
MEANWHILE, IN THE RICHEST COUNTRY IN THE WORLD, PEOPLE MAY SPEND 24 HOURS WAITING TO BE SEEN IN A HOSPITAL EMERGENCY ROOM.

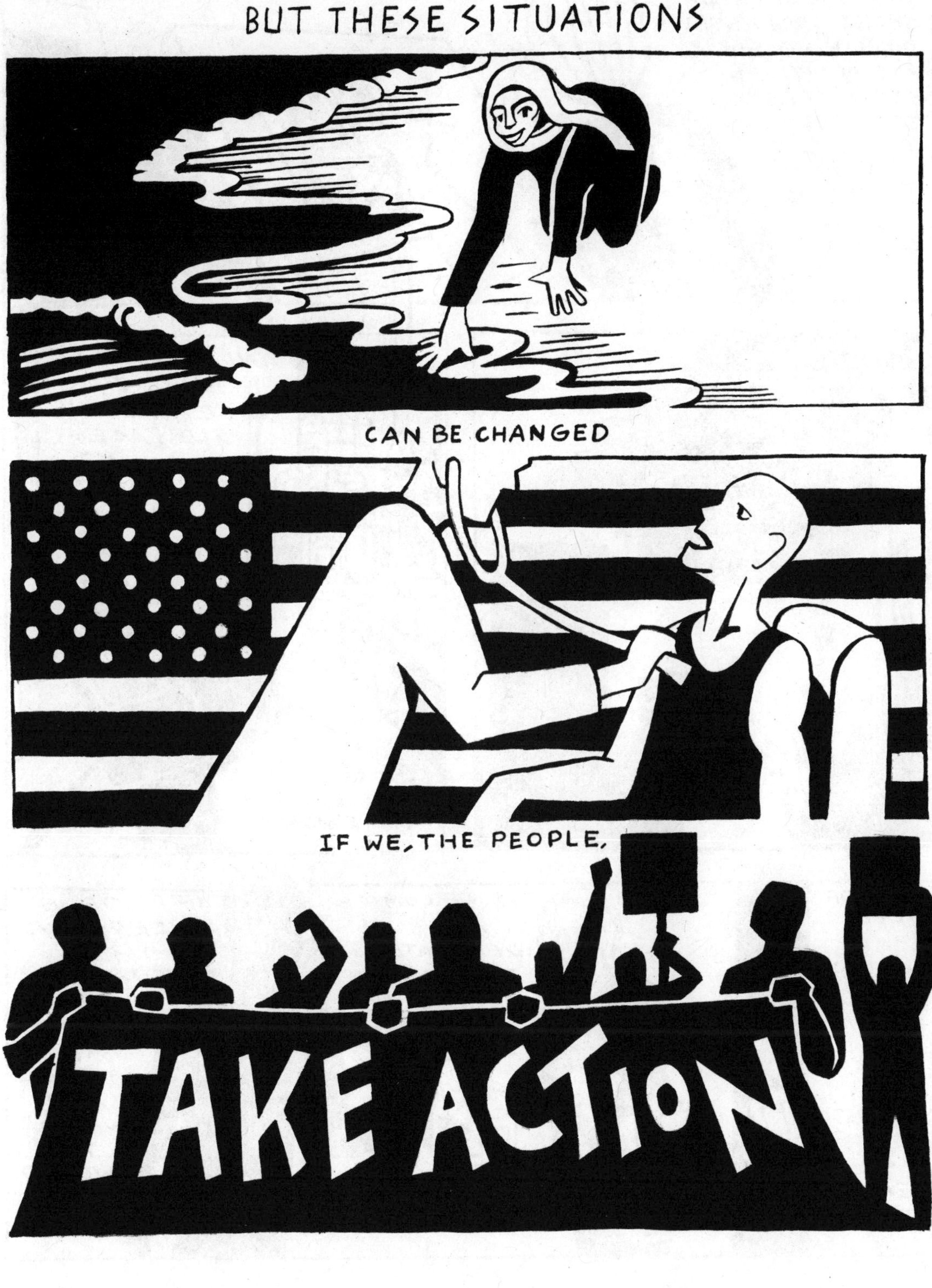
BUT THESE SITUATIONS
CAN BE CHANGED
IF WE, THE PEOPLE,
TAKE ACTION

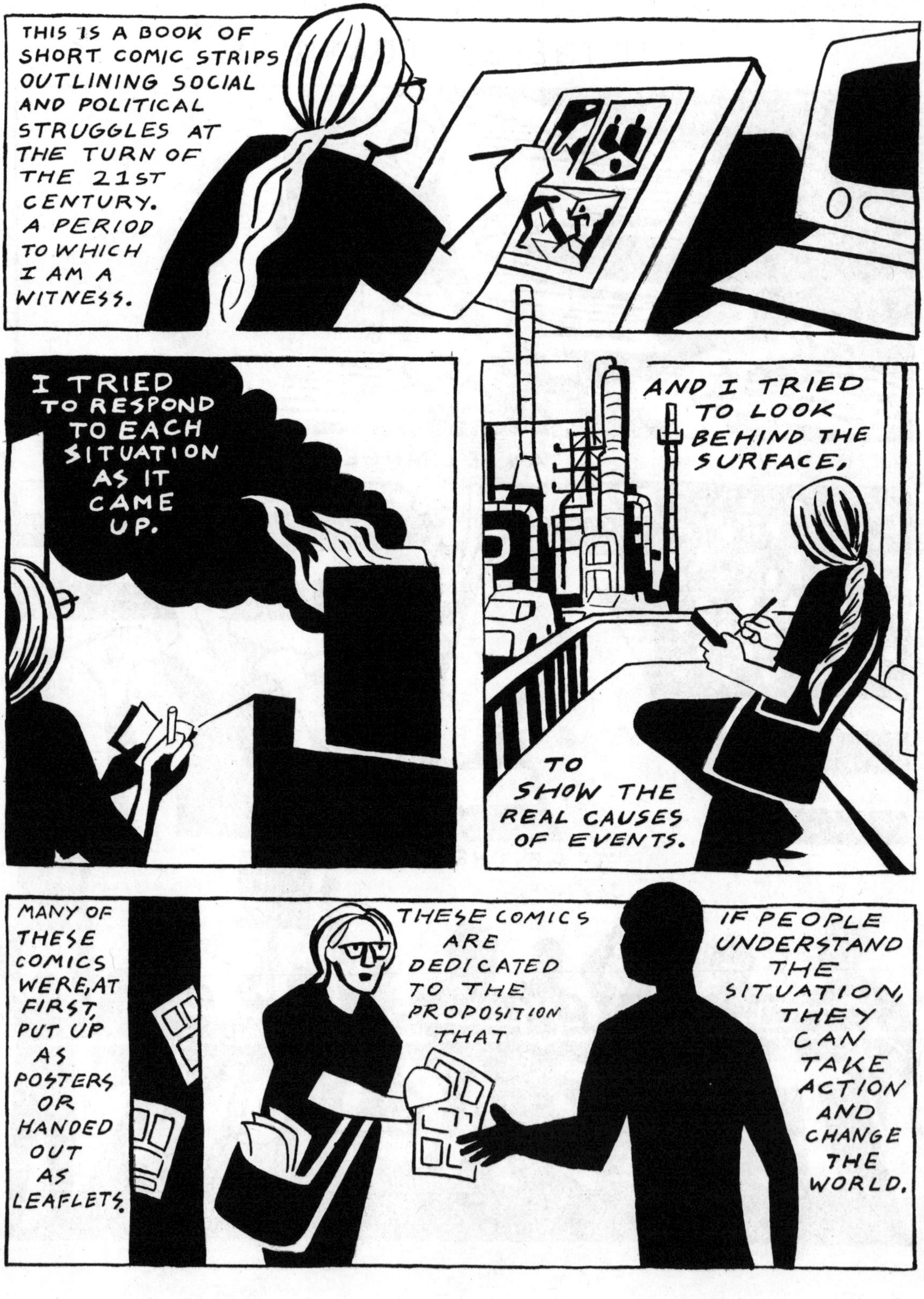
THIS IS A BOOK OF SHORT COMIC STRIPS OUTLINING SOCIAL AND POLITICAL STRUGGLES AT THE TURN OF THE 21ST CENTURY. A PERIOD TO WHICH I AM A WITNESS.
I TRIED TO RESPOND TO EACH SITUATION AS IT CAME UP.
AND I TRIED TO LOOK BEHIND THE SURFACE,
TO SHOW THE REAL CAUSES OF EVENTS.
MANY OF THESE COMICS WERE, AT FIRST, PUT UP AS POSTERS OR HANDED OUT AS LEAFLETS.
THESE COMICS ARE DEDICATED TO THE PROPOSITION THAT
IF PEOPLE UNDERSTAND THE SITUATION, THEY CAN TAKE ACTION AND CHANGE THE WORLD.

Part One:

The New Sixties

THE NEW SIXTIES

I was surprised by the wave of protest that swept the world in the year 2000. I had not expected that so many people, most of them in their twenties, would come out to protest something as abstract as "Corporate Globalization." In the '80s and '90s, I became accustomed to small protests, usually organized around people's immediate survival needs. But it was not just the demographics that surprised me. It was also the type of activity. Hundreds of people were willingly arrested in acts of civil disobedience. And those who were not breaking the law, were very busy doing other things: Making puppets, performing street theater, providing emergency medical care. Everyone was invited to come to mass meetings to plan the days' actions. There were no onlookers.

The so-called "Anti-globalization Movement" was, in fact, the most globalized movement I had ever seen, coordinated over the internet with activists traveling half way around the world to attend demonstrations.

At the height of protests against the Republican Convention in Philadelphia, a young man asked me: "Is this as big as the sixties?"

Above and opposite: A hundred of us were held for five days in a federal prison for protesting a World Bank meeting in Washington, D.C. These drawings were done in that facility.

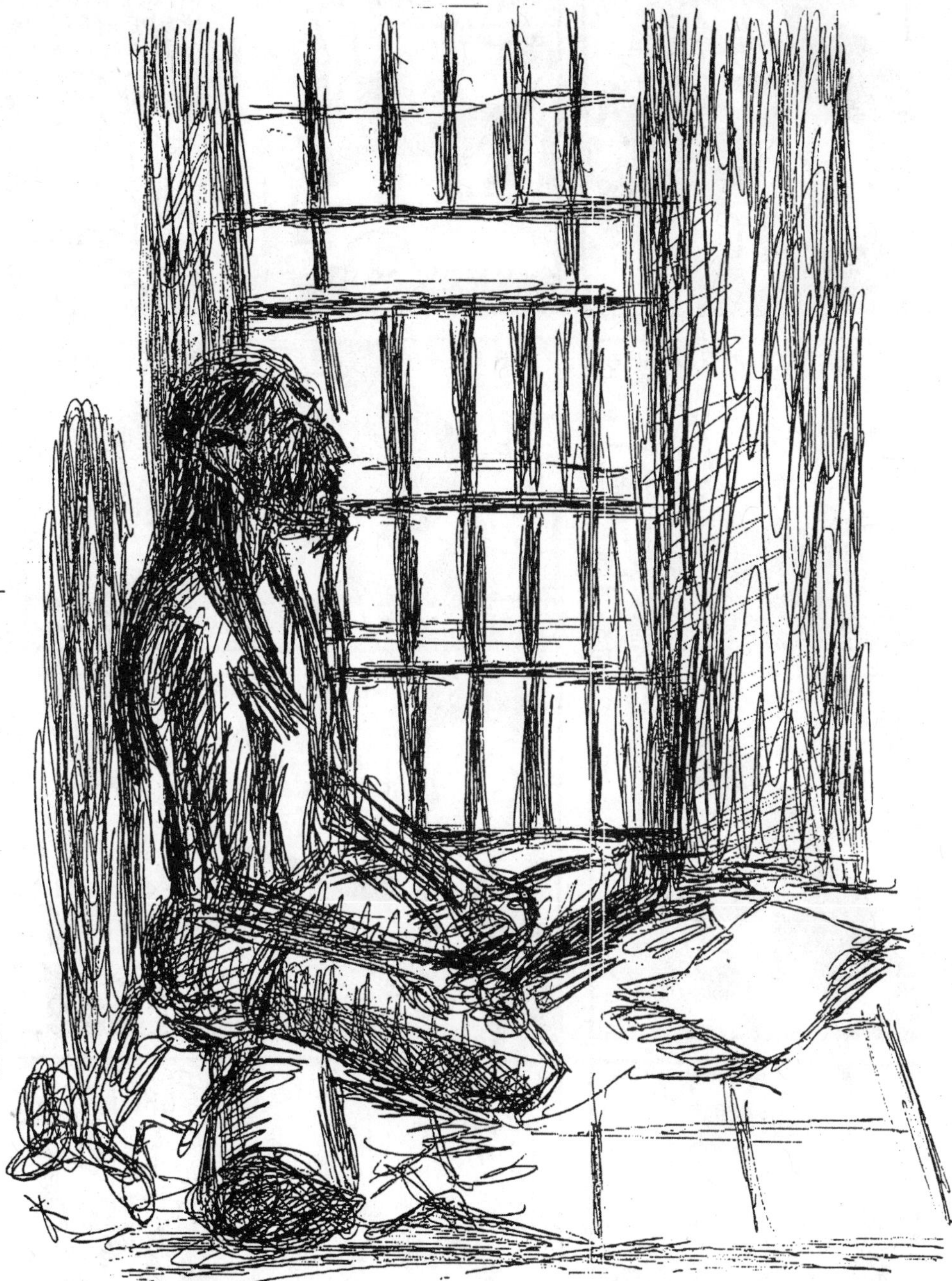

STUDENT STRIKE 2000

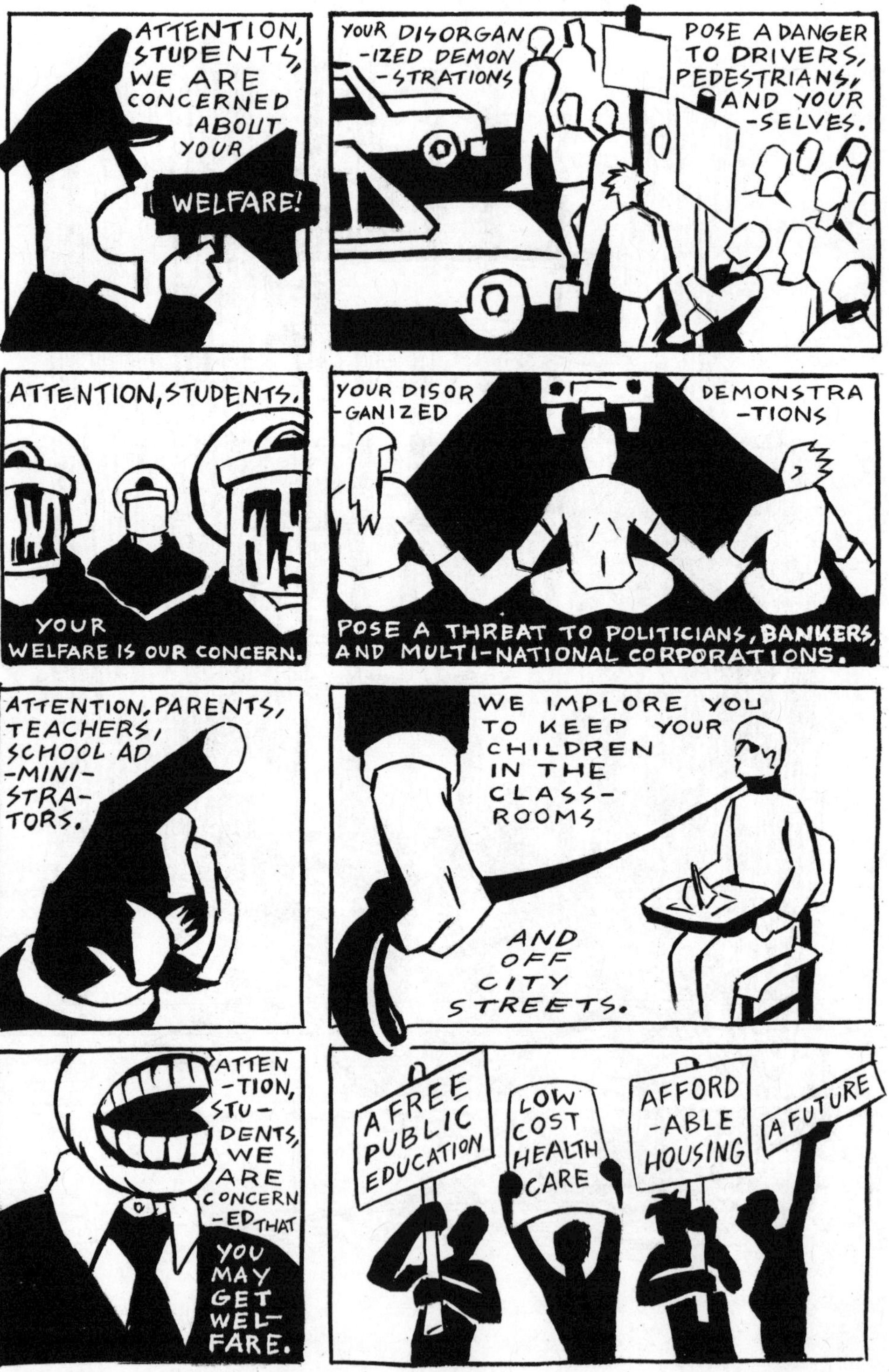
ATTENTION, STUDENTS, WE ARE CONCERNED ABOUT YOUR
WELFARE!
YOUR DISORGAN -IZED DEMON -STRATIONS
POSE A DANGER TO DRIVERS, PEDESTRIANS, AND YOUR -SELVES.
ATTENTION, STUDENTS.
YOUR WELFARE IS OUR CONCERN.
YOUR DISOR -GANIZED
DEMONSTRA -TIONS
POSE A THREAT TO POLITICIANS, BANKERS, AND MULTI-NATIONAL CORPORATIONS.
ATTENTION, PARENTS, TEACHERS, SCHOOL AD -MINI- STRA- TORS.
WE IMPLORE YOU TO KEEP YOUR CHILDREN IN THE CLASS- ROOMS
AND OFF CITY STREETS.
ATTEN -TION, STU- DENTS, WE ARE CONCERN -ED THAT
YOU MAY GET WEL- FARE.
A FREE PUBLIC EDUCATION
LOW COST HEALTH CARE
AFFORD -ABLE HOUSING
A FUTURE

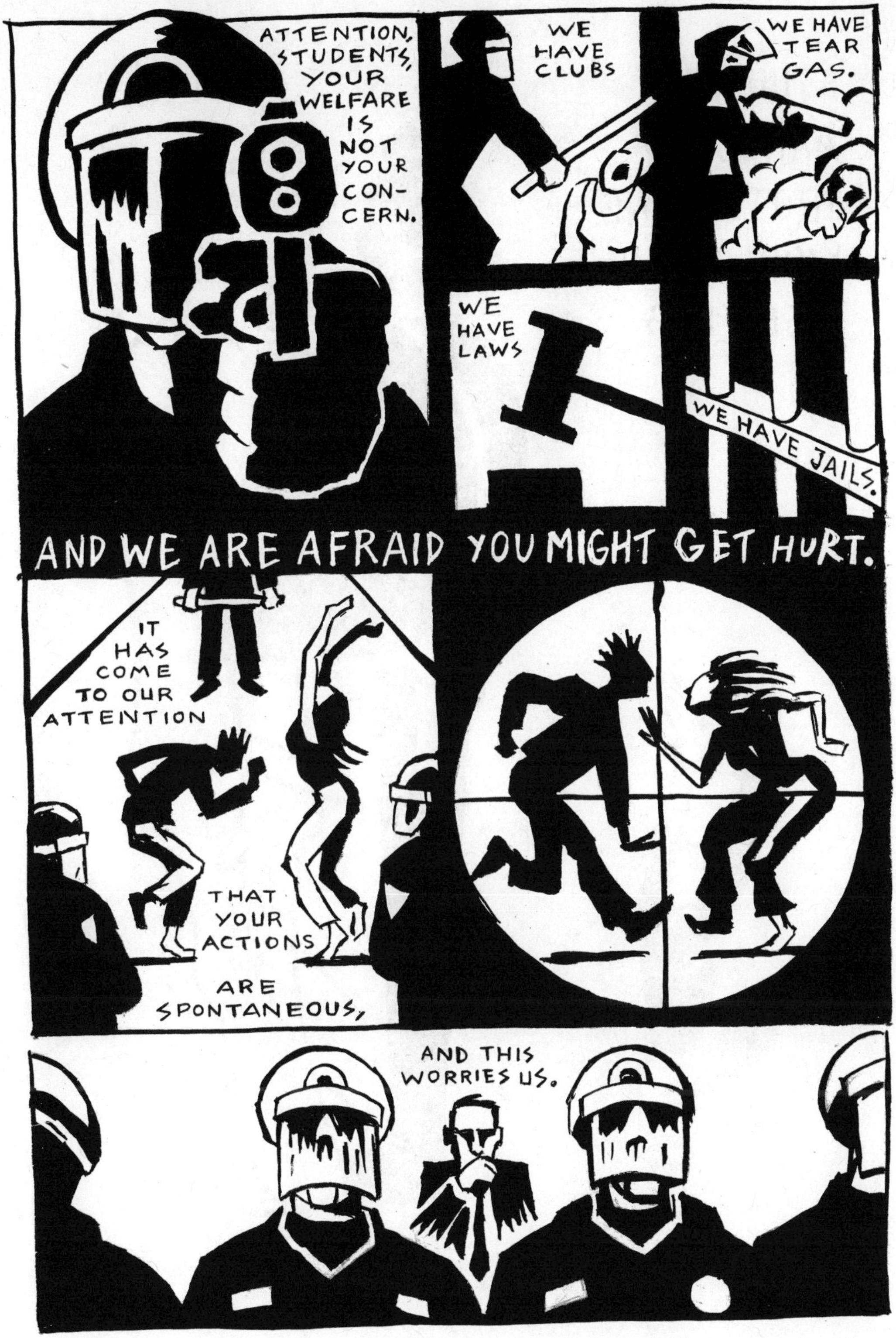
ATTENTION, STUDENTS, YOUR WELFARE IS NOT YOUR CONCERN.
WE HAVE CLUBS
WE HAVE TEAR GAS.
WE HAVE LAWS
WE HAVE JAILS.
AND WE ARE AFRAID YOU MIGHT GET HURT.
IT HAS COME TO OUR ATTENTION
THAT YOUR ACTIONS
ARE SPONTANEOUS,
AND THIS WORRIES US.

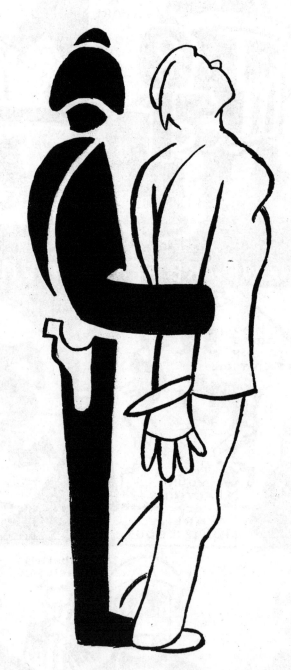

STUDENTS
ARRESTED
PROTESTING
WORLD BANK
MEETING

SETH

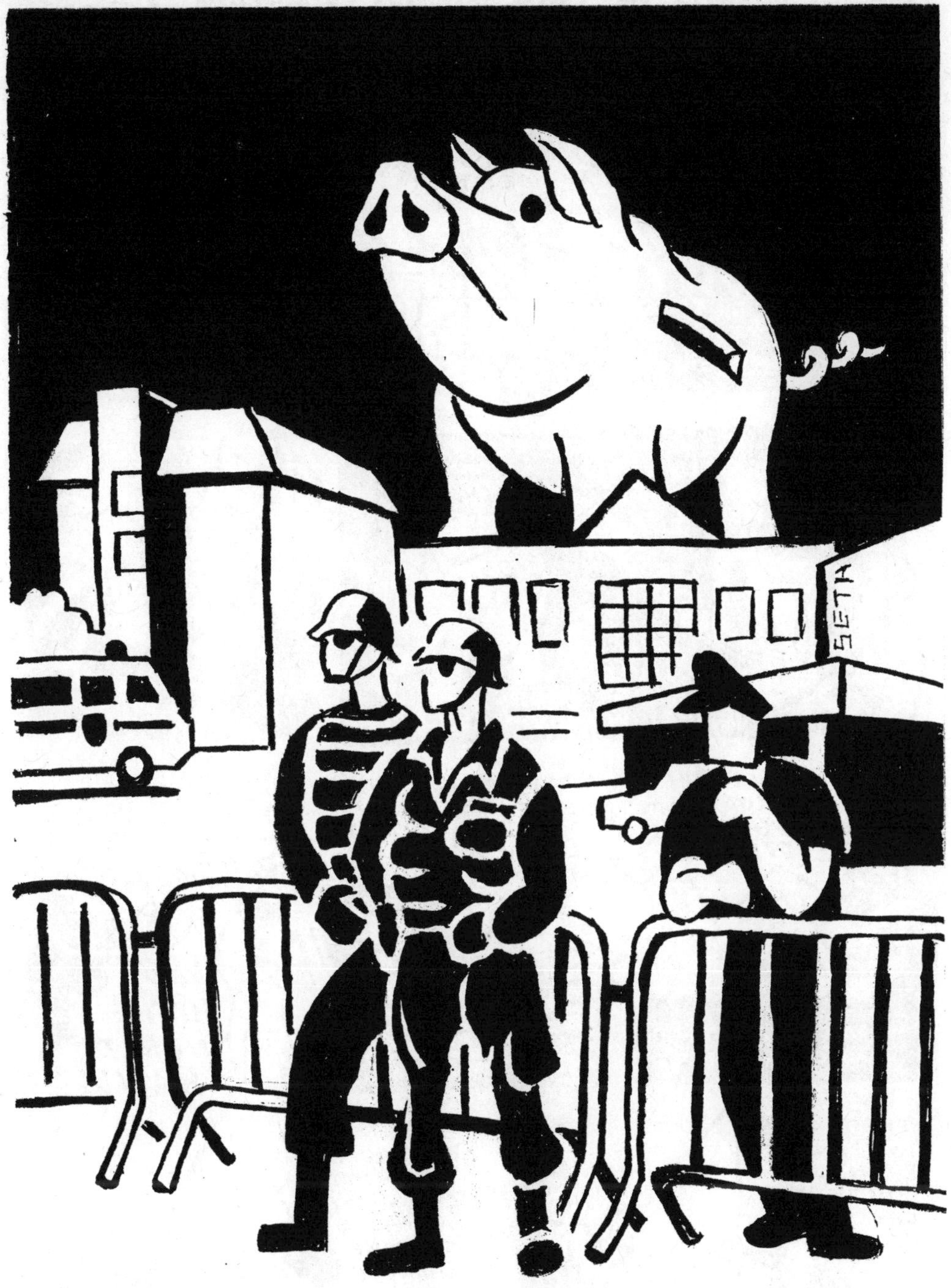
SETH

THE "JOINT TASK FORCE" GUARDING THE WORLD BANK MEETING IN FLORHAM PARK, NEW JERSEY.

WHAT IS THE WORLD BANK ?

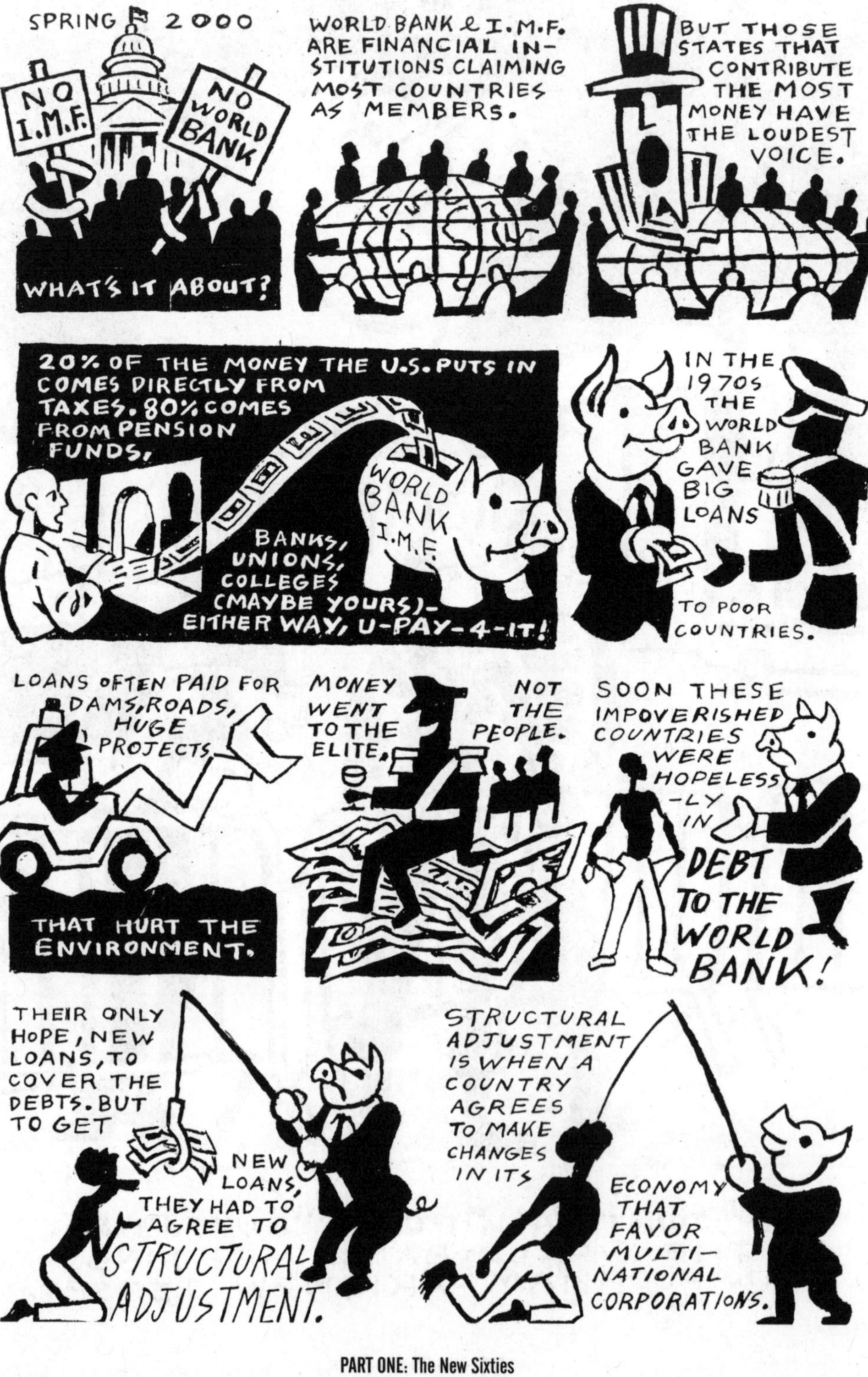
SPRING 2000
NO I.M.F.
NO WORLD BANK
WHAT'S IT ABOUT?
WORLD BANK & I.M.F. ARE FINANCIAL INSTITUTIONS CLAIMING MOST COUNTRIES AS MEMBERS.
BUT THOSE STATES THAT CONTRIBUTE THE MOST MONEY HAVE THE LOUDEST VOICE.
20% OF THE MONEY THE U.S. PUTS IN COMES DIRECTLY FROM TAXES. 80% COMES FROM PENSION FUNDS,
WORLD BANK I.M.F.
BANKS, UNIONS, COLLEGES (MAYBE YOURS)- EITHER WAY, U-PAY-4-IT!
IN THE 1970s THE WORLD BANK GAVE BIG LOANS
TO POOR COUNTRIES.
LOANS OFTEN PAID FOR DAMS, ROADS, HUGE PROJECTS
THAT HURT THE ENVIRONMENT.
MONEY WENT TO THE ELITE,
NOT THE PEOPLE.
SOON THESE IMPOVERISHED COUNTRIES WERE HOPELESS-LY IN
DEBT TO THE WORLD BANK!
THEIR ONLY HOPE, NEW LOANS, TO COVER THE DEBTS. BUT TO GET
NEW LOANS, THEY HAD TO AGREE TO
STRUCTURAL ADJUSTMENT.
STRUCTURAL ADJUSTMENT IS WHEN A COUNTRY AGREES TO MAKE CHANGES IN ITS
ECONOMY THAT FAVOR MULTI-NATIONAL CORPORATIONS.

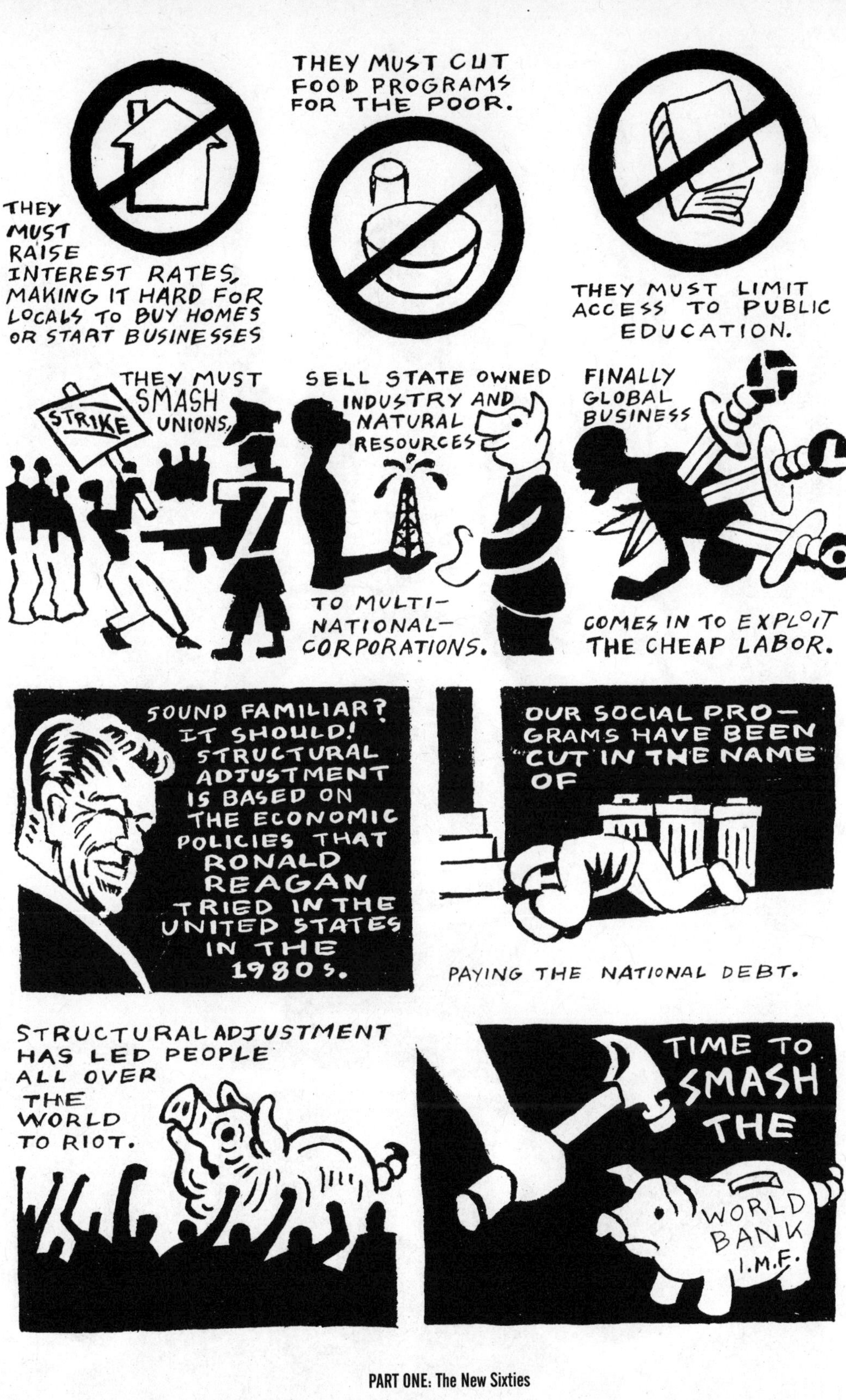
THEY MUST RAISE INTEREST RATES, MAKING IT HARD FOR LOCALS TO BUY HOMES OR START BUSINESSES
THEY MUST CUT FOOD PROGRAMS FOR THE POOR.
THEY MUST LIMIT ACCESS TO PUBLIC EDUCATION.
STRIKE
THEY MUST SMASH UNIONS,
SELL STATE OWNED INDUSTRY AND NATURAL RESOURCES
TO MULTI-NATIONAL-CORPORATIONS.
FINALLY GLOBAL BUSINESS
COMES IN TO EXPLOIT THE CHEAP LABOR.
SOUND FAMILIAR? IT SHOULD! STRUCTURAL ADJUSTMENT IS BASED ON THE ECONOMIC POLICIES THAT RONALD REAGAN TRIED IN THE UNITED STATES IN THE 1980s.
OUR SOCIAL PROGRAMS HAVE BEEN CUT IN THE NAME OF
PAYING THE NATIONAL DEBT.
STRUCTURAL ADJUSTMENT HAS LED PEOPLE ALL OVER THE WORLD TO RIOT.
TIME TO SMASH THE
WORLD BANK I.M.F.

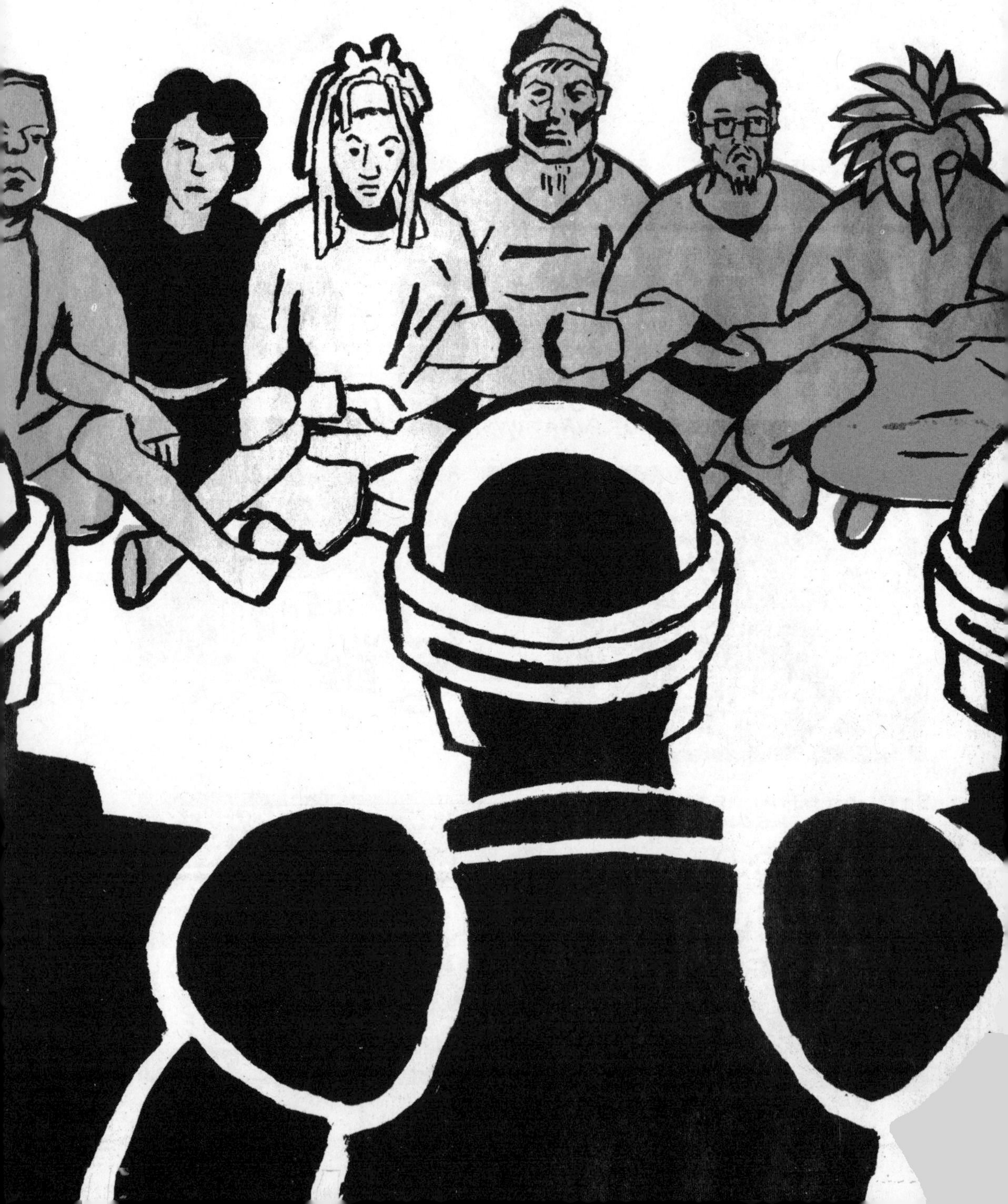

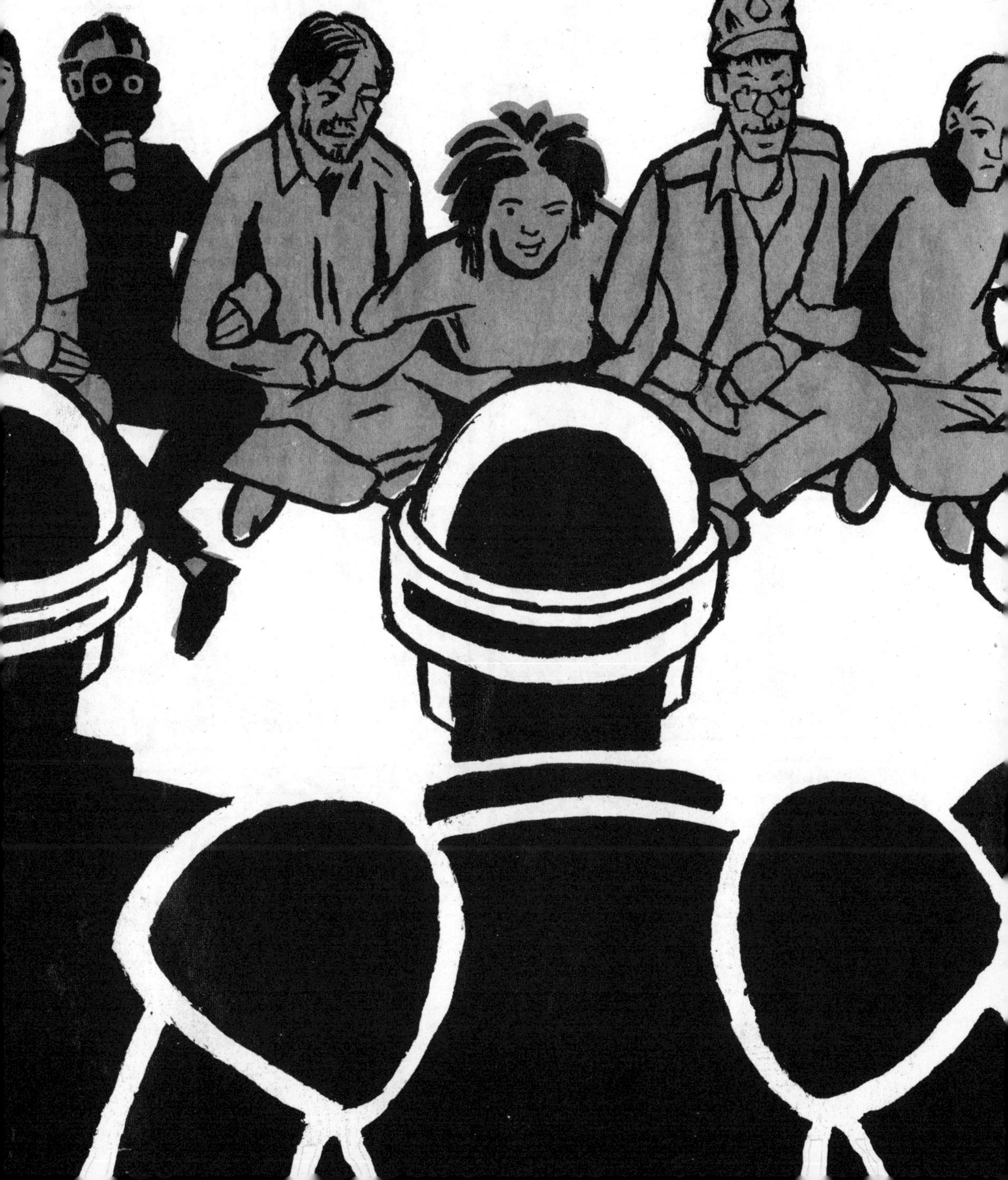

A CALL TO ACTION

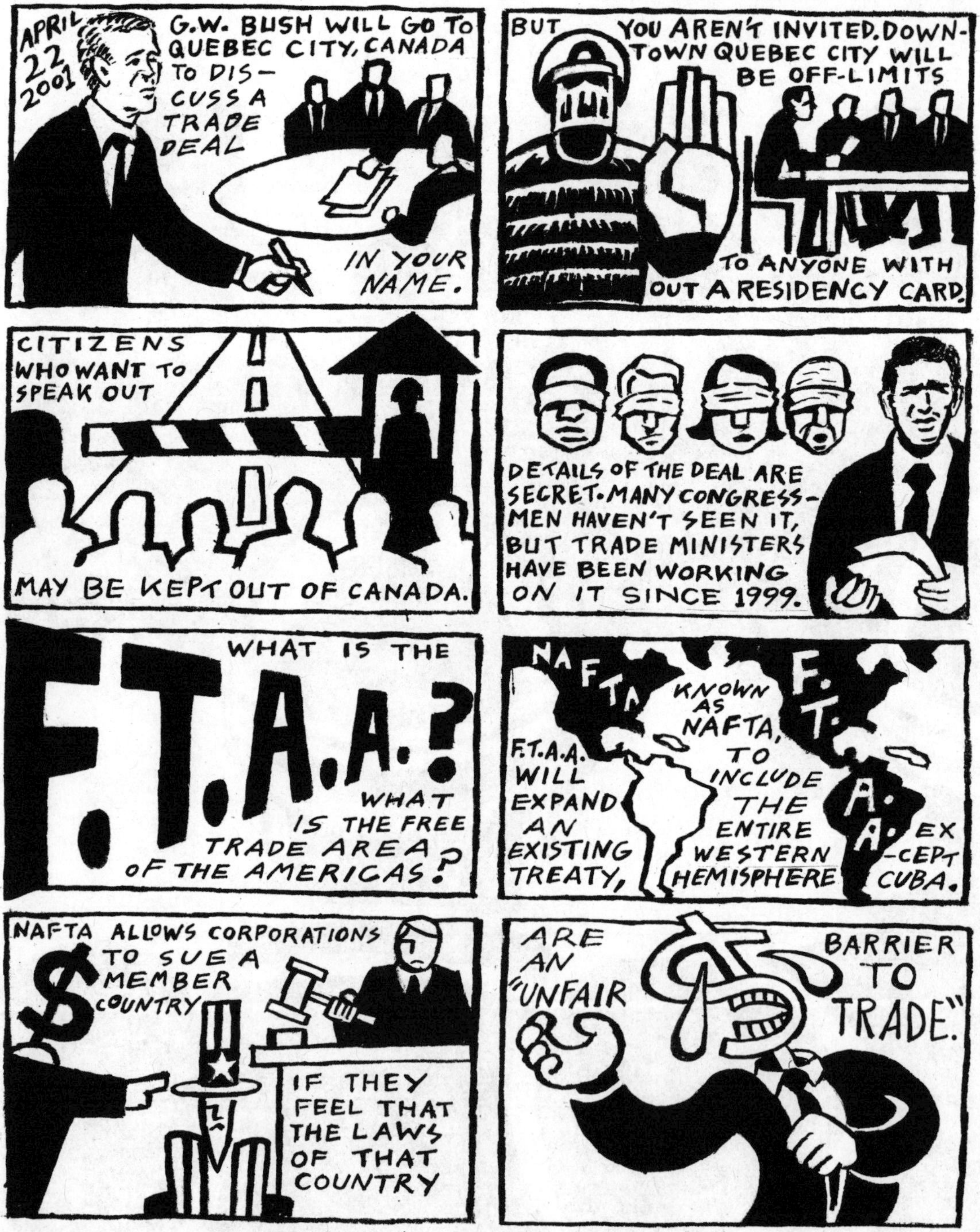

APRIL 22 2001
G.W. BUSH WILL GO TO QUEBEC CITY, CANADA TO DIS-CUSS A TRADE DEAL
IN YOUR NAME.
BUT
YOU AREN'T INVITED. DOWN-TOWN QUEBEC CITY WILL BE OFF-LIMITS
TO ANYONE WITH OUT A RESIDENCY CARD.
CITIZENS WHO WANT TO SPEAK OUT
MAY BE KEPT OUT OF CANADA.
DETAILS OF THE DEAL ARE SECRET. MANY CONGRESS-MEN HAVEN'T SEEN IT, BUT TRADE MINISTERS HAVE BEEN WORKING ON IT SINCE 1999.
WHAT IS THE
F.T.A.A.?
WHAT IS THE FREE TRADE AREA OF THE AMERICAS?
NAFTA
F.T.A.A.
F.T.A.A. WILL EXPAND AN EXISTING TREATY,
KNOWN AS NAFTA,
TO INCLUDE THE ENTIRE WESTERN HEMISPHERE
EX-CEPT CUBA.
NAFTA ALLOWS CORPORATIONS TO SUE A MEMBER COUNTRY
IF THEY FEEL THAT THE LAWS OF THAT COUNTRY
ARE AN "UNFAIR
BARRIER TO TRADE."

FOR EXAMPLE, THE U.S. BASED METAL-CLAD GROUP,
USED NAFTA
TO FORCE MEXICO TO ACCEPT A TOXIC WASTE DUMP.
NAFTA MAY MAKE CANADA
SELL WHOLE LAKES TO A WATER EXPORT COMPANY.
SINCE NAFTA
MILLIONS OF JOBS HAVE LEFT THE U.S. & CANADA AS FACTORIES
WENT TO MEXICO.
THIS DIDN'T HELP THE MEXICANS. SINCE NAFTA,
8 MILLION MEXICANS HAVE FALLEN OUT OF THE MIDDLE CLASS.
FTAA MAY FORCE COUNTRIES TO USE
GENETICALLY ALTERED FOOD,
FORCE PRIVATIZATION OF PUBLIC SCHOOLS,
McSCHOOL'S
ALLOW COMPANIES TO PATENT NATURALLY GROWING HERBS,
AND KEEP POOR COUNTRIES FROM MAKING
AFFORDABLE MED'S.
WE ARE GOING NORTH TO PROTEST THIS DEAL, WHETHER G.W. BUSH WANTS US THERE OR NOT. COME WITH US. THIS DEAL WILL AFFECT YOU, YOUR FAMILY, YOUR COMMUNITY. YOU HAVE EVERY RIGHT TO SPEAK OUT.

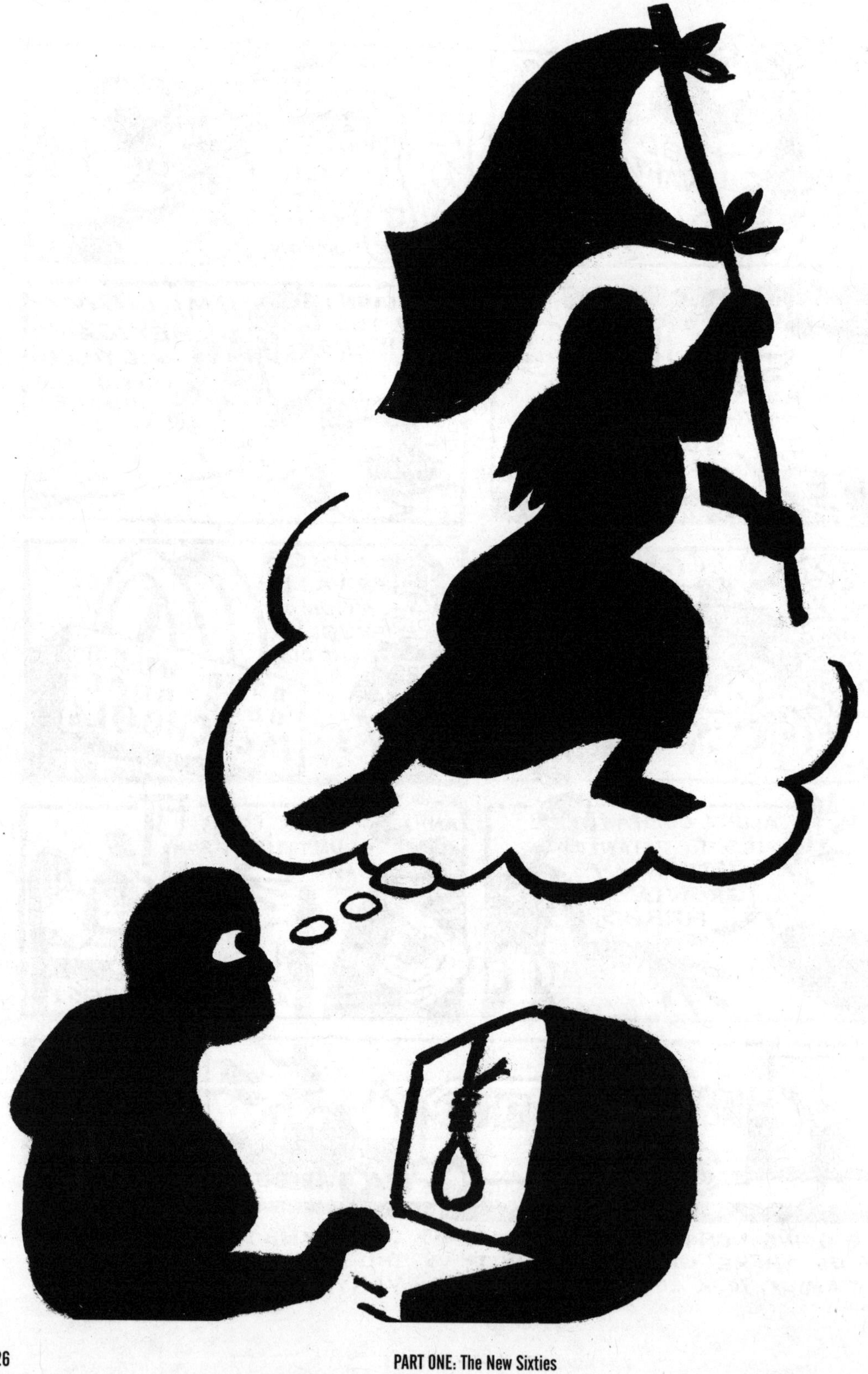

SO, YOU WANT A NEW SIXTIES....

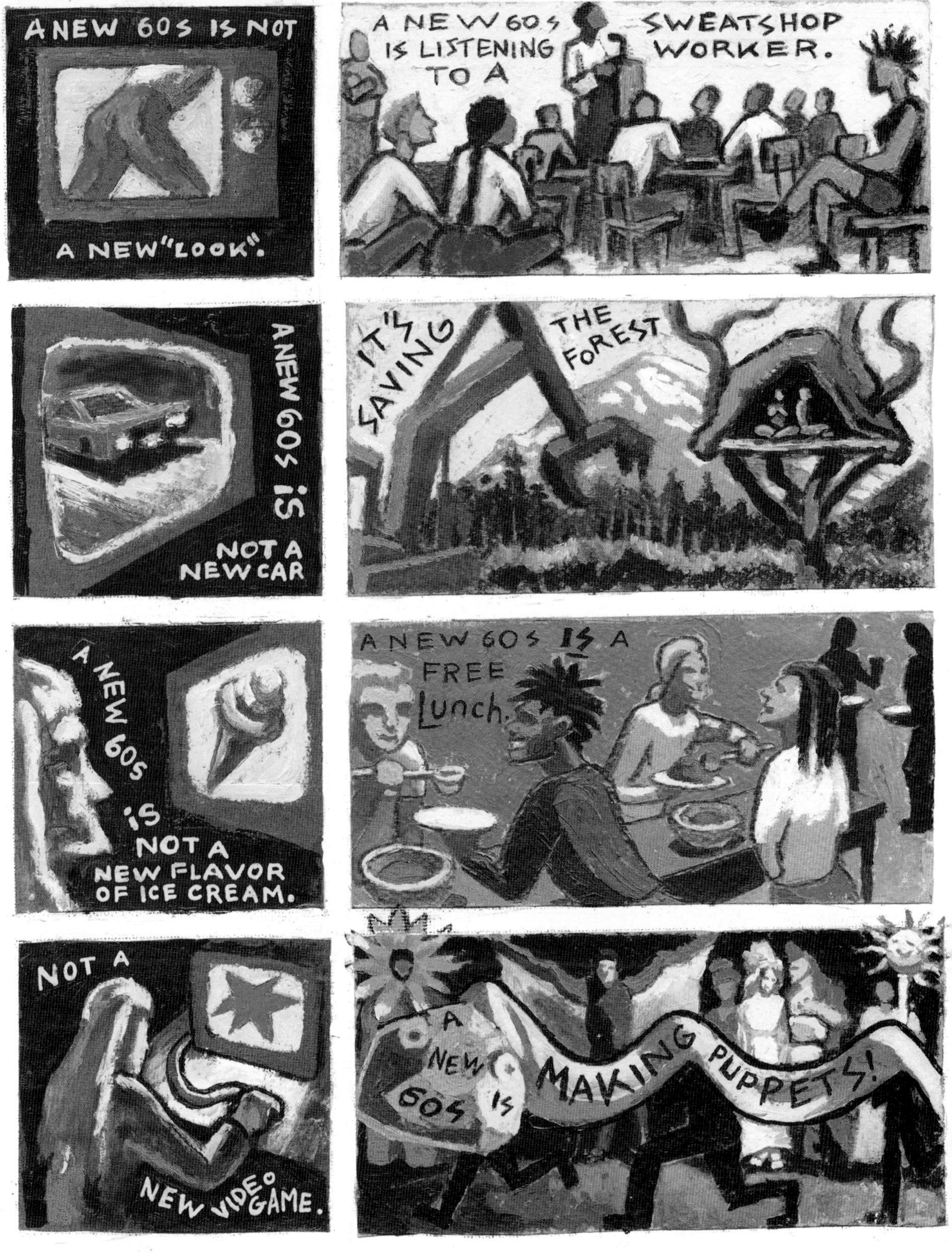
A NEW 60S IS NOT
A NEW "LOOK".
A NEW 60S IS LISTENING TO A
SWEATSHOP WORKER.
A NEW 60S IS
NOT A NEW CAR
IT'S SAVING
THE FOREST
A NEW 60S
IS
NOT A NEW FLAVOR OF ICE CREAM.
A NEW 60S IS A FREE Lunch.
NOT A
NEW VIDEO GAME.
A NEW 60S IS MAKING PUPPETS!

A NEW SIXTIES IS NOT A NEW DANCE.

A NEW SIXTIES IS PEOPLE BLOCKING TRAFFIC.

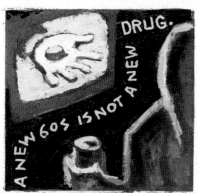
A NEW 60s IS NOT A NEW DRUG.

it is RUNNING IN THE STREETS.

A NEW 60s IS NOT A NEW BAND.

A NEW 60s IS

SINGING IN JAIL.

YOU CAN'T WATCH IT! YOU CAN'T BUY IT!

YOU CAN LIVE IT, IF YOU ARE READY TO TAKE THE RISK

SETH

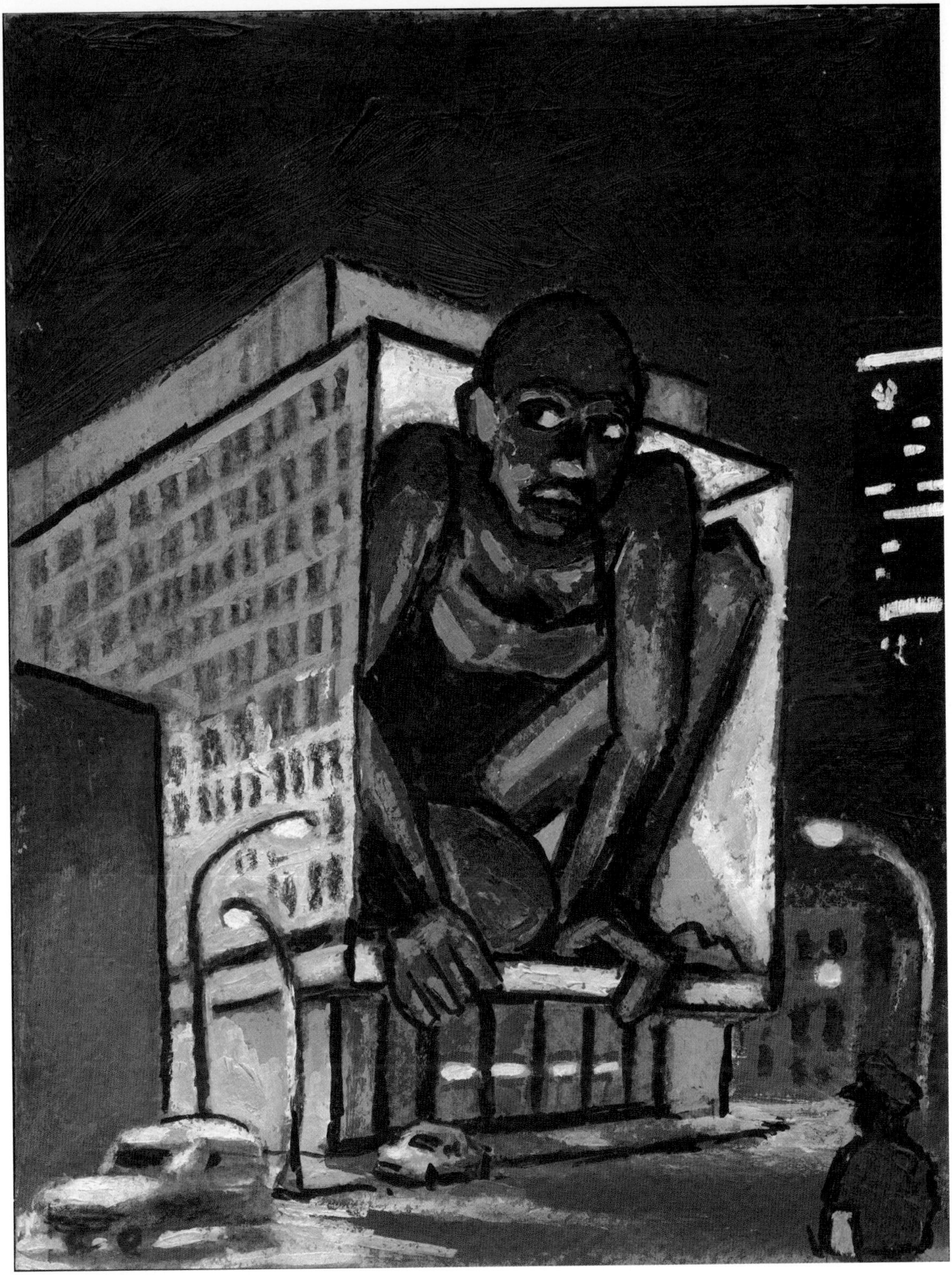

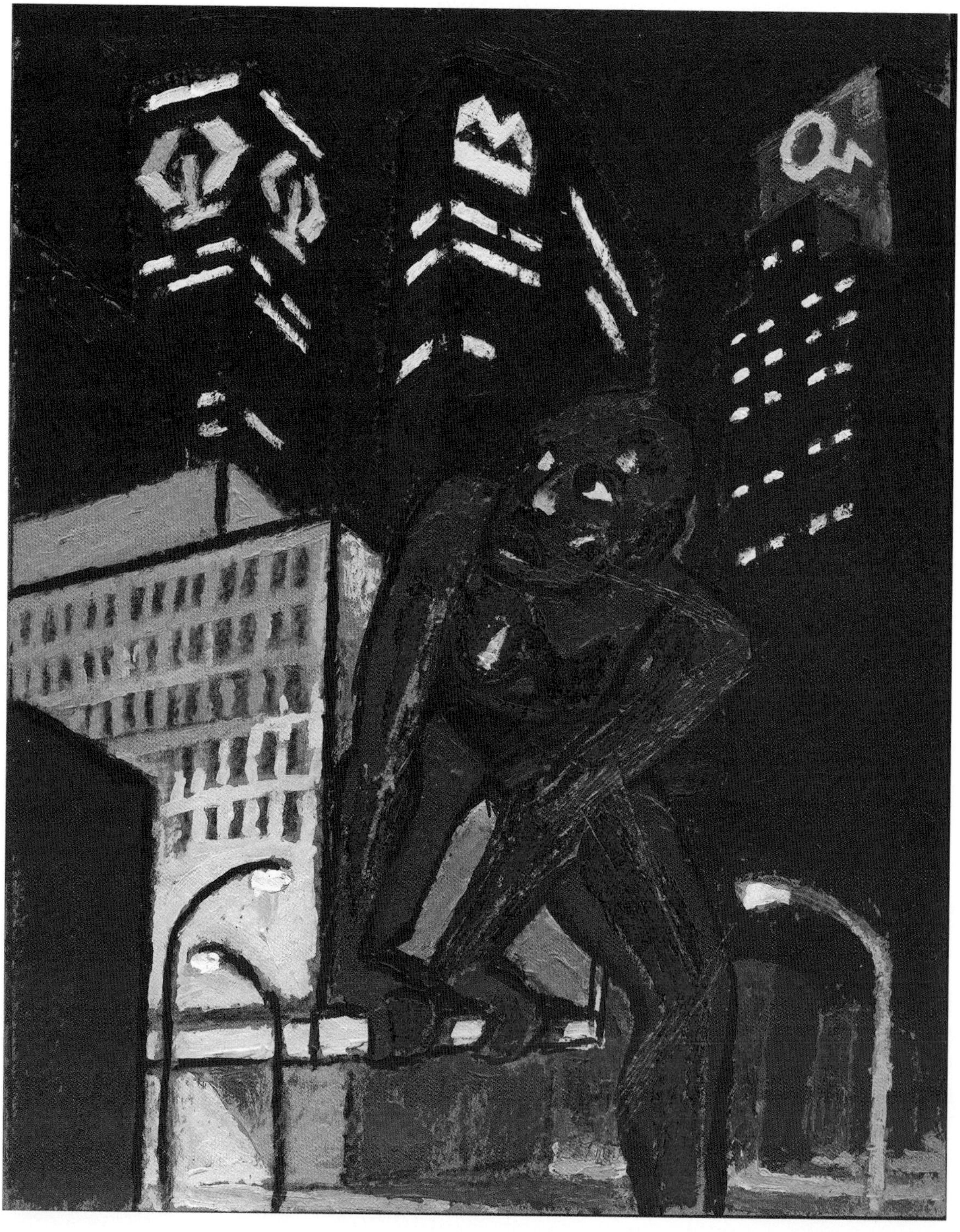

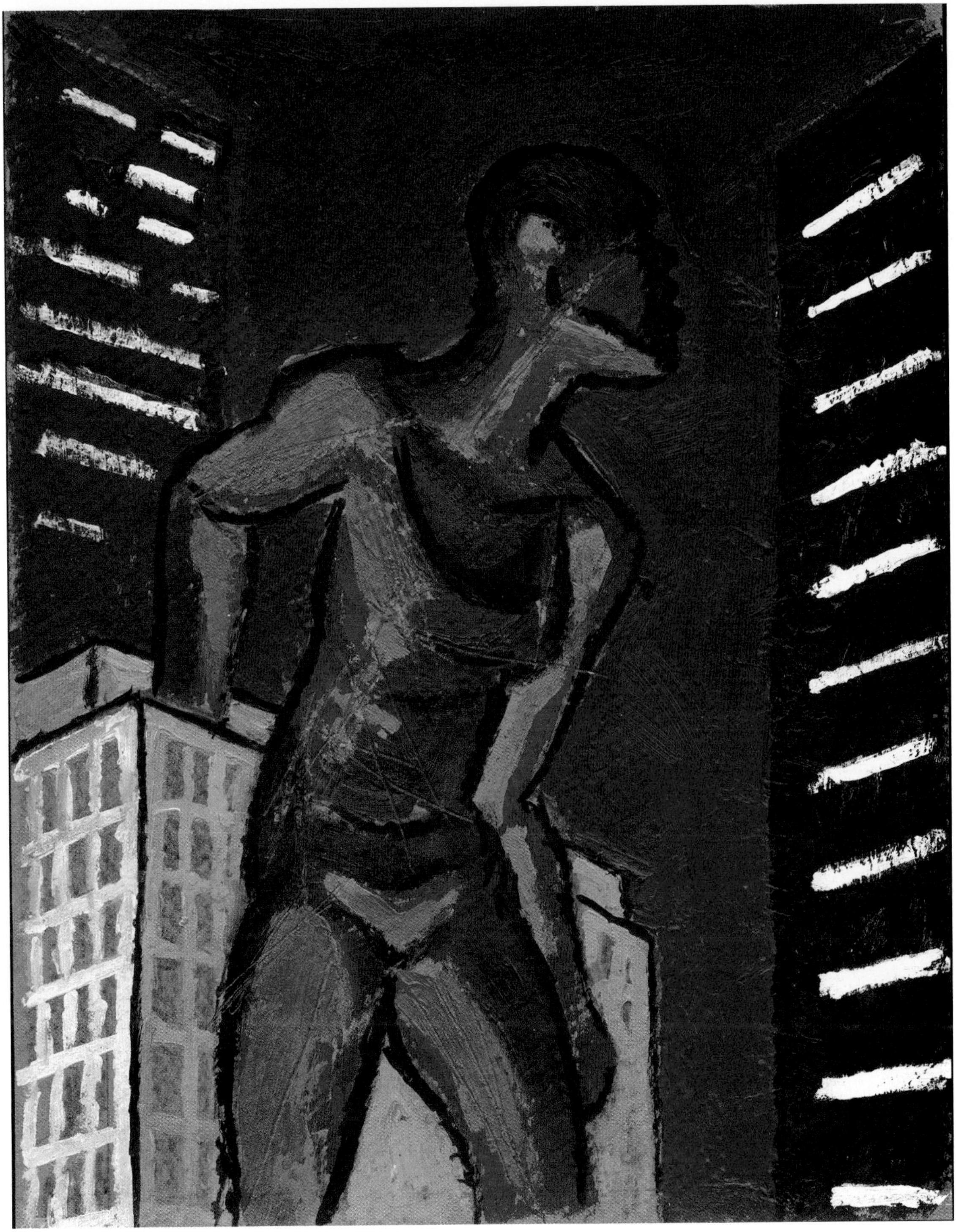

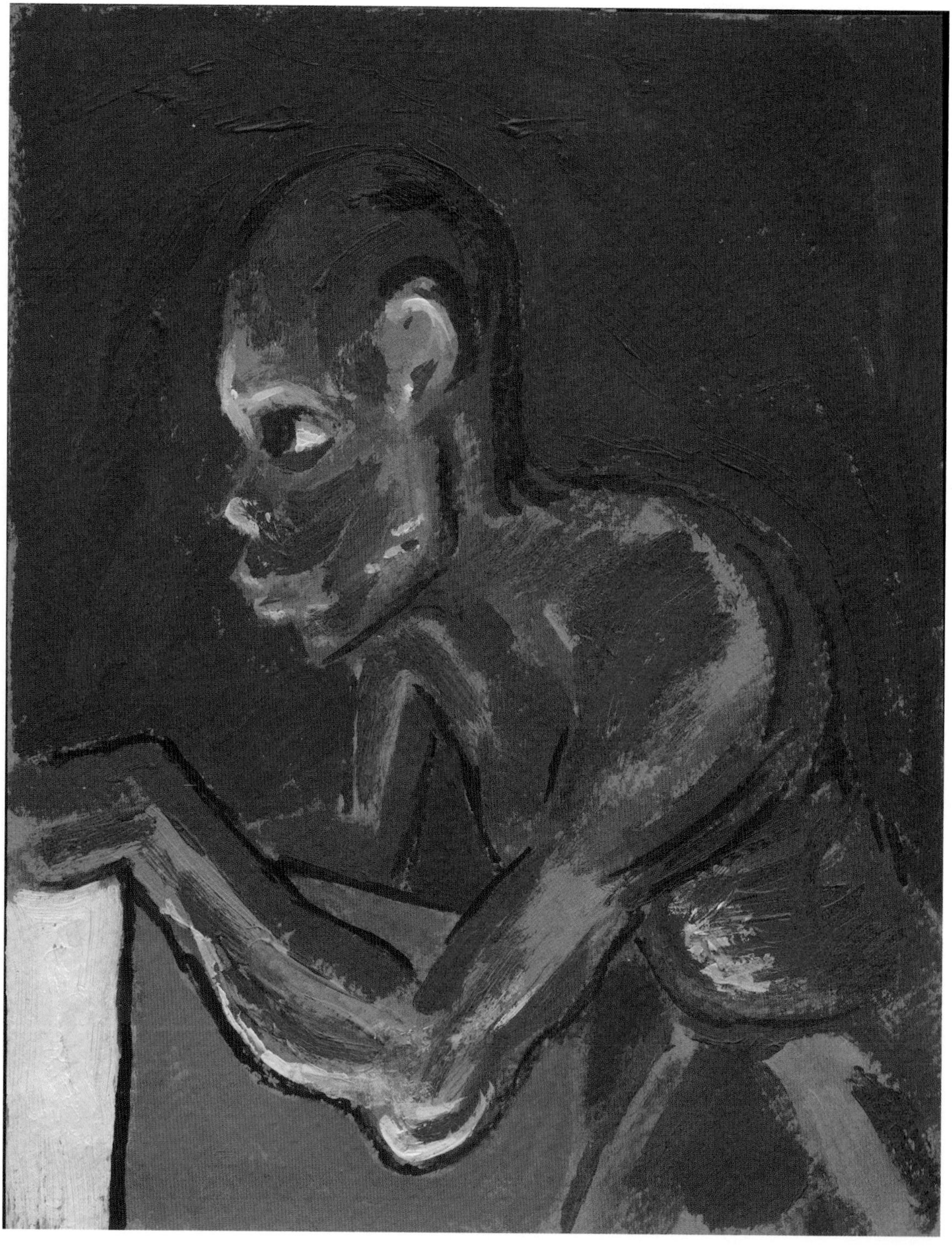

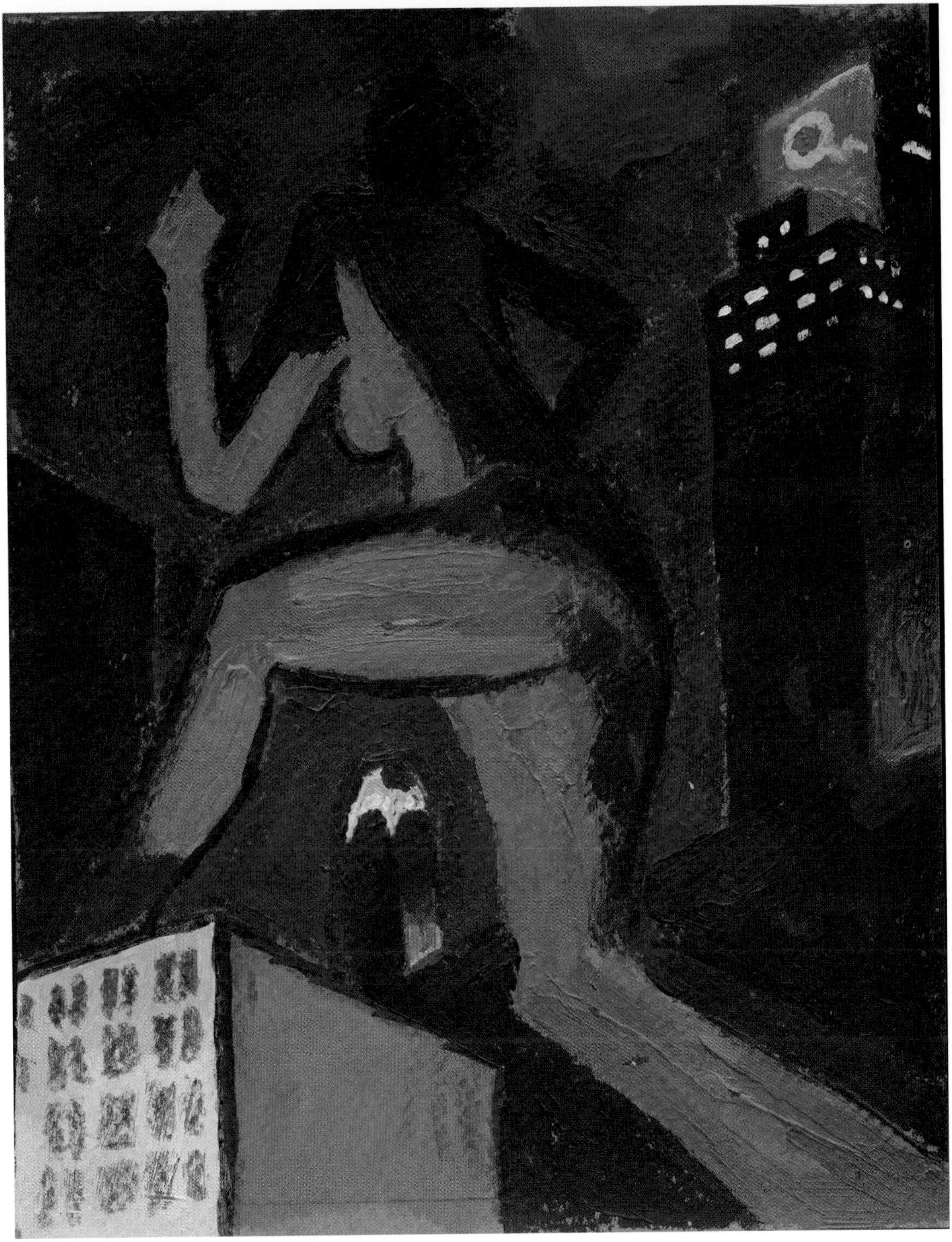

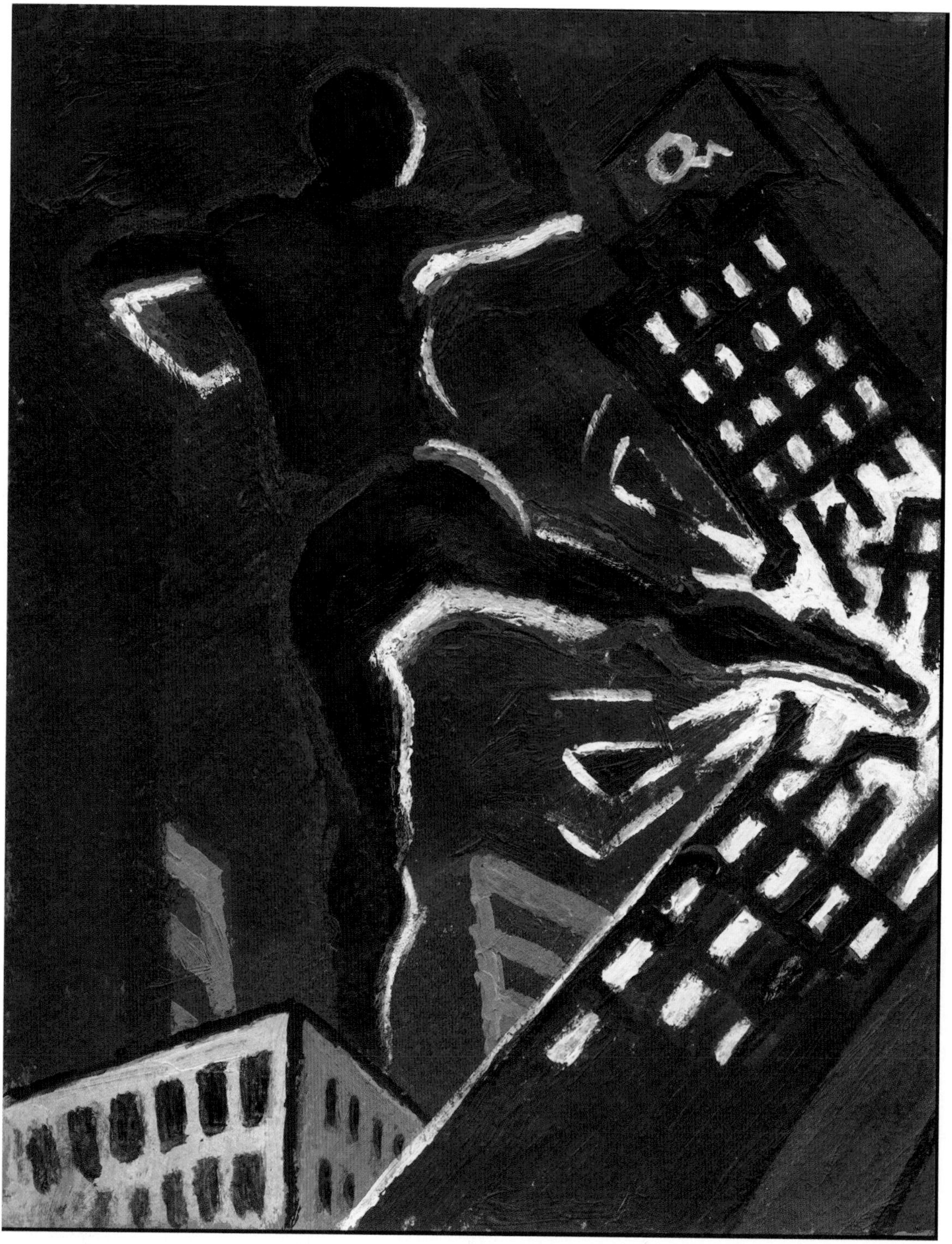

Part Two:

9-11 Armageddon

9-11 ARMAGEDDON

It has become a cliché to say that September 11th changed Americans forever. But how were we changed?

For many years, Americans had been oblivious to their country's foreign policy. How many Americans knew that their government had overthrown the democratically elected governments of Iran or Guatemala or Chile ? If you knew that the United States was invading Grenada, you were probably a member of that tiny minority who objected to the war.

Americans were apathetic and, perhaps, with good reason. People had jobs to get to, bills to pay, careers to pursue, families to raise. Who could be so idle, whose life could be so empty, that they worry about events on the other side of the world?

Then, one day, we found out that what we didn't know could hurt us. For two weeks everything in New York city came to a screeching halt. No one went in to work. Everyone's to-do list became irrelevant. People milled around Union Square trying to make sense of it.

Hundreds stood in line at the Javitz Center hoping for the opportunity to volunteer in the "rescue" effort at Ground Zero. Suddenly, digging through toxic debris had become the most coveted position in this competitive city. And all the while this huge pillar of smoke, a Biblical metaphor, hung in the southern sky.

When TV talking heads say that we changed on September 11th, they usually mean that we became a nation of flag waiving super-patriots. The Right definitely took advantage of these events to push their agenda, and they got away with a lot. Their attitude was crass and exploitative. At times they could barely conceal their glee. A sign I saw in Austin that fall read, "Avenge September 11th! Unleash the dogs of war! Have a nice day!"

But I think that something else may have changed. Something deeper and more subtle. It may take a while for that to become apparent.

This page: Quick sketch of the World Trade Center as it burned.
Opposite: Sketch of the ruins of Ground Zero.

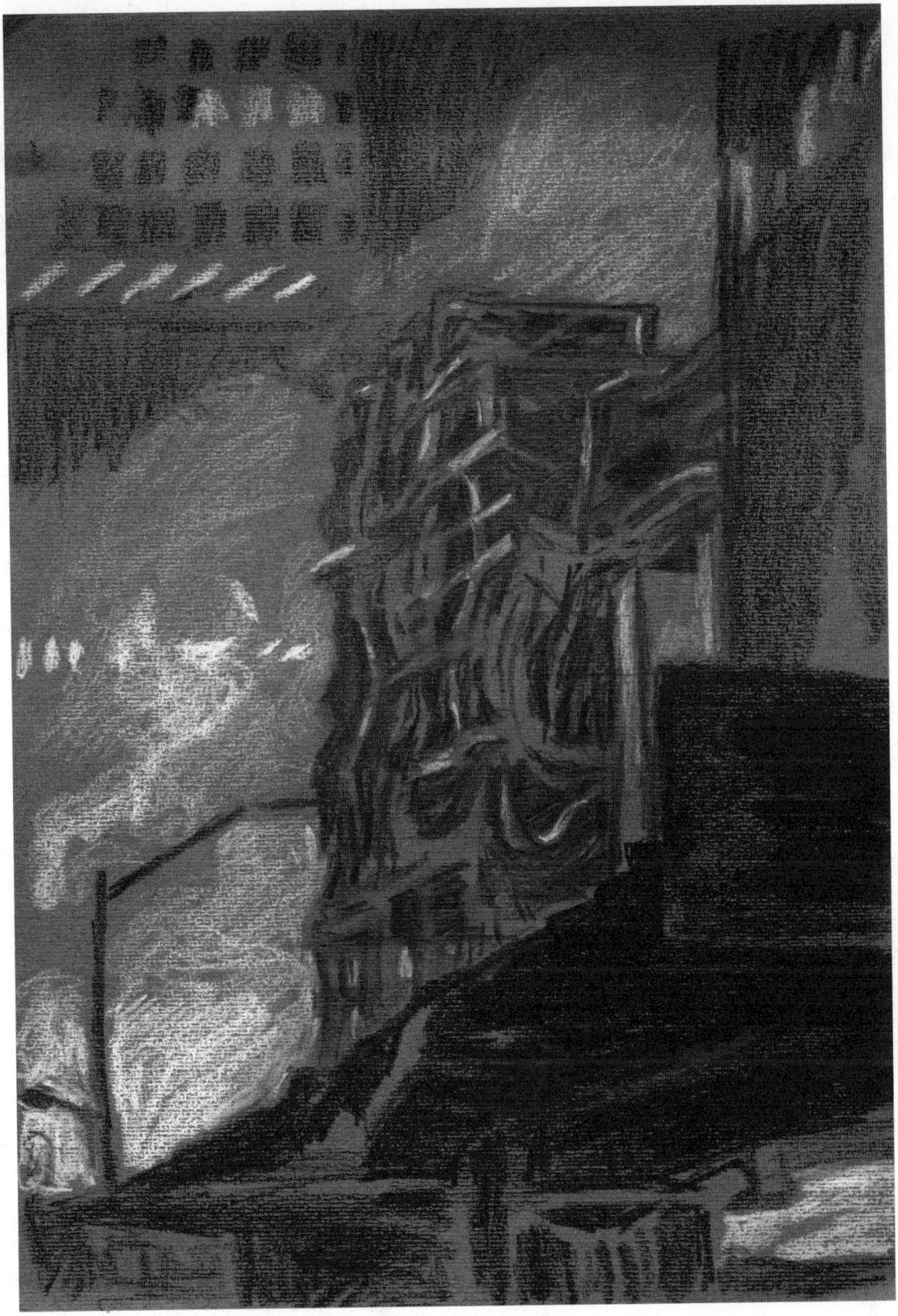

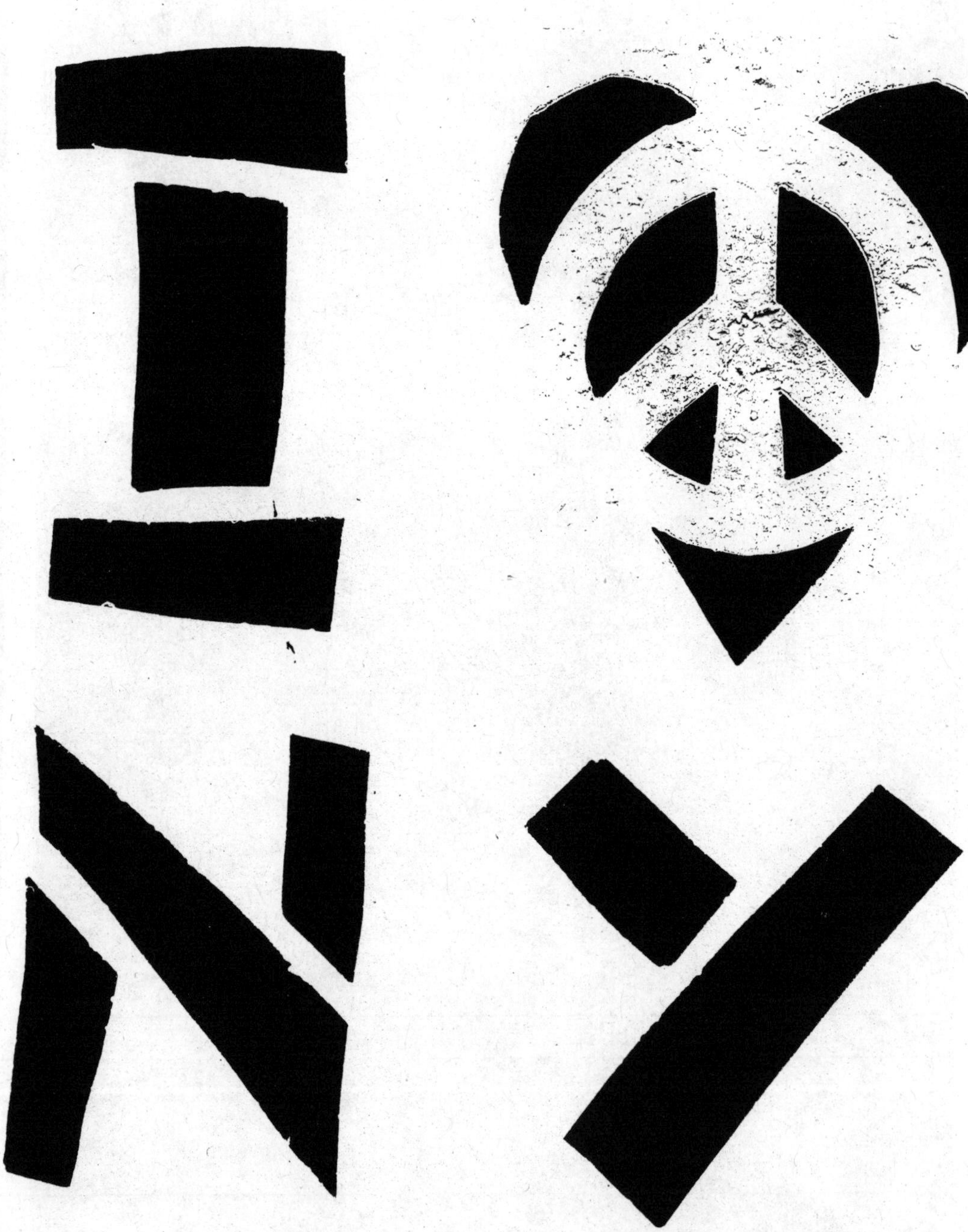

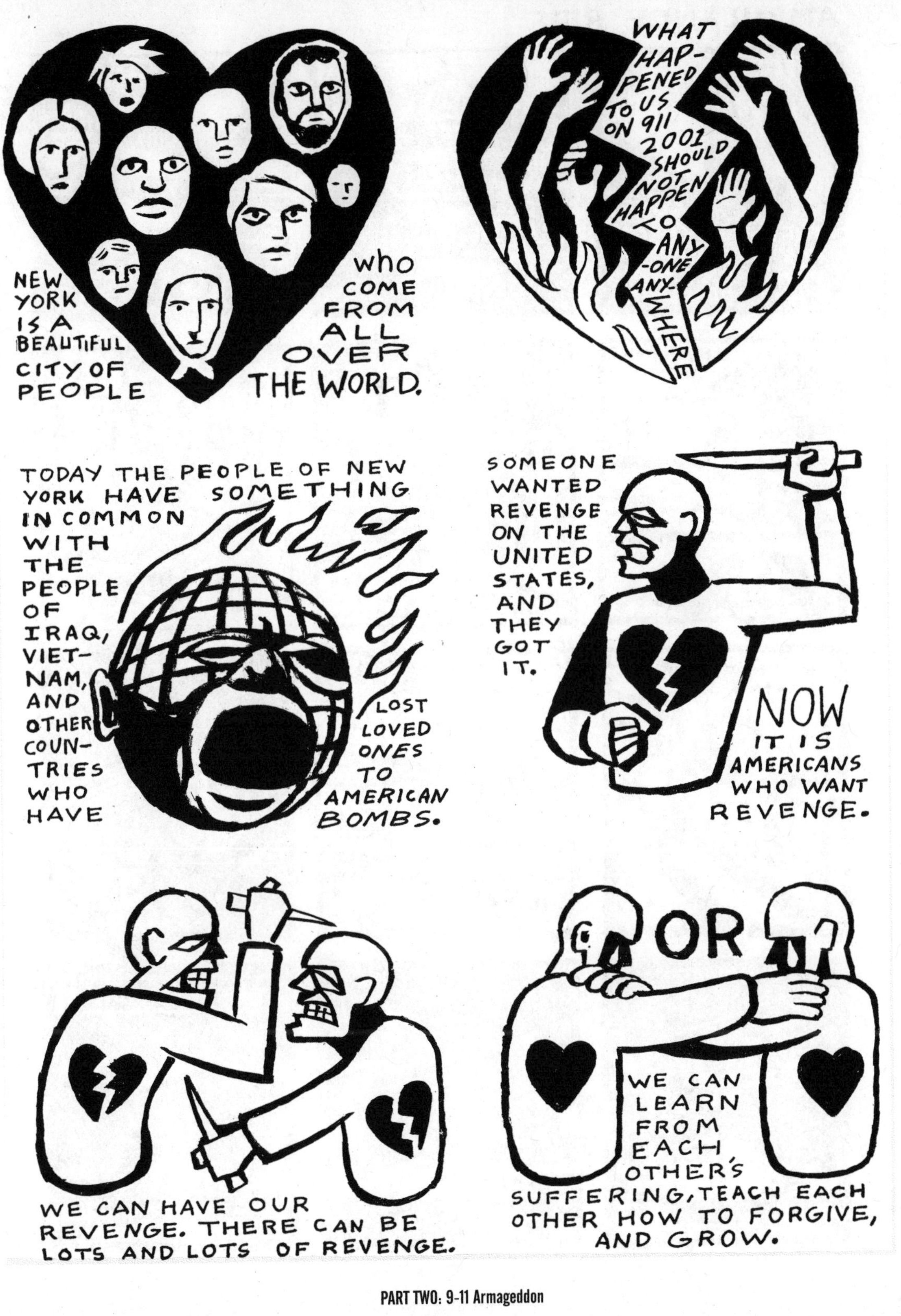
NEW YORK IS A BEAUTIFUL CITY OF PEOPLE
WHO COME FROM ALL OVER THE WORLD.
WHAT HAPPENED TO US ON 911 2001 SHOULD NOT HAPPEN TO ANY-ONE ANY-WHERE
TODAY THE PEOPLE OF NEW YORK HAVE SOMETHING IN COMMON WITH THE PEOPLE OF IRAQ, VIET-NAM, AND OTHER COUN-TRIES WHO HAVE
LOST LOVED ONES TO AMERICAN BOMBS.
SOMEONE WANTED REVENGE ON THE UNITED STATES, AND THEY GOT IT.
NOW IT IS AMERICANS WHO WANT REVENGE.
WE CAN HAVE OUR REVENGE. THERE CAN BE LOTS AND LOTS OF REVENGE.
OR
WE CAN LEARN FROM EACH OTHER'S SUFFERING, TEACH EACH OTHER HOW TO FORGIVE, AND GROW.

AMBULANCE RIDE

A STONE'S THROW AWAY FROM THE WASHINGTON MONUMENT, SOME ONE IS BLEEDING.
NOT FAR FROM THE CAPITAL,
A MAN IS DYING.
AN AMBULANCE ARRIVES.
D.C. GENERAL HOSPITAL IS ONLY BLOCKS AWAY,
A STATE OF THE ART FACILITY
THE ONLY HOSPITAL SERVING
D.C.'S POOR.
BUT D.C. GENERAL IS CLOSED, BY ORDER
OF MAYOR "BOW TIE".
THE AM-BULANCE TAKES A ½-HR. RIDE
THROUGH D.C.
TO HOWARD
UNIVERSITY HOSPITAL.
BUT HOWARD IS FULL-UP WITH CASES THAT WOULD HAVE GONE
AMBULANCE
TO D.C. GENERAL.
THE RIDE CONTINUES.
RSITY HOSPITAL

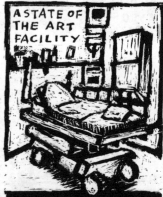

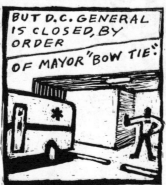

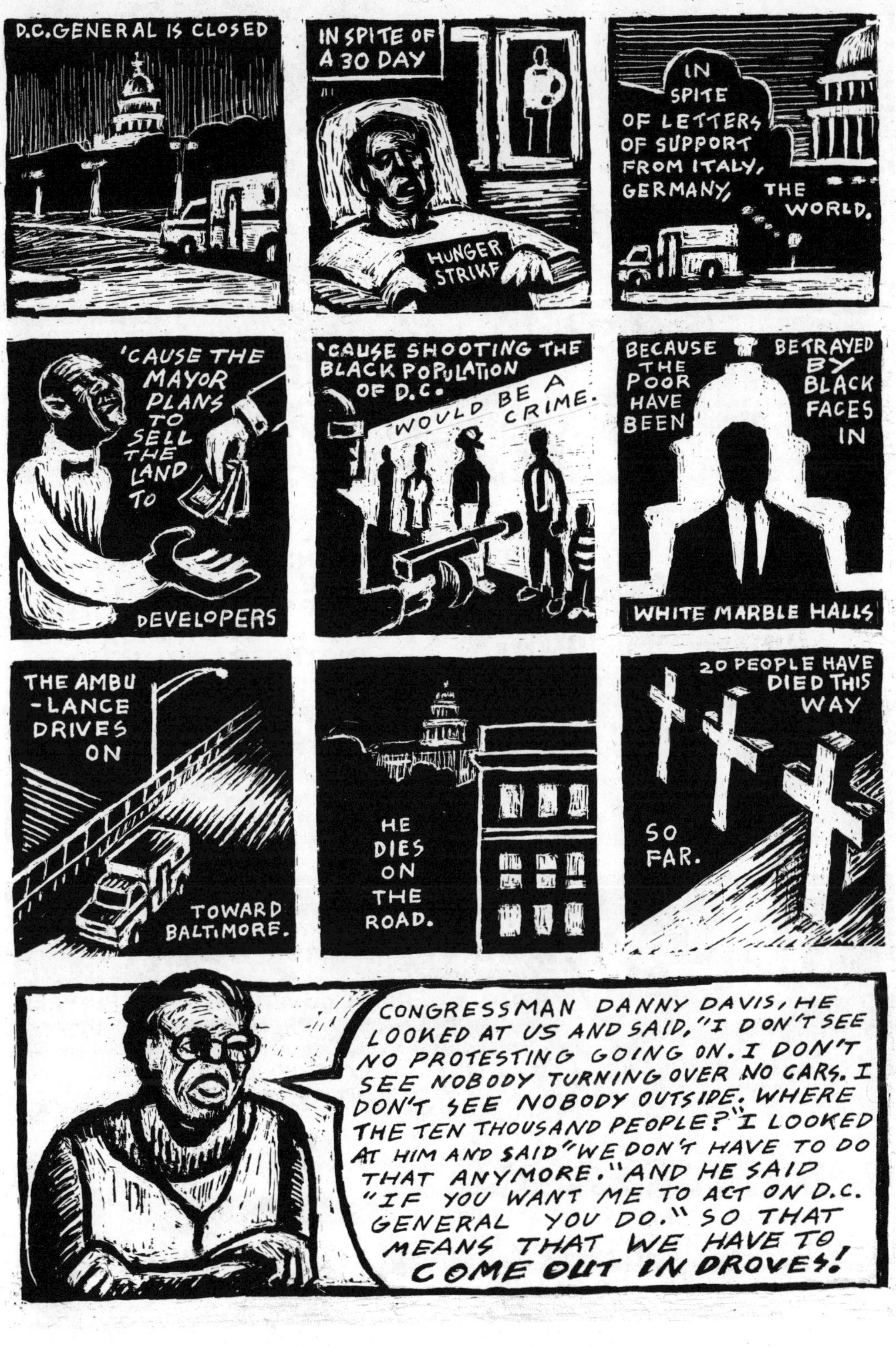
D.C.GENERAL IS CLOSED
IN SPITE OF A 30 DAY
HUNGER STRIKE
IN SPITE OF LETTERS OF SUPPORT FROM ITALY, GERMANY, THE WORLD.
'CAUSE THE MAYOR PLANS TO SELL THE LAND TO
DEVELOPERS
'CAUSE SHOOTING THE BLACK POPULATION OF D.C.
WOULD BE A CRIME.
BECAUSE THE POOR HAVE BEEN
BETRAYED BY BLACK FACES IN
WHITE MARBLE HALLS
THE AMBU-LANCE DRIVES ON
TOWARD BALTIMORE.
HE DIES ON THE ROAD.
20 PEOPLE HAVE DIED THIS WAY
SO FAR.
CONGRESSMAN DANNY DAVIS, HE LOOKED AT US AND SAID, "I DON'T SEE NO PROTESTING GOING ON. I DON'T SEE NOBODY TURNING OVER NO CARS. I DON'T SEE NOBODY OUTSIDE. WHERE THE TEN THOUSAND PEOPLE?" I LOOKED AT HIM AND SAID "WE DON'T HAVE TO DO THAT ANYMORE." AND HE SAID "IF YOU WANT ME TO ACT ON D.C. GENERAL YOU DO." SO THAT MEANS THAT WE HAVE TO COME OUT IN DROVES!

9-11-2001, AN ATTACK ON THE PENTAGON LEFT MANY DEAD, OTHERS WOUNDED.

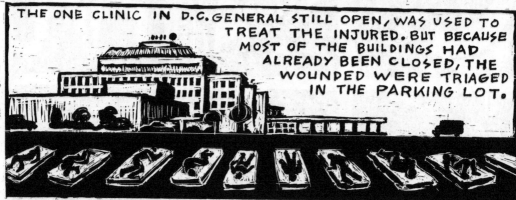

THE ONE CLINIC IN D.C. GENERAL STILL OPEN, WAS USED TO TREAT THE INJURED. BUT BECAUSE MOST OF THE BUILDINGS HAD ALREADY BEEN CLOSED, THE WOUNDED WERE TRIAGED IN THE PARKING LOT.

D.C. GENERAL WAS THE ONLY FACILITY IN D.C. EQUIPPED TO DEAL WITH GERM WARFARE, SO IT WAS REOPENED FOR ONE DAY TO CHECK GOVERNMENT EMPLOYEES FOR ANTHRAX. THE MAYOR WAS FIRST IN LINE. WHY IS IT THAT POLITICIANS, WHO ARE FIRST TO WAVE THE FLAG, ARE FIRST TO TAKE WHAT PEOPLE NEED? WE NEED A NEW TYPE OF PATRIOTISM THAT PUTS THE HEALTH OF THE PEOPLE AHEAD OF THE HEALTH OF THE STATE.

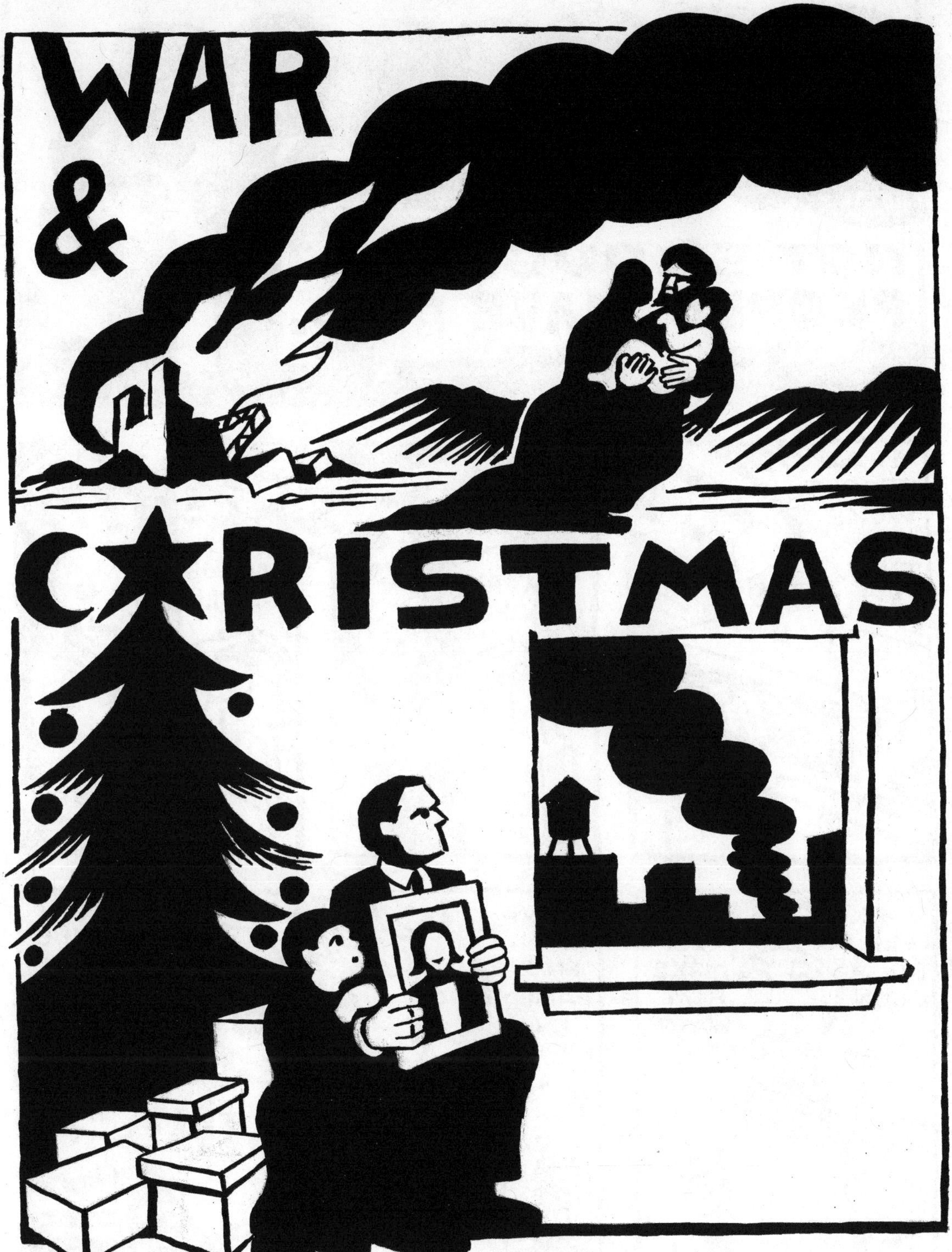
WAR
&
CHRISTMAS

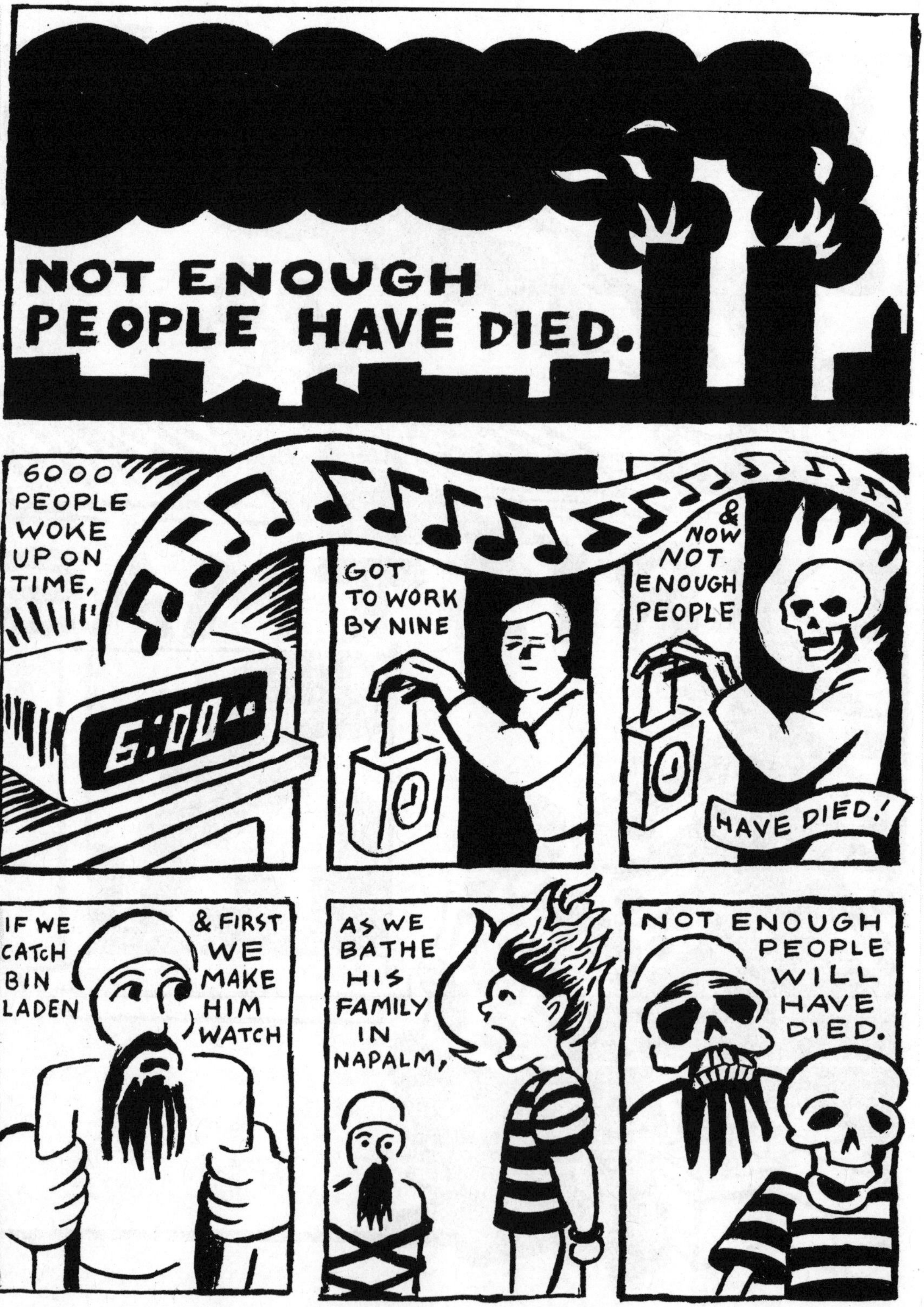

NOT ENOUGH PEOPLE HAVE DIED.
6000 PEOPLE WOKE UP ON TIME,
6:00
GOT TO WORK BY NINE
& NOW NOT ENOUGH PEOPLE
HAVE DIED!
IF WE CATCH BIN LADEN
& FIRST WE MAKE HIM WATCH
AS WE BATHE HIS FAMILY IN NAPALM,
NOT ENOUGH PEOPLE WILL HAVE DIED.

IF WE CAPTURE ALL THE TERRORISTS,

TOR-TURE THEM TO DEATH

ON T.V. NOT ENOUGH PEOPLE WILL DIE.

IF WE KILL ALL THE ARABS

AND THEIR CHILDREN AND THEIR CHILDREN'S CHILDREN,

NOT ENOUGH PEOPLE WILL HAVE DIED.

WE HAVE TO GO AFTER EVERYONE WHO'S EVER GIVEN MONEY TO TERROR-ISTS.

LET'S START WITH RONALD REAGAN.

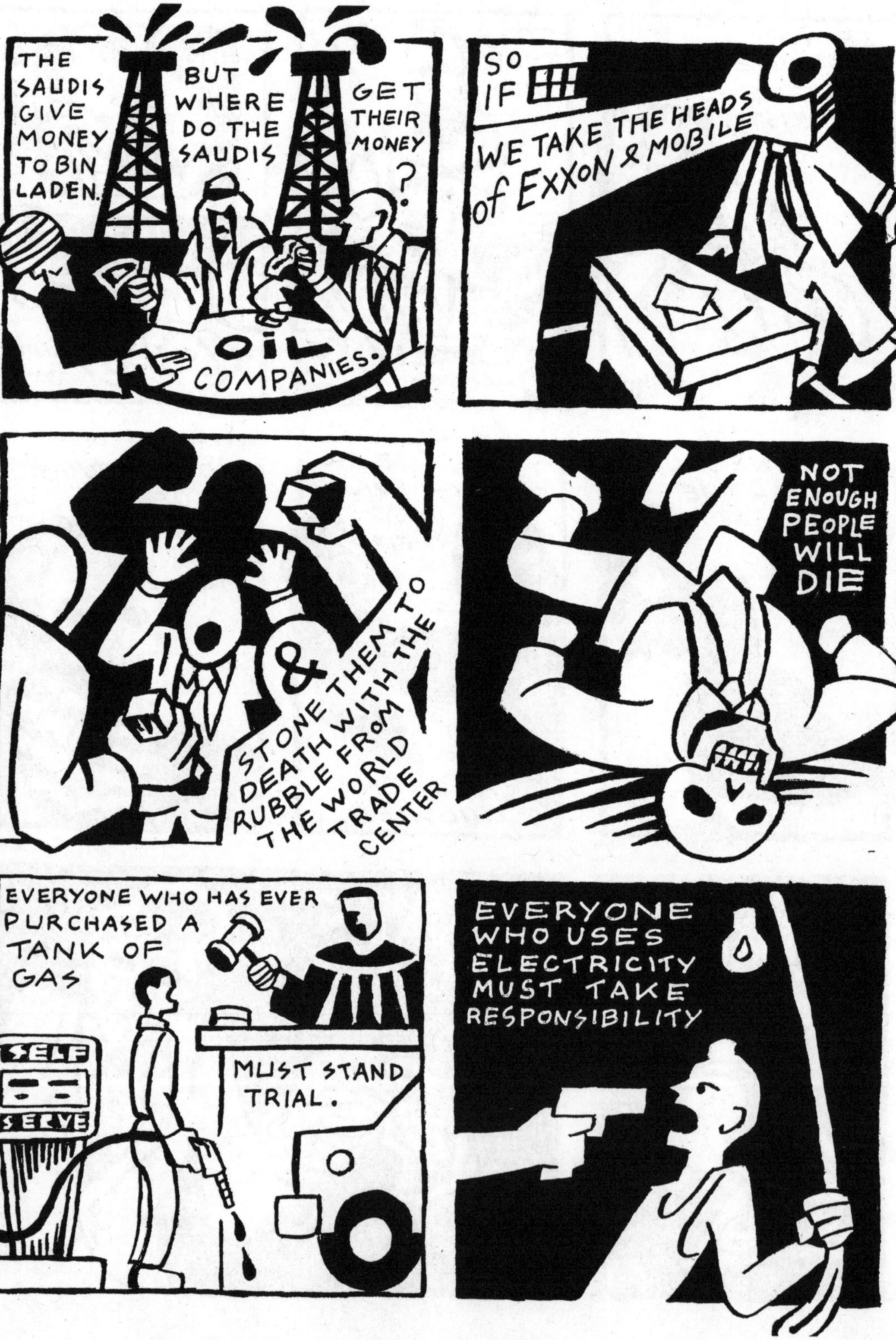
THE SAUDIS GIVE MONEY TO BIN LADEN.
BUT WHERE DO THE SAUDIS
GET THEIR MONEY?
OIL COMPANIES.
SO IF
WE TAKE THE HEADS of EXXON & MOBILE
& STONE THEM TO DEATH WITH THE RUBBLE FROM THE WORLD TRADE CENTER
NOT ENOUGH PEOPLE WILL DIE
EVERYONE WHO HAS EVER PURCHASED A TANK OF GAS
MUST STAND TRIAL.
SELF SERVE
EVERYONE WHO USES ELECTRICITY MUST TAKE RESPONSIBILITY

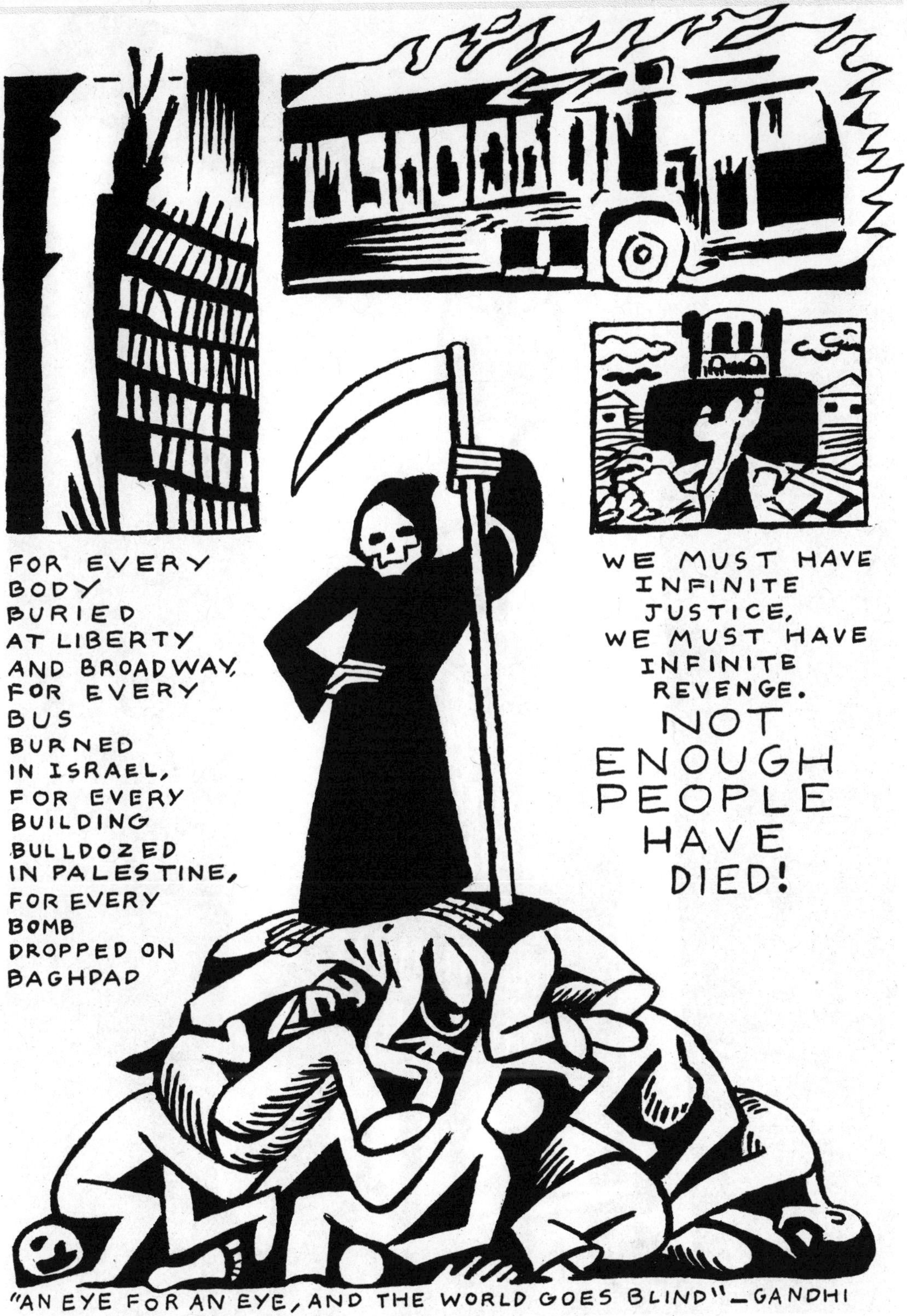
FOR EVERY BODY BURIED AT LIBERTY AND BROADWAY, FOR EVERY BUS BURNED IN ISRAEL, FOR EVERY BUILDING BULLDOZED IN PALESTINE, FOR EVERY BOMB DROPPED ON BAGHDAD
WE MUST HAVE INFINITE JUSTICE, WE MUST HAVE INFINITE REVENGE.
NOT ENOUGH PEOPLE HAVE DIED!
"AN EYE FOR AN EYE, AND THE WORLD GOES BLIND" _GANDHI

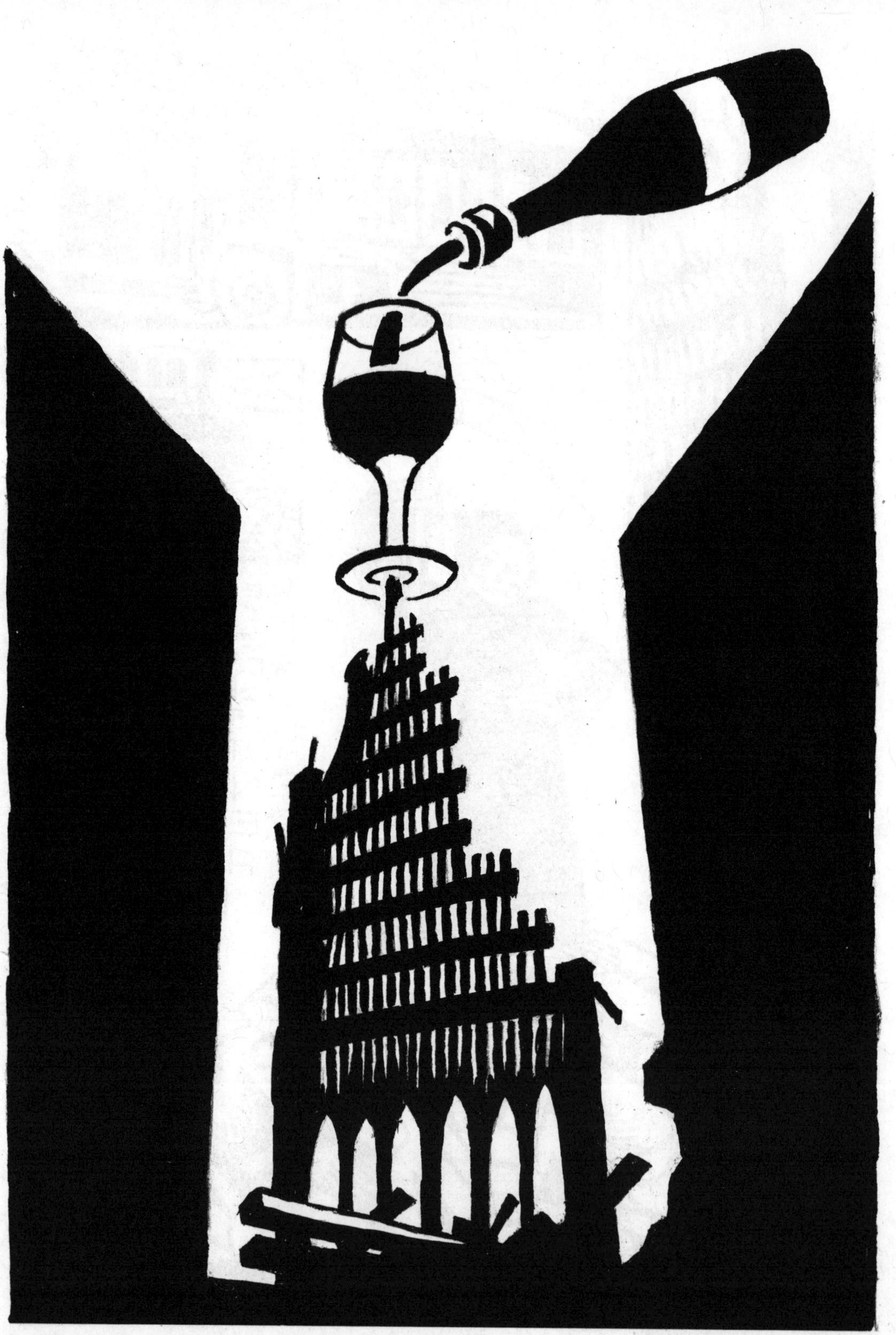

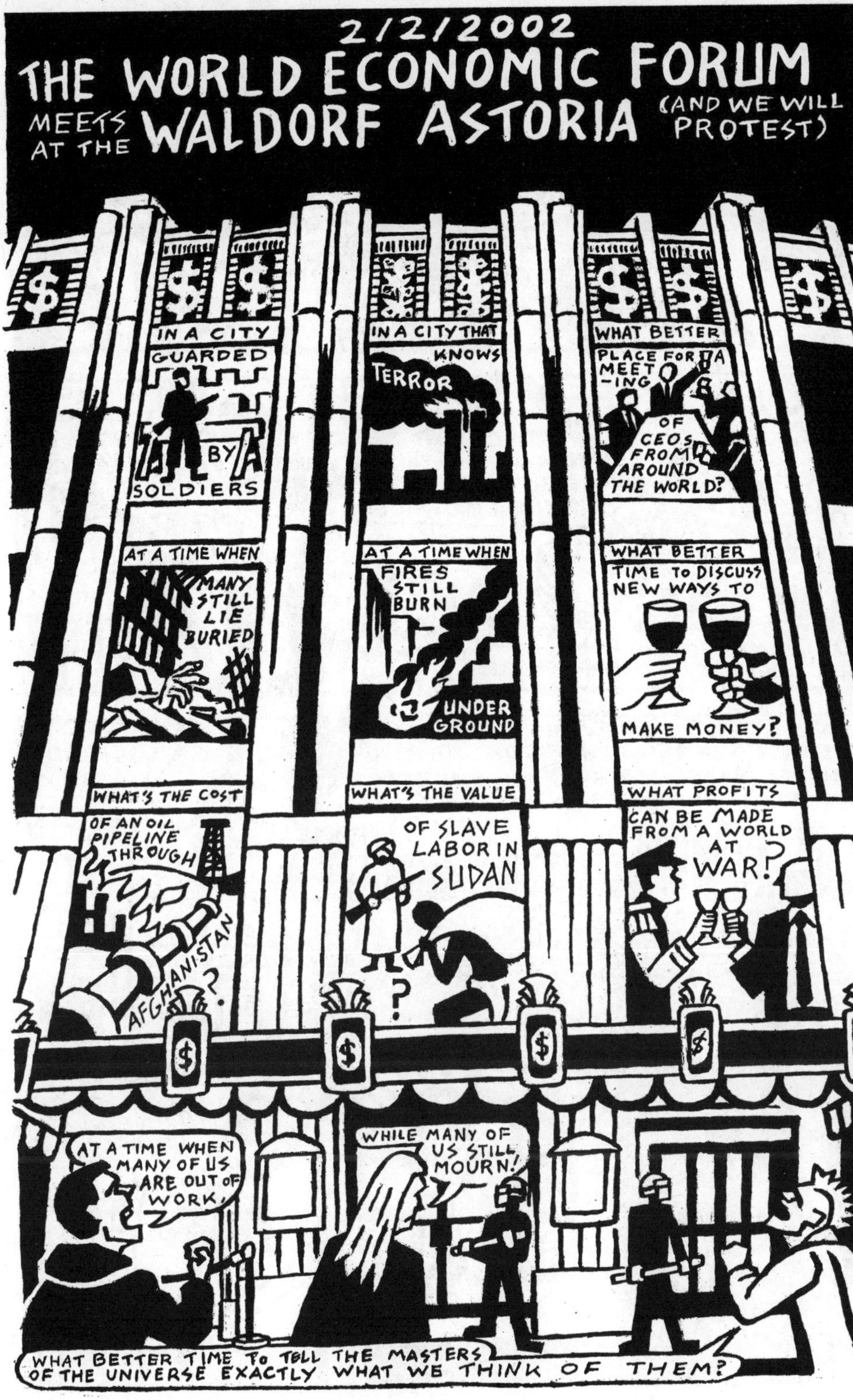
2/2/2002
THE WORLD ECONOMIC FORUM
MEETS AT THE WALDORF ASTORIA (AND WE WILL PROTEST)
IN A CITY GUARDED BY SOLDIERS
IN A CITY THAT KNOWS TERROR
WHAT BETTER PLACE FOR A MEET-ING OF CEOS FROM AROUND THE WORLD?
AT A TIME WHEN MANY STILL LIE BURIED
AT A TIME WHEN FIRES STILL BURN UNDER GROUND
WHAT BETTER TIME TO DISCUSS NEW WAYS TO MAKE MONEY?
WHAT'S THE COST OF AN OIL PIPELINE THROUGH AFGHANISTAN?
WHAT'S THE VALUE OF SLAVE LABOR IN SUDAN ?
WHAT PROFITS CAN BE MADE FROM A WORLD AT WAR?
AT A TIME WHEN MANY OF US ARE OUT OF WORK,
WHILE MANY OF US STILL MOURN!
WHAT BETTER TIME TO TELL THE MASTERS OF THE UNIVERSE EXACTLY WHAT WE THINK OF THEM?

DOWNSIZING THE HEROES

SETH 2004

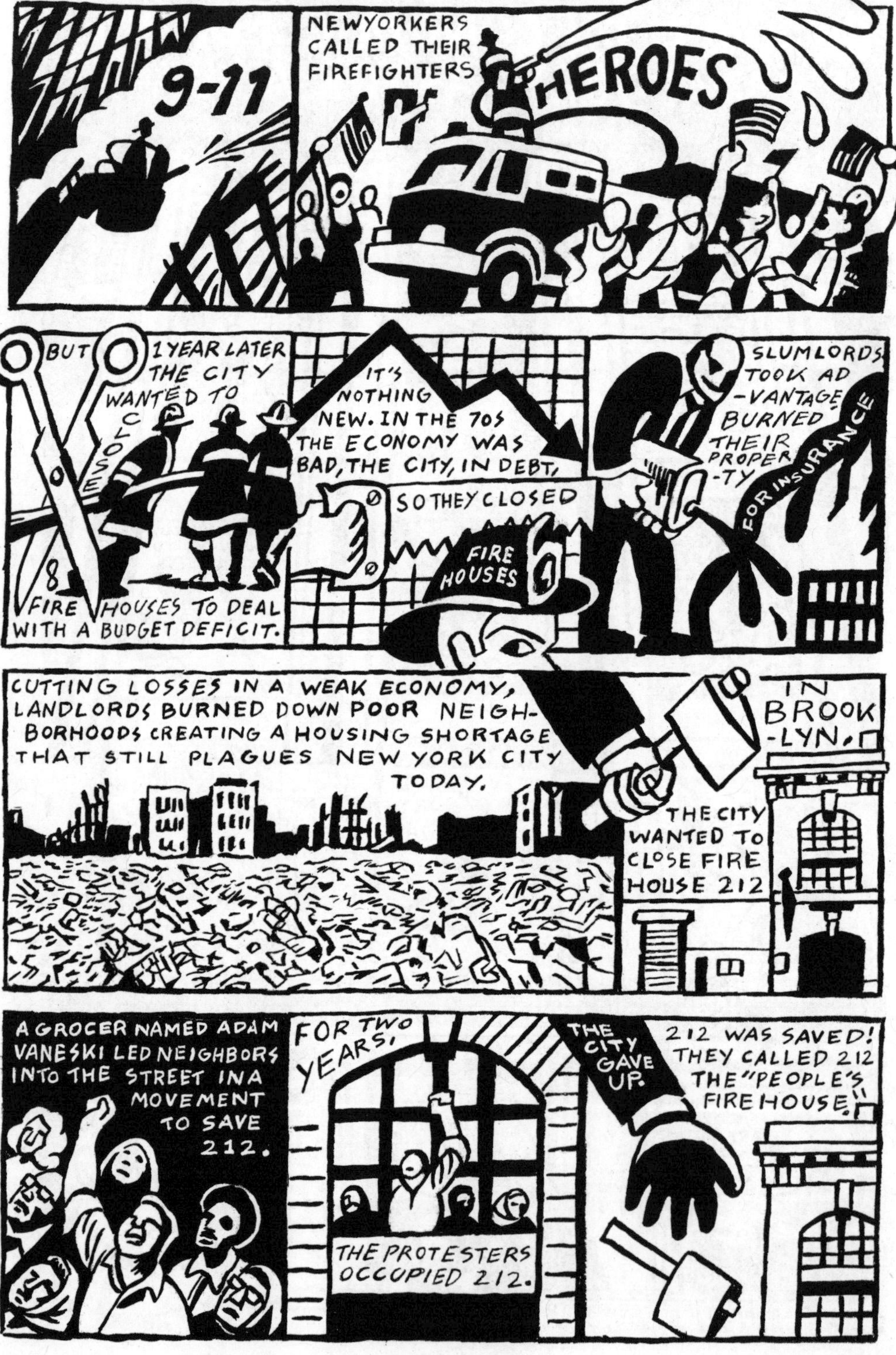

9-11
NEWYORKERS CALLED THEIR FIREFIGHTERS
HEROES
BUT 1 YEAR LATER THE CITY WANTED TO CLOSE 8 FIRE HOUSES TO DEAL WITH A BUDGET DEFICIT.
IT'S NOTHING NEW. IN THE 70S THE ECONOMY WAS BAD, THE CITY, IN DEBT,
SO THEY CLOSED
FIRE HOUSES
SLUMLORDS TOOK AD-VANTAGE, BURNED THEIR PROPER-TY
FOR INSURANCE
CUTTING LOSSES IN A WEAK ECONOMY, LANDLORDS BURNED DOWN POOR NEIGH-BORHOODS CREATING A HOUSING SHORTAGE THAT STILL PLAGUES NEW YORK CITY TODAY.
IN BROOK-LYN,
THE CITY WANTED TO CLOSE FIRE HOUSE 212
A GROCER NAMED ADAM VANESKI LED NEIGHBORS INTO THE STREET IN A MOVEMENT TO SAVE 212.
FOR TWO YEARS,
THE PROTESTERS OCCUPIED 212.
THE CITY GAVE UP.
212 WAS SAVED! THEY CALLED 212 THE "PEOPLE'S FIRE HOUSE."

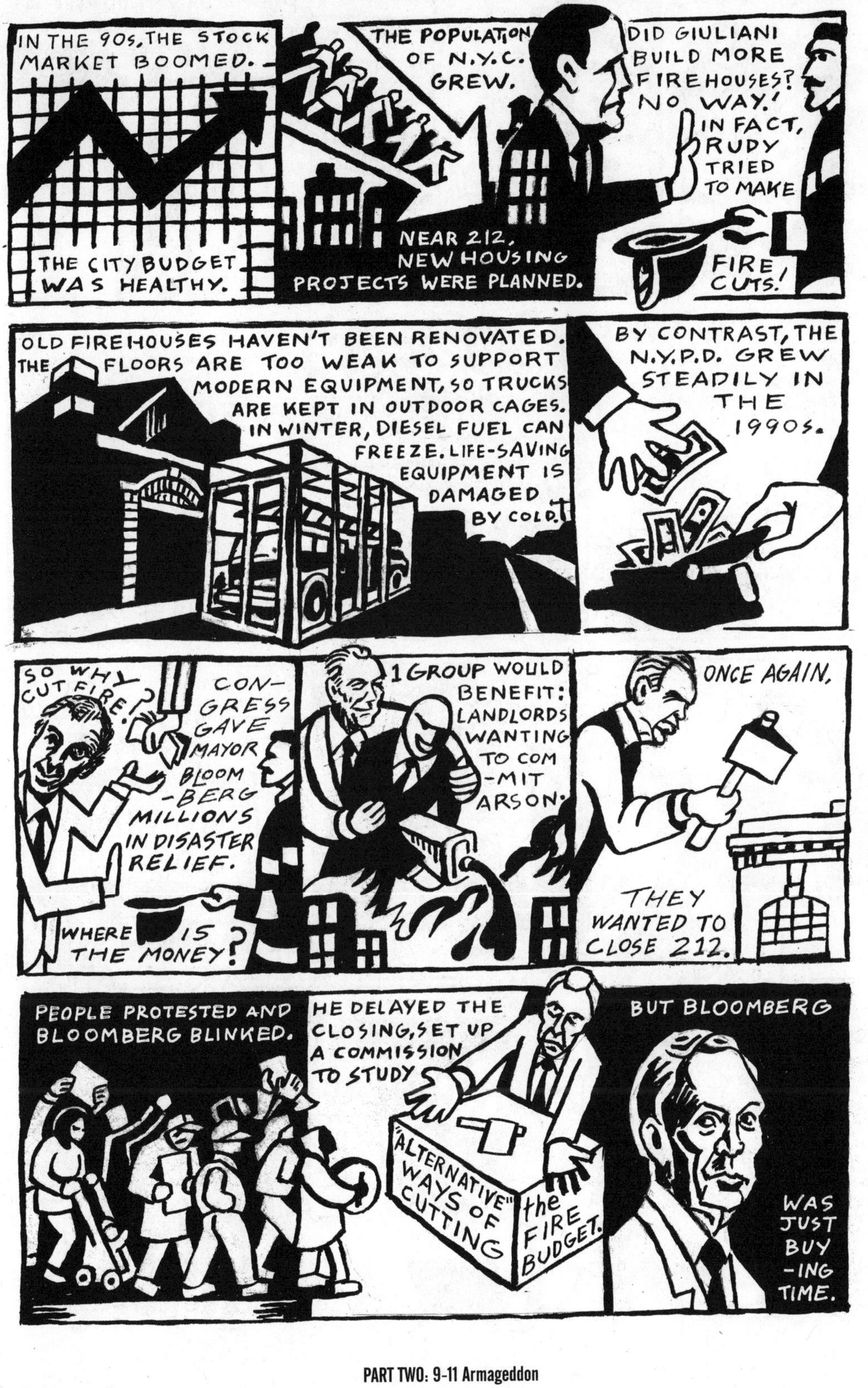
IN THE 90s, THE STOCK MARKET BOOMED.
THE CITY BUDGET WAS HEALTHY.
THE POPULATION OF N.Y.C. GREW.
NEAR 212, NEW HOUSING PROJECTS WERE PLANNED.
DID GIULIANI BUILD MORE FIREHOUSES? NO WAY!
IN FACT, RUDY TRIED TO MAKE
FIRE CUTS!
OLD FIREHOUSES HAVEN'T BEEN RENOVATED. THE FLOORS ARE TOO WEAK TO SUPPORT MODERN EQUIPMENT, SO TRUCKS ARE KEPT IN OUTDOOR CAGES. IN WINTER, DIESEL FUEL CAN FREEZE. LIFE-SAVING EQUIPMENT IS DAMAGED BY COLD.
BY CONTRAST, THE N.Y.P.D. GREW STEADILY IN THE 1990s.
SO WHY CUT FIRE?
CONGRESS GAVE MAYOR BLOOMBERG MILLIONS IN DISASTER RELIEF.
WHERE IS THE MONEY?
1 GROUP WOULD BENEFIT: LANDLORDS WANTING TO COMMIT ARSON.
ONCE AGAIN,
THEY WANTED TO CLOSE 212.
PEOPLE PROTESTED AND BLOOMBERG BLINKED.
HE DELAYED THE CLOSING, SET UP A COMMISSION TO STUDY
"ALTERNATIVE" WAYS OF CUTTING
the FIRE BUDGET.
BUT BLOOMBERG
WAS JUST BUYING TIME.

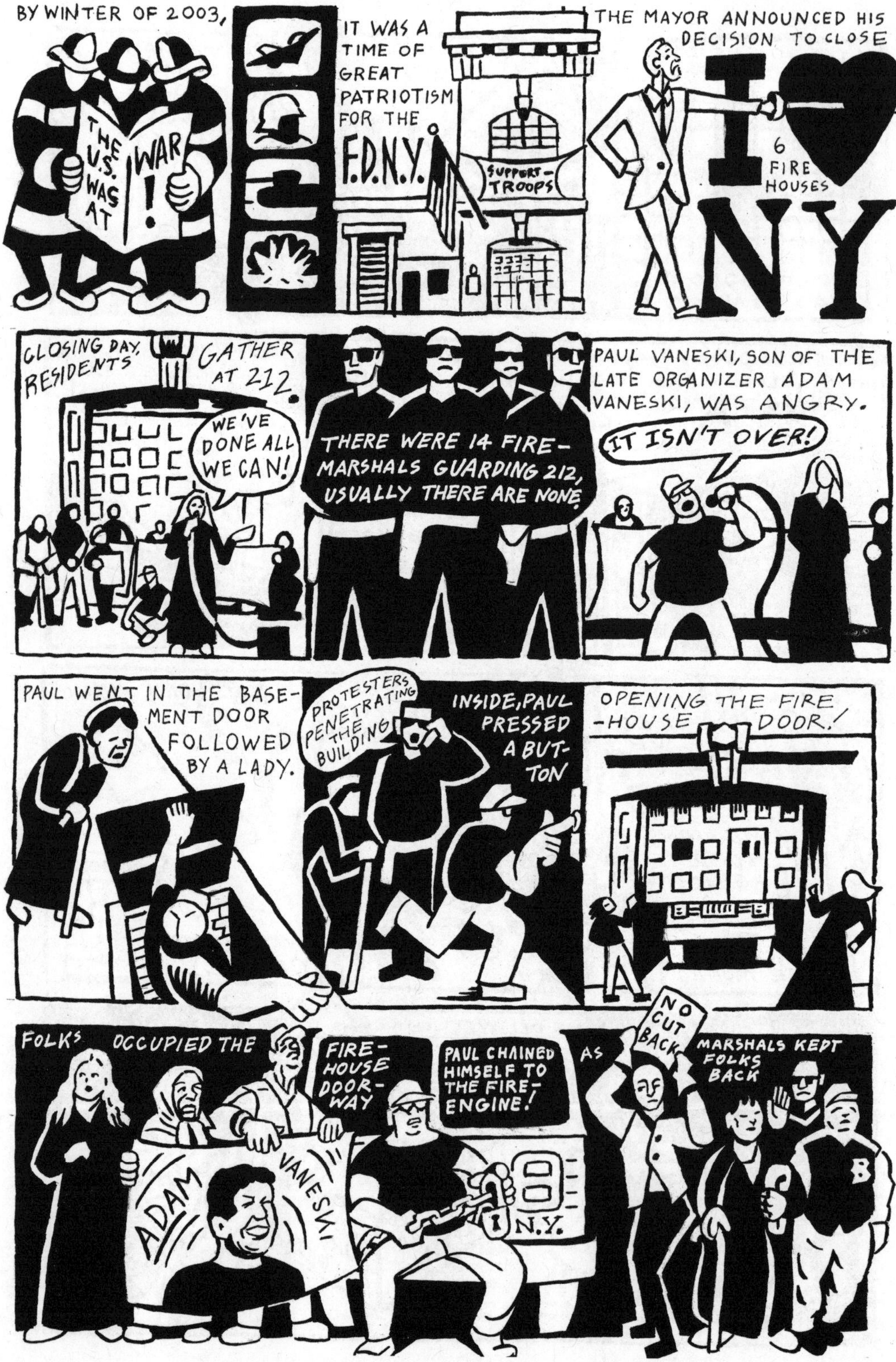
BY WINTER OF 2003,
THE U.S. WAS AT WAR!
IT WAS A TIME OF GREAT PATRIOTISM FOR THE F.D.N.Y.
SUPPORT TROOPS
THE MAYOR ANNOUNCED HIS DECISION TO CLOSE
I ♥ NY
6 FIRE HOUSES
CLOSING DAY, RESIDENTS GATHER AT 212.
WE'VE DONE ALL WE CAN!
THERE WERE 14 FIRE-MARSHALS GUARDING 212, USUALLY THERE ARE NONE.
PAUL VANESKI, SON OF THE LATE ORGANIZER ADAM VANESKI, WAS ANGRY.
IT ISN'T OVER!
PAUL WENT IN THE BASE-MENT DOOR FOLLOWED BY A LADY.
PROTESTERS PENETRATING THE BUILDING
INSIDE, PAUL PRESSED A BUT-TON
OPENING THE FIRE-HOUSE DOOR!
FOLKS OCCUPIED THE
FIRE-HOUSE DOOR-WAY
ADAM VANESKI
PAUL CHAINED HIMSELF TO THE FIRE-ENGINE!
N.Y.
AS
NO CUT BACK
MARSHALS KEPT FOLKS BACK

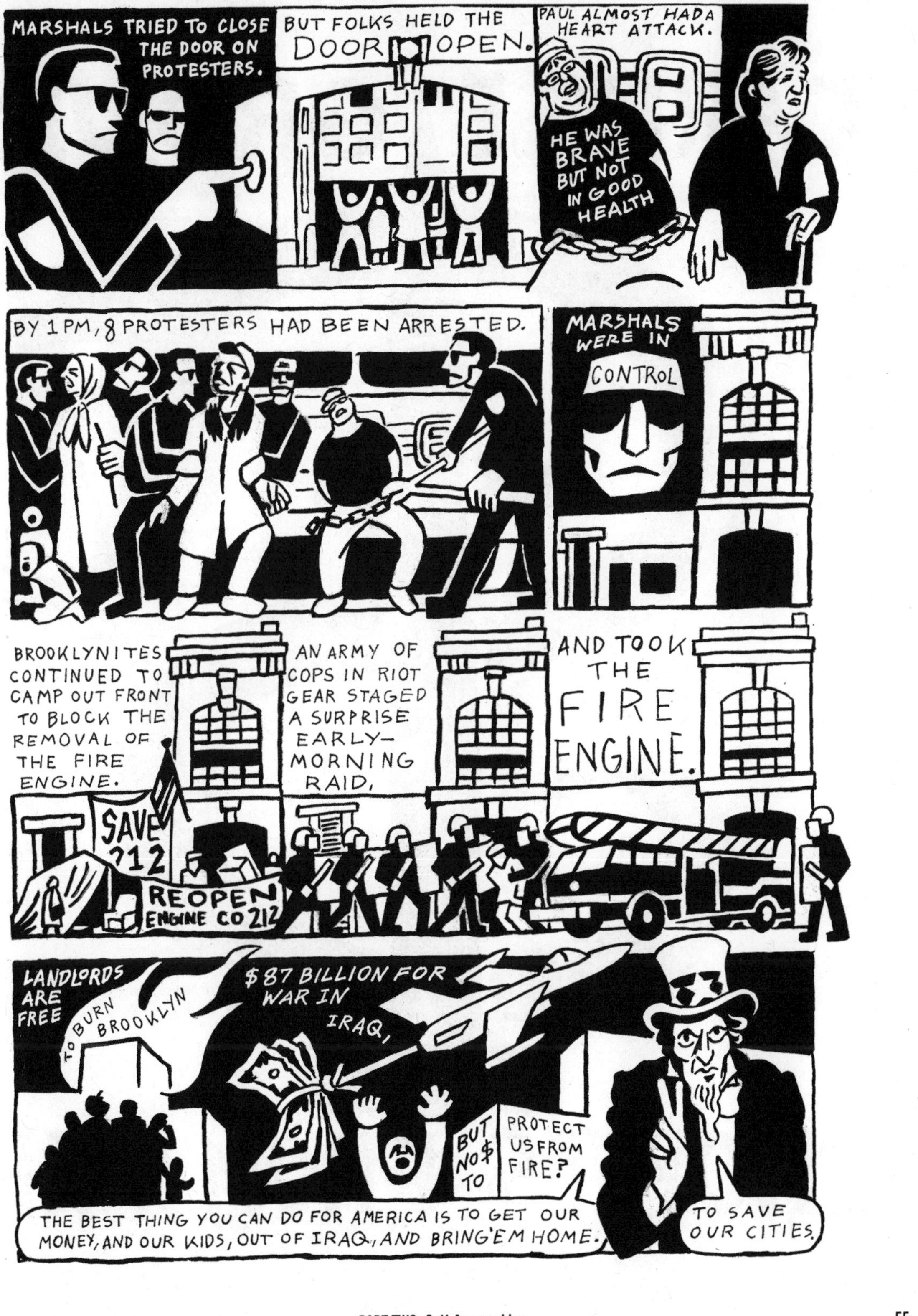
MARSHALS TRIED TO CLOSE THE DOOR ON PROTESTERS.
BUT FOLKS HELD THE DOOR OPEN.
PAUL ALMOST HAD A HEART ATTACK.
HE WAS BRAVE BUT NOT IN GOOD HEALTH
BY 1 PM, 8 PROTESTERS HAD BEEN ARRESTED.
MARSHALS WERE IN CONTROL
BROOKLYNITES CONTINUED TO CAMP OUT FRONT TO BLOCK THE REMOVAL OF THE FIRE ENGINE.
SAVE 212
REOPEN ENGINE CO 212
AN ARMY OF COPS IN RIOT GEAR STAGED A SURPRISE EARLY-MORNING RAID,
AND TOOK THE FIRE ENGINE.
LANDLORDS ARE FREE
TO BURN BROOKLYN
$87 BILLION FOR WAR IN IRAQ,
BUT NO $ TO
PROTECT US FROM FIRE?
THE BEST THING YOU CAN DO FOR AMERICA IS TO GET OUR MONEY, AND OUR KIDS, OUT OF IRAQ, AND BRING'EM HOME.
TO SAVE OUR CITIES.

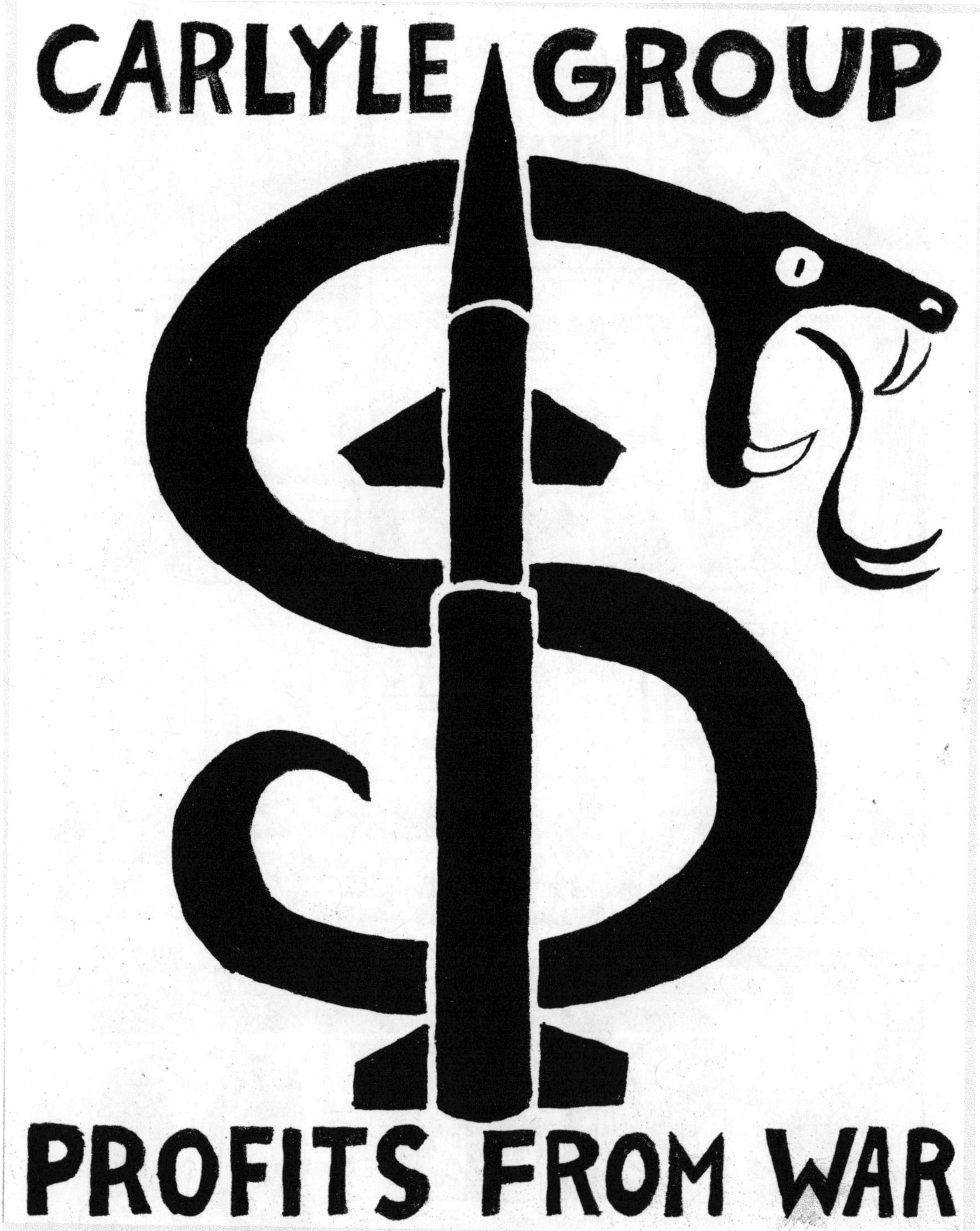
CARLYLE GROUP
PROFITS FROM WAR

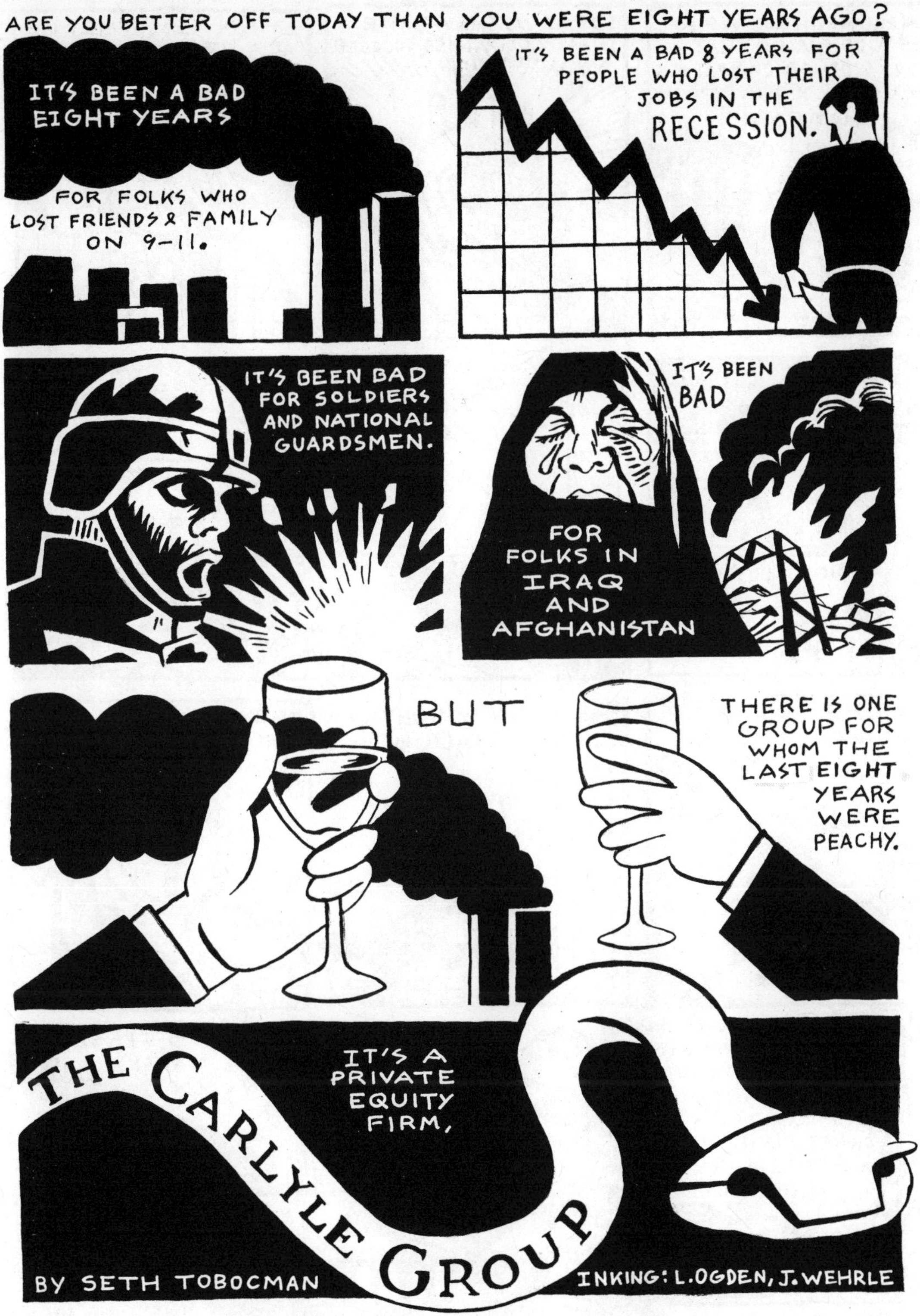
ARE YOU BETTER OFF TODAY THAN YOU WERE EIGHT YEARS AGO?
IT'S BEEN A BAD EIGHT YEARS
FOR FOLKS WHO LOST FRIENDS & FAMILY ON 9-11.
IT'S BEEN A BAD 8 YEARS FOR PEOPLE WHO LOST THEIR JOBS IN THE RECESSION.
IT'S BEEN BAD FOR SOLDIERS AND NATIONAL GUARDSMEN.
IT'S BEEN BAD
FOR FOLKS IN IRAQ AND AFGHANISTAN
BUT
THERE IS ONE GROUP FOR WHOM THE LAST EIGHT YEARS WERE PEACHY.
THE CARLYLE GROUP
IT'S A PRIVATE EQUITY FIRM,
BY SETH TOBOCMAN
INKING: L.OGDEN, J.WEHRLE

A PRIVATE EQUITY FIRM IS A COMPANY THAT BUYS OTHER COMPANIES — USUALLY FAILING COMPANIES.

IDEALLY, THEY MAKE THESE COMPANIES SUCCEED,

THEN SELL THEM AT A PROFIT.

CARLYLE PREFERS TO BUY COMPANIES THAT DO BUSINESS WITH THE GOVERNMENT.

1989, THE BERLIN WALL FELL. THE COLD WAR WAS OVER. THE MILITARY BUDGET WAS CUT. HARD TIMES FOR WAR RELATED INDUSTRIES.

CARLYLE BOUGHT UP MILITARY COMPANIES DIRT CHEAP.

THEY BOUGHT VAUGHT AIR CRAFT.

THEY BOUGHT U.S.I.S., WHO DO BACKGROUND CHECKS ON AIR-LINE EMPLOYEES.

THEY BOUGHT B.D.M., A COMPANY WORKING WITH THE GOVERNMENT OF SAUDI ARABIA. B.D.M., IN TURN OWNED VINNELL, A MERCENARY CORPORATION.

WHO GUARD SAUDI OIL FIELDS.

CARLYLE BOUGHT UNITED DEFENSE INDUSTRIES, WOULD-BE MAKERS OF A GIANT CANNON CALLED THE CRUSADER.

IT WAS TOO BIG, TOO HEAVY, FOR MODERN WARFARE.

THE ARMY DIDN'T WANT THE CRUSADER.

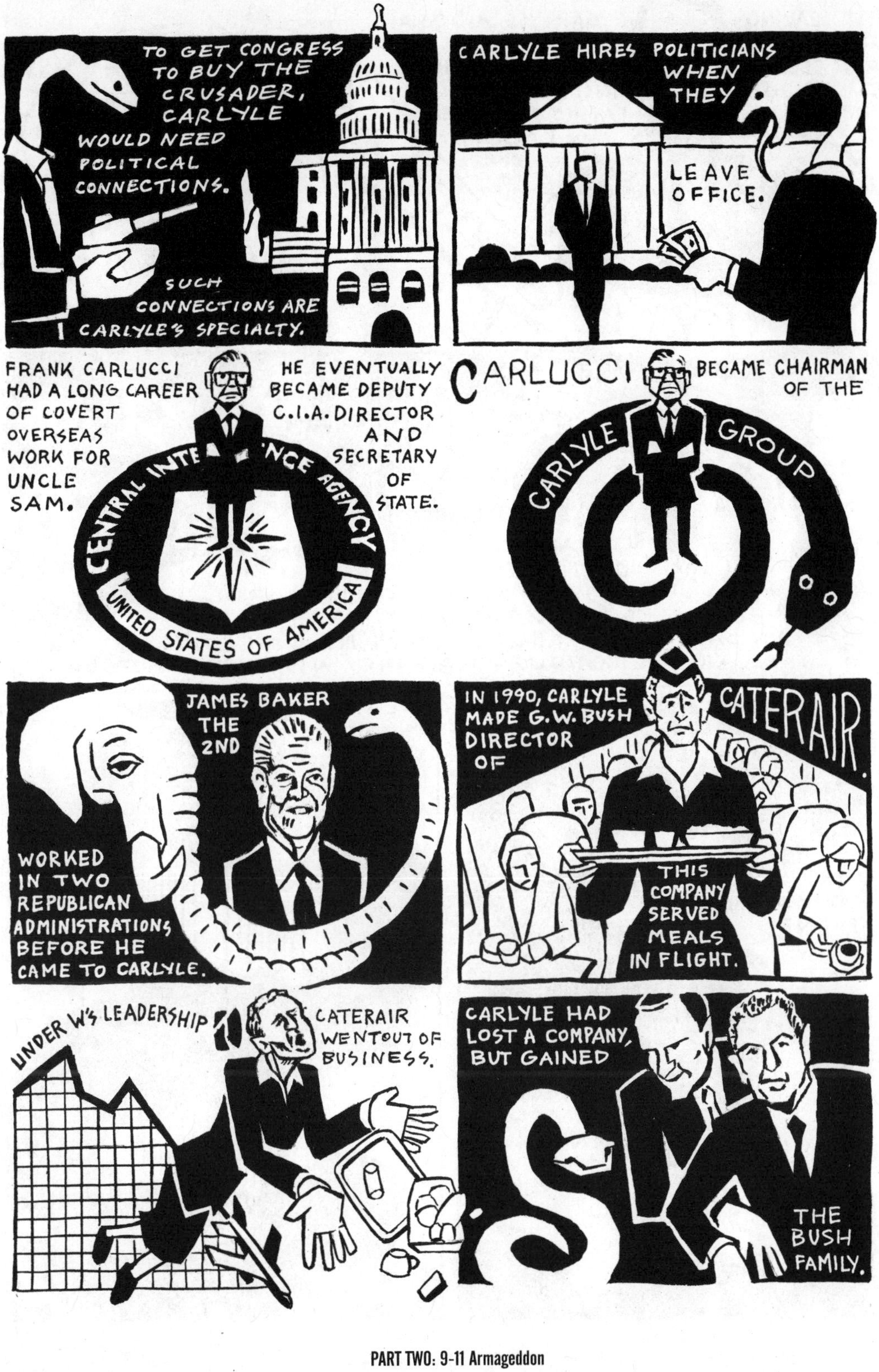
TO GET CONGRESS TO BUY THE CRUSADER, CARLYLE WOULD NEED POLITICAL CONNECTIONS.
SUCH CONNECTIONS ARE CARLYLE'S SPECIALTY.
CARLYLE HIRES POLITICIANS WHEN THEY
LEAVE OFFICE.
FRANK CARLUCCI HAD A LONG CAREER OF COVERT OVERSEAS WORK FOR UNCLE SAM.
HE EVENTUALLY BECAME DEPUTY C.I.A. DIRECTOR AND SECRETARY OF STATE.
CENTRAL INTE
NCE AGENCY
UNITED STATES OF AMERICA
CARLUCCI BECAME CHAIRMAN OF THE
CARLYLE GROUP
JAMES BAKER THE 2ND
WORKED IN TWO REPUBLICAN ADMINISTRATIONS BEFORE HE CAME TO CARLYLE.
IN 1990, CARLYLE MADE G.W. BUSH DIRECTOR OF
CATERAIR.
THIS COMPANY SERVED MEALS IN FLIGHT.
UNDER W'S LEADERSHIP
CATERAIR WENTOUT OF BUSINESS.
CARLYLE HAD LOST A COMPANY, BUT GAINED
THE BUSH FAMILY.

AFTER LEAVING OFFICE, GEORGE SENIOR BECAME A CARLYLE BOARD MEMBER.

CARLYLE ALSO HAS DEALINGS WITH MANY WEALTHY SAUDIS INCLUDING THE FAMILY OF OSAMA BIN LADEN.

CARLYLE GROUP

AND SO, ON THE MORNING OF SEPTEMBER 11th 2001, GEORGE BUSH SENIOR AND THE BROTHER OF OSAMA BIN LADEN WERE BOTH ATTENDING A MEETING OF THE CARLYLE GROUP AT A FANCY WASHINGTON HOTEL.

DID THESE MEN KNOW WHAT WAS ABOUT TO HAPPEN?

WE MAY NEVER KNOW THE ANSWER.

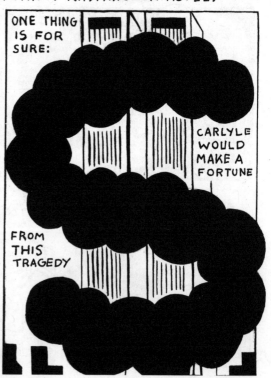

ONE THING IS FOR SURE:

CARLYLE WOULD MAKE A FORTUNE

FROM THIS TRAGEDY

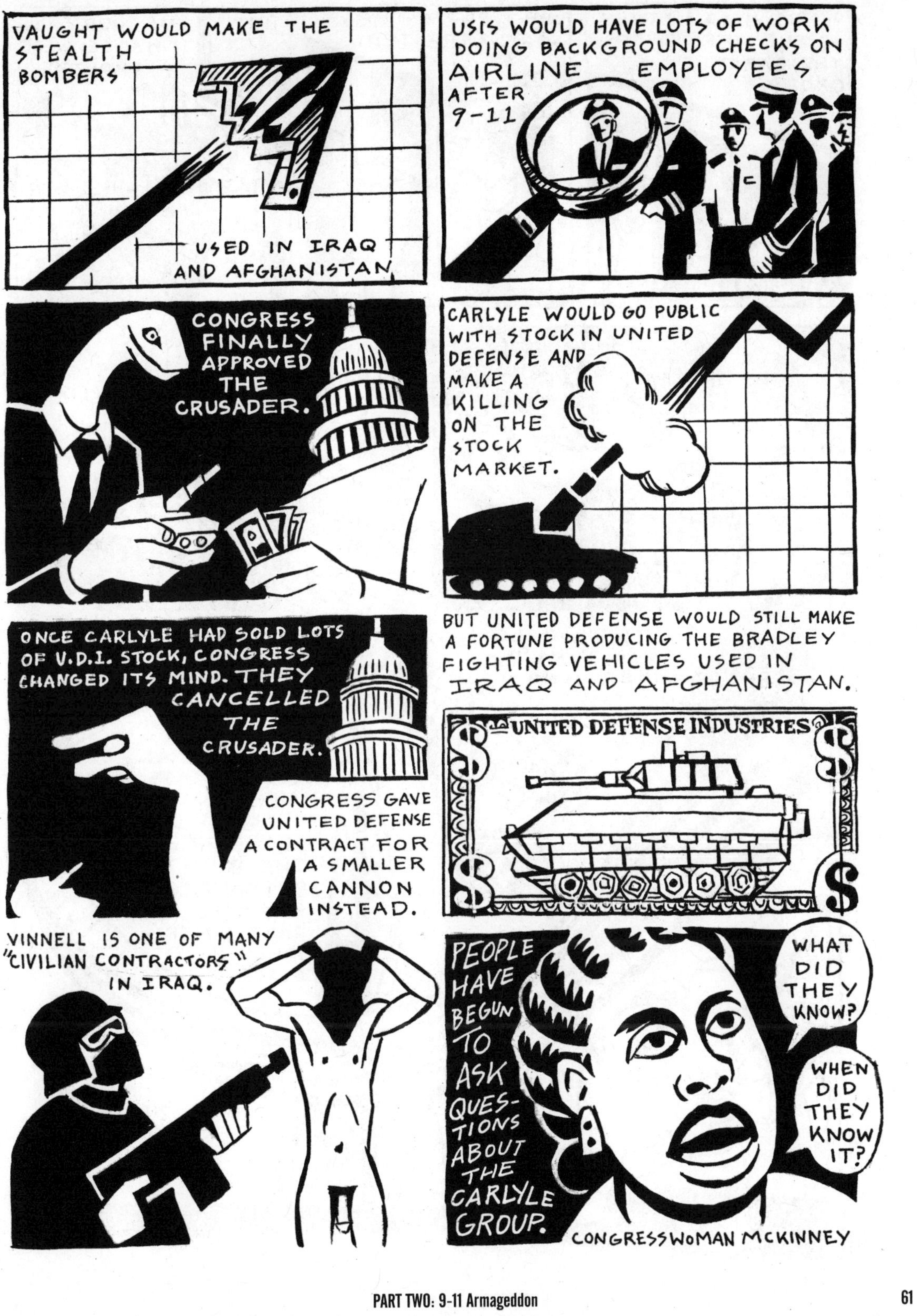
VAUGHT WOULD MAKE THE STEALTH BOMBERS
USED IN IRAQ AND AFGHANISTAN
USIS WOULD HAVE LOTS OF WORK DOING BACKGROUND CHECKS ON AIRLINE EMPLOYEES AFTER 9-11
CONGRESS FINALLY APPROVED THE CRUSADER.
CARLYLE WOULD GO PUBLIC WITH STOCK IN UNITED DEFENSE AND MAKE A KILLING ON THE STOCK MARKET.
ONCE CARLYLE HAD SOLD LOTS OF V.D.I. STOCK, CONGRESS CHANGED ITS MIND. THEY CANCELLED THE CRUSADER.
CONGRESS GAVE UNITED DEFENSE A CONTRACT FOR A SMALLER CANNON INSTEAD.
BUT UNITED DEFENSE WOULD STILL MAKE A FORTUNE PRODUCING THE BRADLEY FIGHTING VEHICLES USED IN IRAQ AND AFGHANISTAN.
UNITED DEFENSE INDUSTRIES
VINNELL IS ONE OF MANY "CIVILIAN CONTRACTORS" IN IRAQ.
PEOPLE HAVE BEGUN TO ASK QUESTIONS ABOUT THE CARLYLE GROUP.
WHAT DID THEY KNOW?
WHEN DID THEY KNOW IT?
CONGRESSWOMAN MCKINNEY

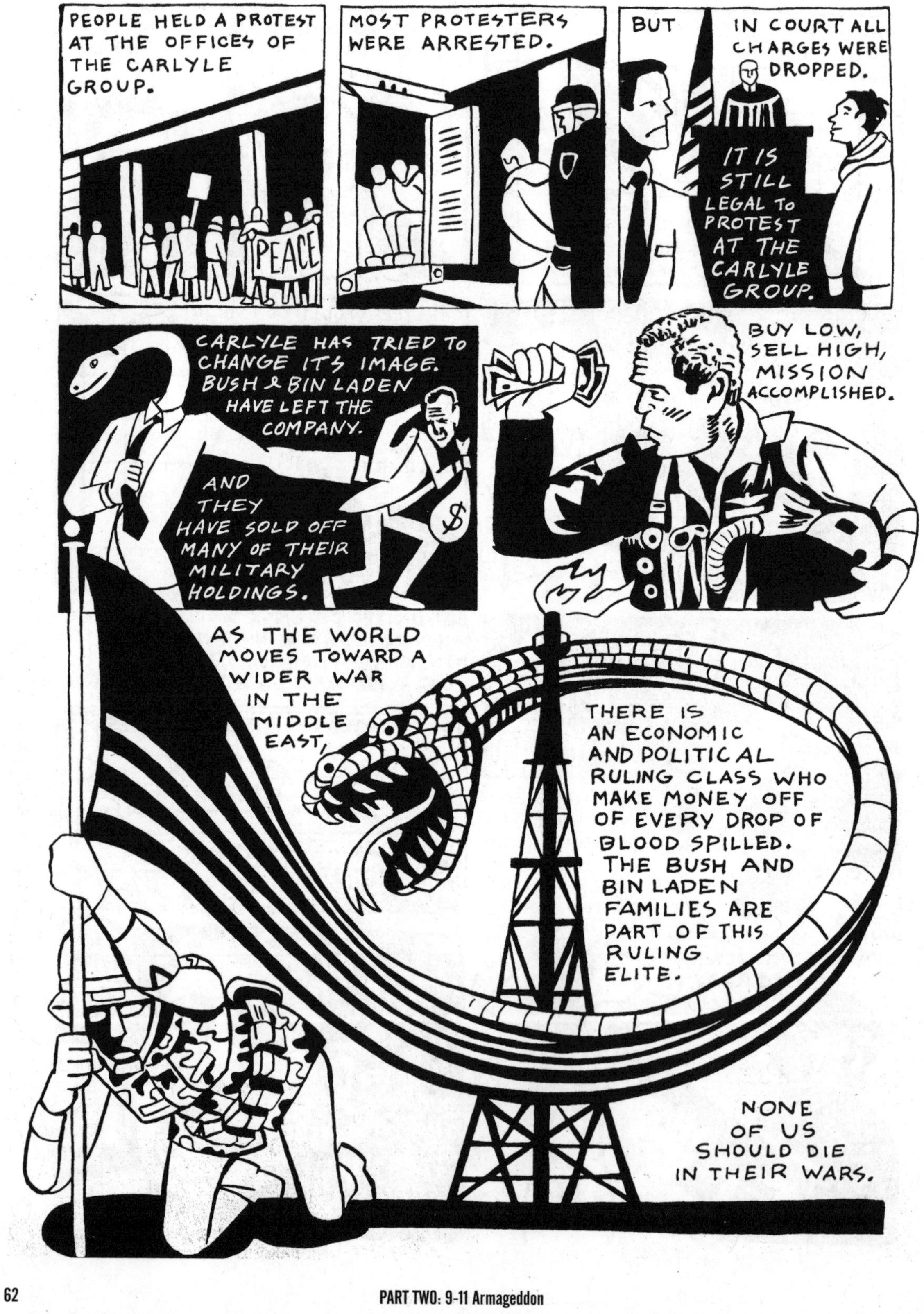
PEOPLE HELD A PROTEST AT THE OFFICES OF THE CARLYLE GROUP.
PEACE
MOST PROTESTERS WERE ARRESTED.
BUT
IN COURT ALL CHARGES WERE DROPPED.
IT IS STILL LEGAL TO PROTEST AT THE CARLYLE GROUP.
CARLYLE HAS TRIED TO CHANGE ITS IMAGE. BUSH & BIN LADEN HAVE LEFT THE COMPANY.
AND THEY HAVE SOLD OFF MANY OF THEIR MILITARY HOLDINGS.
$
BUY LOW, SELL HIGH, MISSION ACCOMPLISHED.
AS THE WORLD MOVES TOWARD A WIDER WAR IN THE MIDDLE EAST,
THERE IS AN ECONOMIC AND POLITICAL RULING CLASS WHO MAKE MONEY OFF OF EVERY DROP OF BLOOD SPILLED. THE BUSH AND BIN LADEN FAMILIES ARE PART OF THIS RULING ELITE.
NONE OF US SHOULD DIE IN THEIR WARS.

Part Three:

No Blood For Oil!

NO BLOOD FOR OIL!

Hillary Clinton, John Edwards, and other leading democrats have finally come around to opposing the war in Iraq. At least verbally. But there were many people who opposed it before it started. Many people stood on street corners with signs, while others yelled "Kill 'em all!" out their car windows.

In 2002, I worked with a group called "No Blood For Oil" that was staging weekly and, sometimes, daily vigils in front of the U.N. to try to convince them not to support Bush's war plans. I formed an affinity group with other artists, called "World War 3 Arts In Action," which took on the job of providing the protesters with signs and banners. World War 3 Arts In Action would go on to provide visuals to a number of different antiwar groups.

The vast majority of people in the world have always been against this war, and they have now been joined by the majority of Americans. Only one question remains: In this country, which claims to export democracy, will the government act on the will of the people?

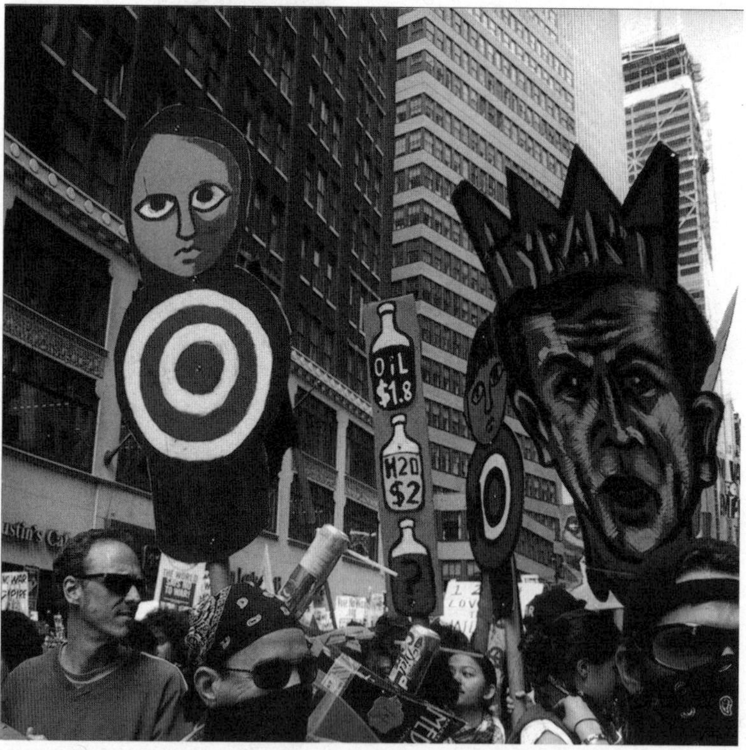

OiL
$1.8
H2O
$2

Above: Antiwar march with signs by World War 3 Arts In Action, and king's head by Christopher Cardinale. Photo by Christopher Cardinale.
Opposite: Placard at peace march. Photo by Christopher Cardinale.

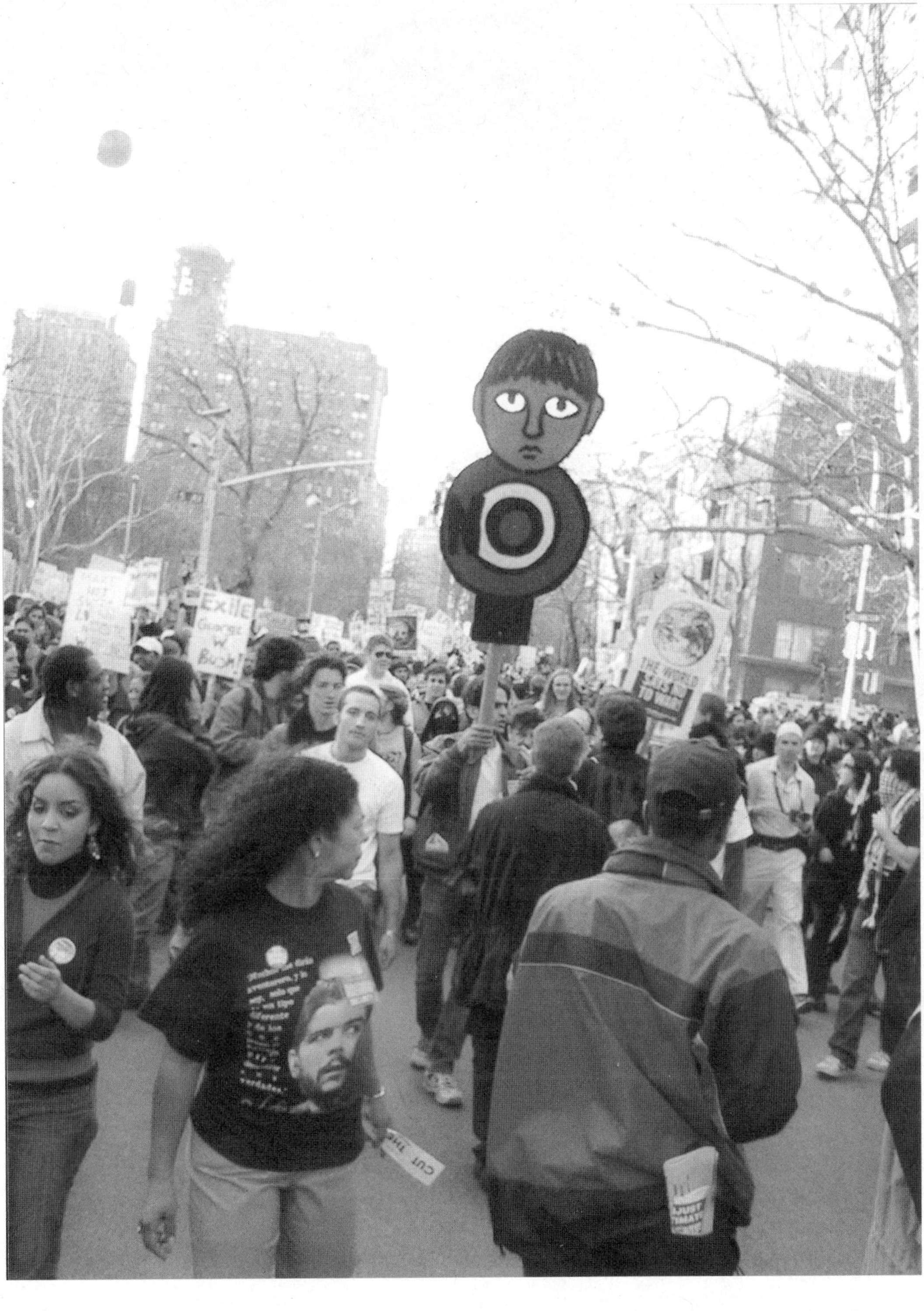
EXILE
George W Bush!

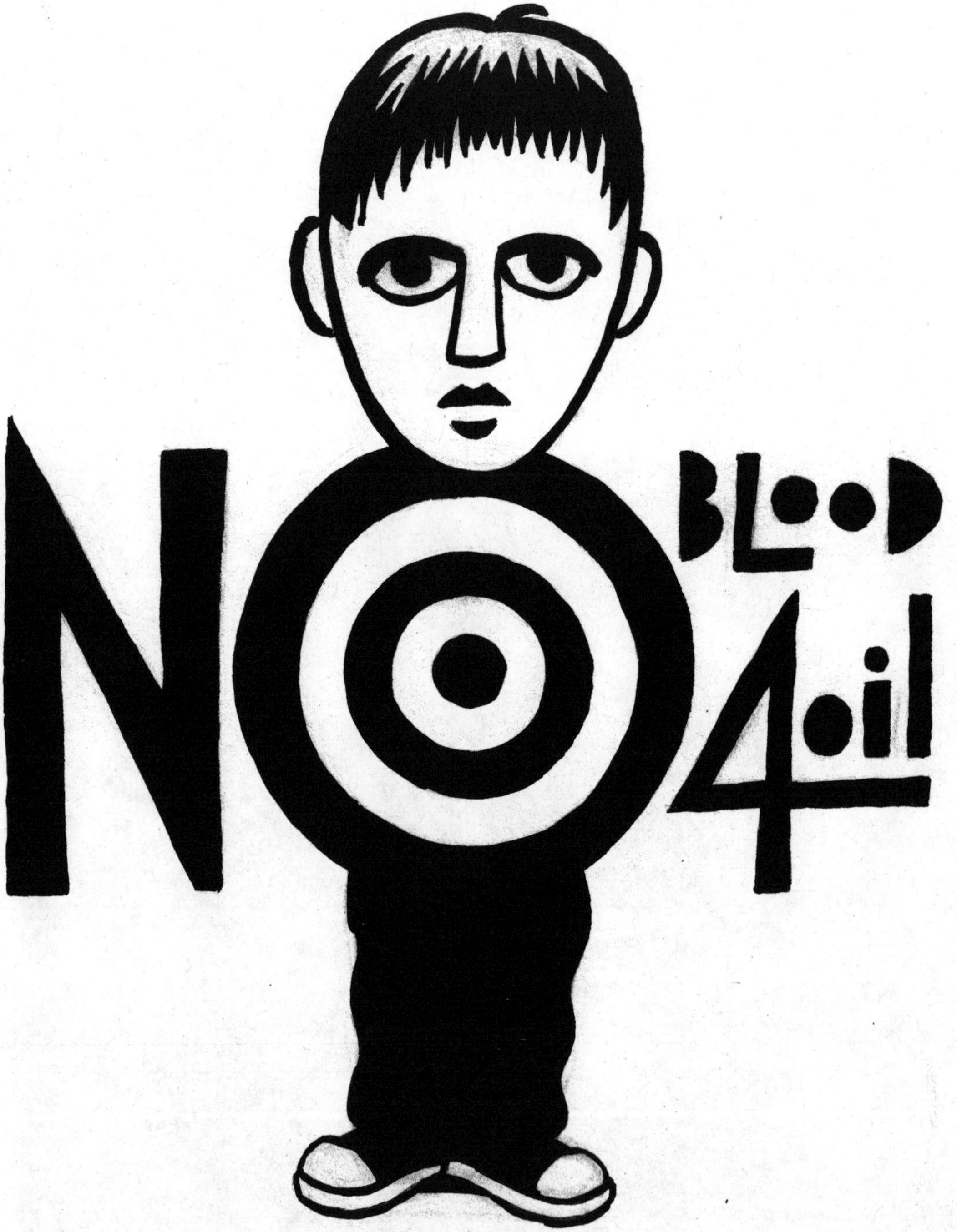
NO
BLOOD
4oil
SETH 2003

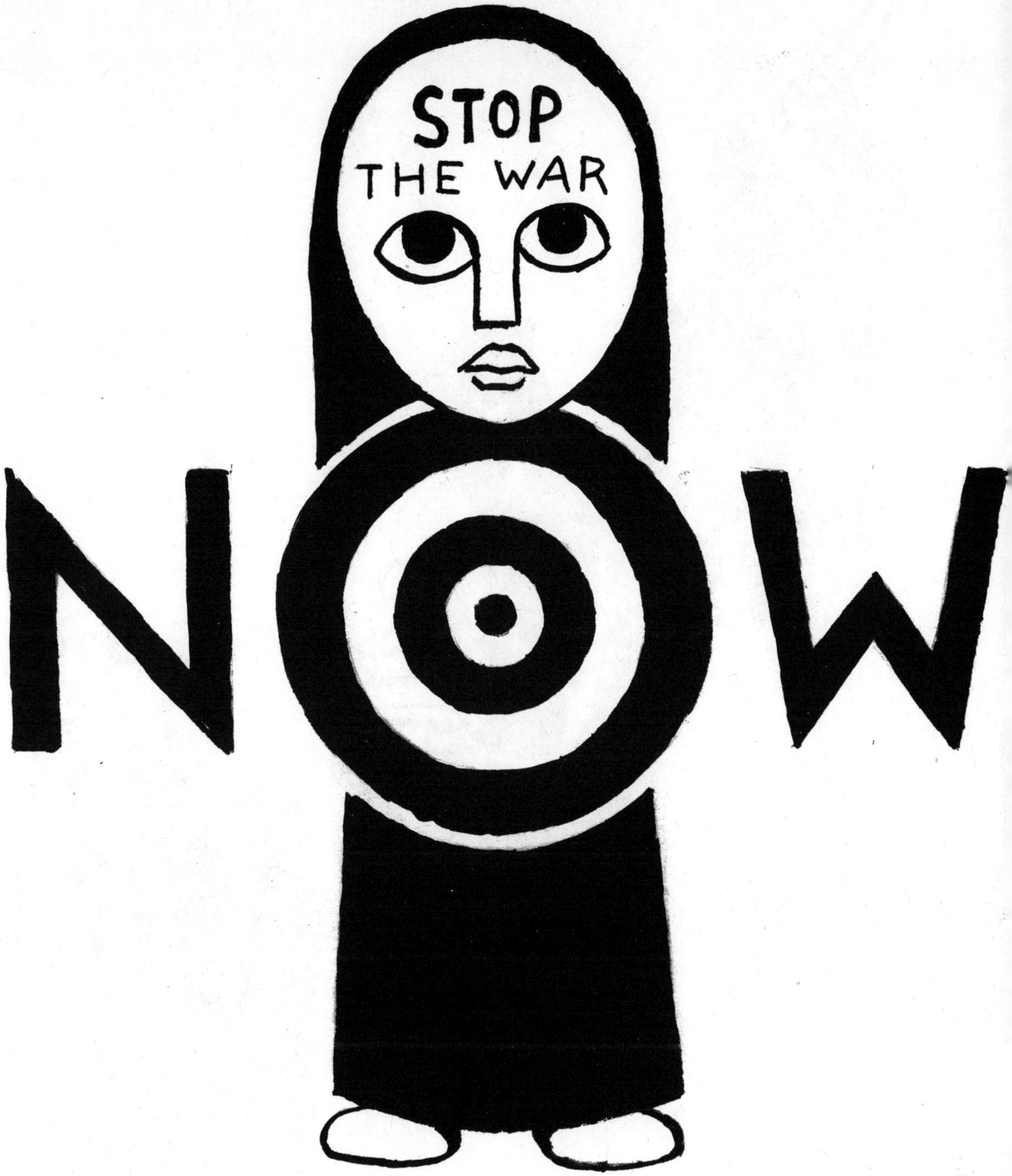
STOP
THE WAR
NOW

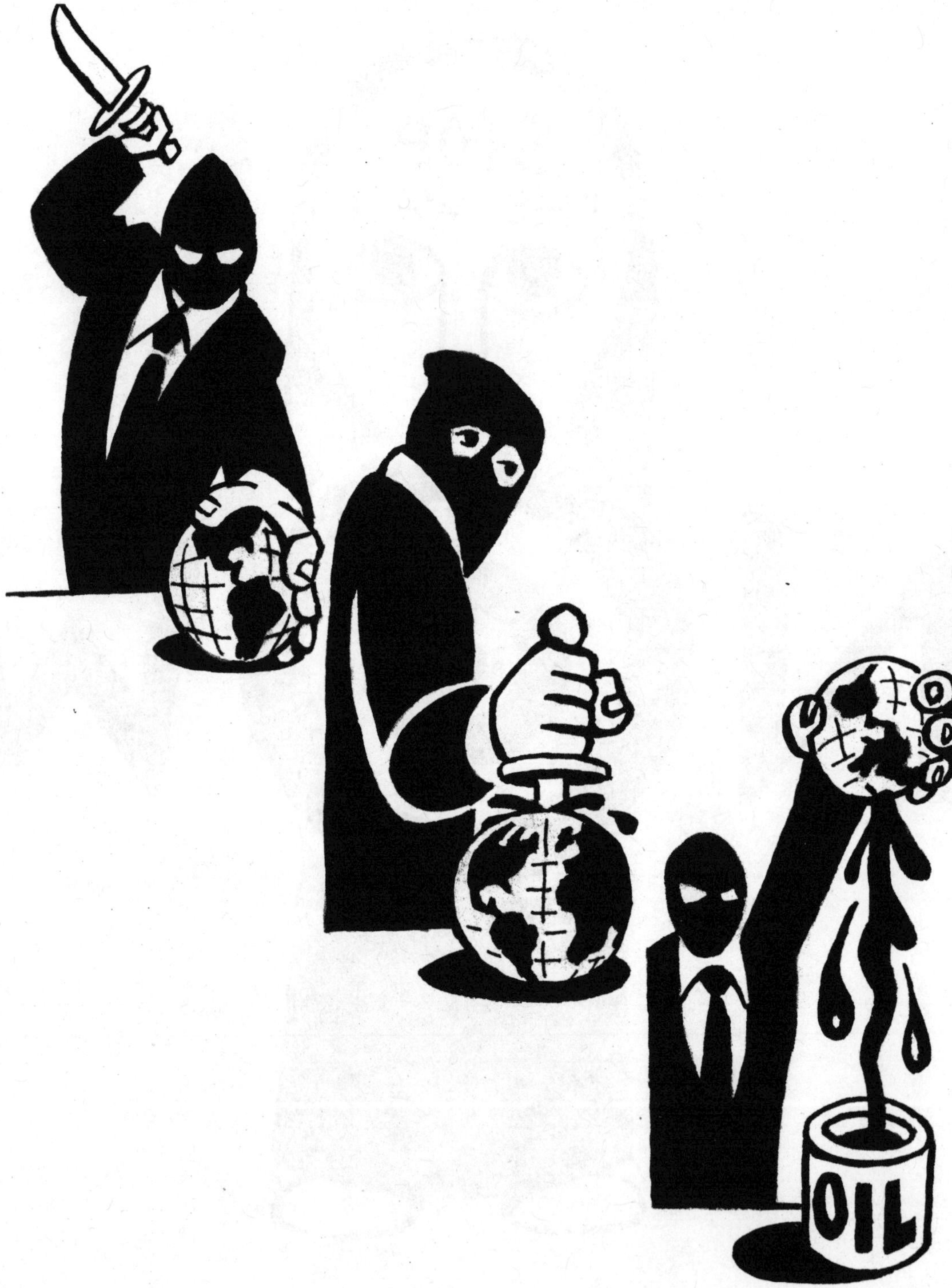
OIL

NAKEDNESS AND POWER

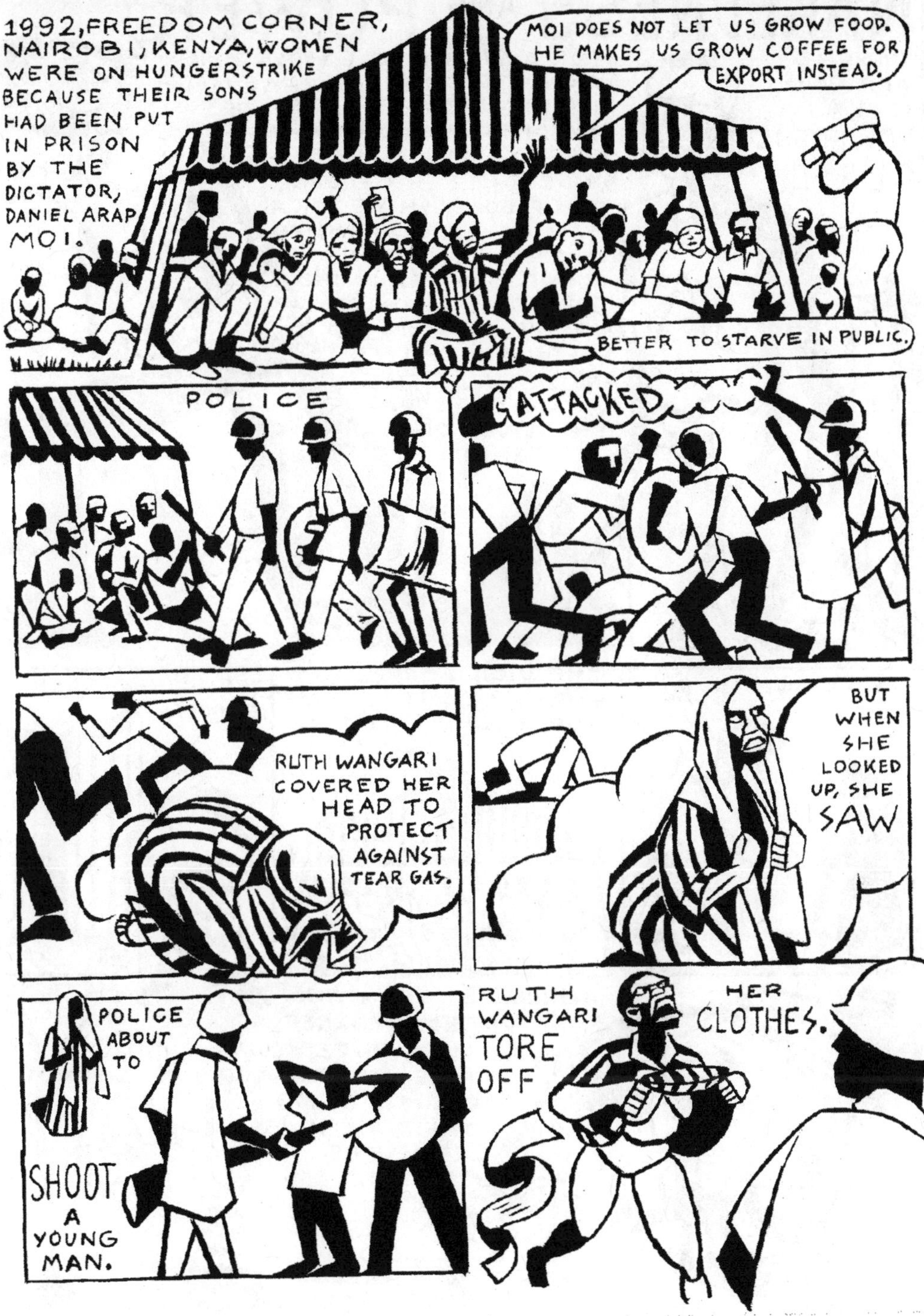

1992, FREEDOM CORNER, NAIROBI, KENYA, WOMEN WERE ON HUNGERSTRIKE BECAUSE THEIR SONS HAD BEEN PUT IN PRISON BY THE DICTATOR, DANIEL ARAP MOI.
MOI DOES NOT LET US GROW FOOD. HE MAKES US GROW COFFEE FOR EXPORT INSTEAD.
BETTER TO STARVE IN PUBLIC.
POLICE
ATTACKED
RUTH WANGARI COVERED HER HEAD TO PROTECT AGAINST TEAR GAS.
BUT WHEN SHE LOOKED UP, SHE SAW
POLICE ABOUT TO
SHOOT A YOUNG MAN.
RUTH WANGARI TORE OFF
HER CLOTHES.

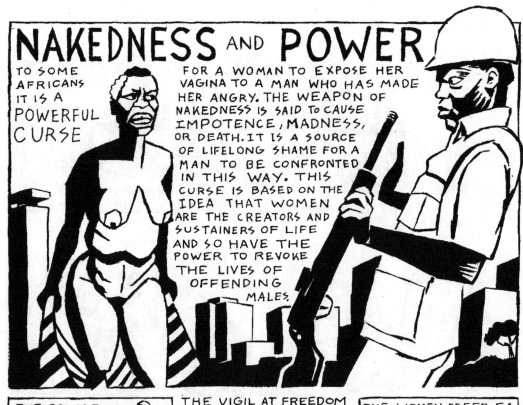

NAKEDNESS AND POWER

TO SOME AFRICANS IT IS A POWERFUL CURSE FOR A WOMAN TO EXPOSE HER VAGINA TO A MAN WHO HAS MADE HER ANGRY. THE WEAPON OF NAKEDNESS IS SAID TO CAUSE IMPOTENCE, MADNESS, OR DEATH. IT IS A SOURCE OF LIFELONG SHAME FOR A MAN TO BE CONFRONTED IN THIS WAY. THIS CURSE IS BASED ON THE IDEA THAT WOMEN ARE THE CREATORS AND SUSTAINERS OF LIFE AND SO HAVE THE POWER TO REVOKE THE LIVES OF OFFENDING MALES.

THE POLICE FLED.

THE VIGIL AT FREEDOM CORNER CONTINUED FOR A WHOLE YEAR.

THE WOMEN FREED 51 PRISONERS.

INSPIRED BY THE ACTION AT FREEDOM CORNER, FARMERS RIPPED OUT COFFEE AND PLANTED FOOD TO FEED THEIR FAMILIES. THE LANDLESS POOR ALSO SEIZED LAND ON WHICH TO GROW FOOD.

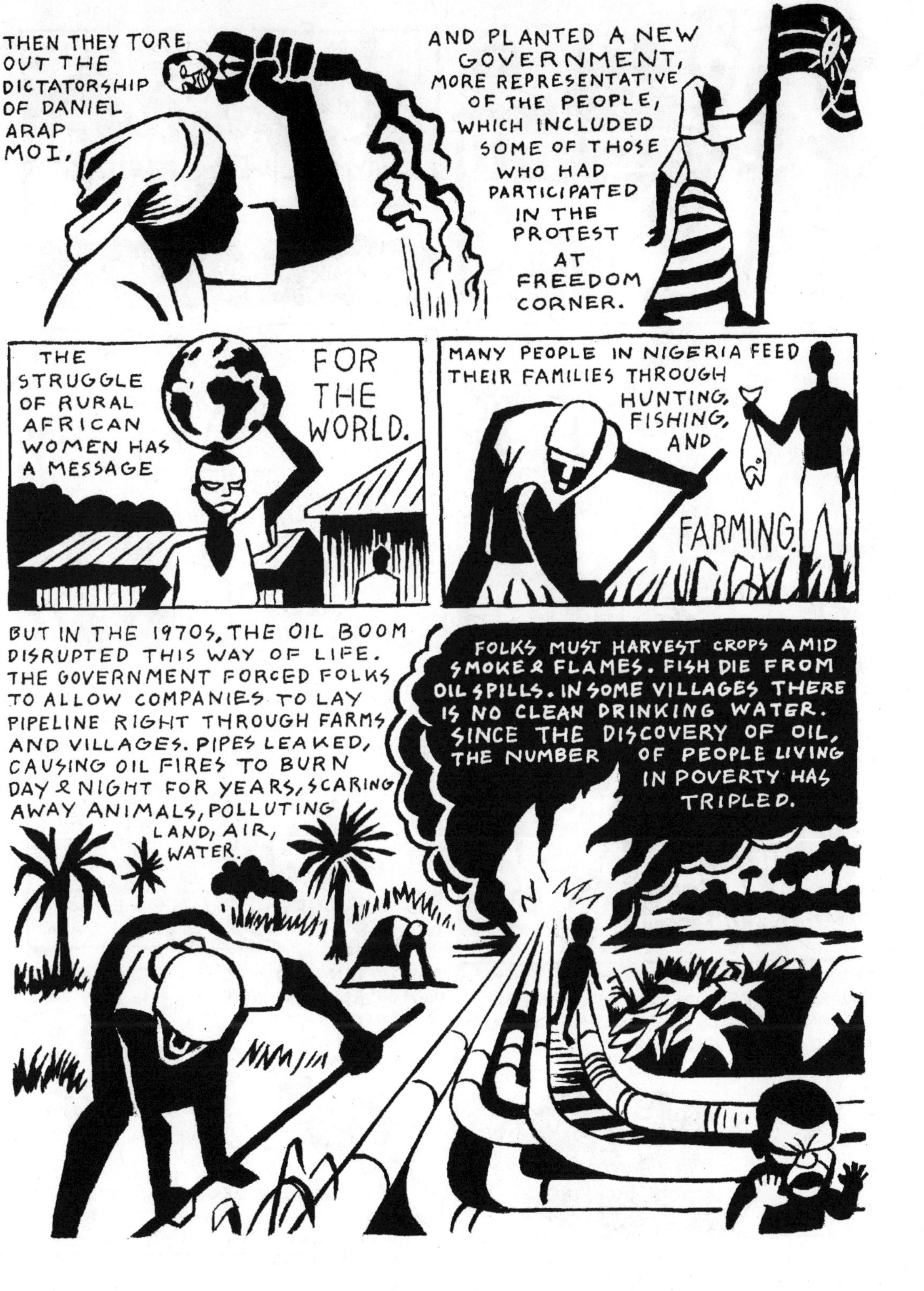

THEN THEY TORE OUT THE DICTATORSHIP OF DANIEL ARAP MOI,
AND PLANTED A NEW GOVERNMENT, MORE REPRESENTATIVE OF THE PEOPLE, WHICH INCLUDED SOME OF THOSE WHO HAD PARTICIPATED IN THE PROTEST AT FREEDOM CORNER.
THE STRUGGLE OF RURAL AFRICAN WOMEN HAS A MESSAGE
FOR THE WORLD.
MANY PEOPLE IN NIGERIA FEED THEIR FAMILIES THROUGH HUNTING, FISHING, AND
FARMING.
BUT IN THE 1970S, THE OIL BOOM DISRUPTED THIS WAY OF LIFE. THE GOVERNMENT FORCED FOLKS TO ALLOW COMPANIES TO LAY PIPELINE RIGHT THROUGH FARMS AND VILLAGES. PIPES LEAKED, CAUSING OIL FIRES TO BURN DAY & NIGHT FOR YEARS, SCARING AWAY ANIMALS, POLLUTING LAND, AIR, WATER.
FOLKS MUST HARVEST CROPS AMID SMOKE & FLAMES. FISH DIE FROM OIL SPILLS. IN SOME VILLAGES THERE IS NO CLEAN DRINKING WATER. SINCE THE DISCOVERY OF OIL, THE NUMBER OF PEOPLE LIVING IN POVERTY HAS TRIPLED.

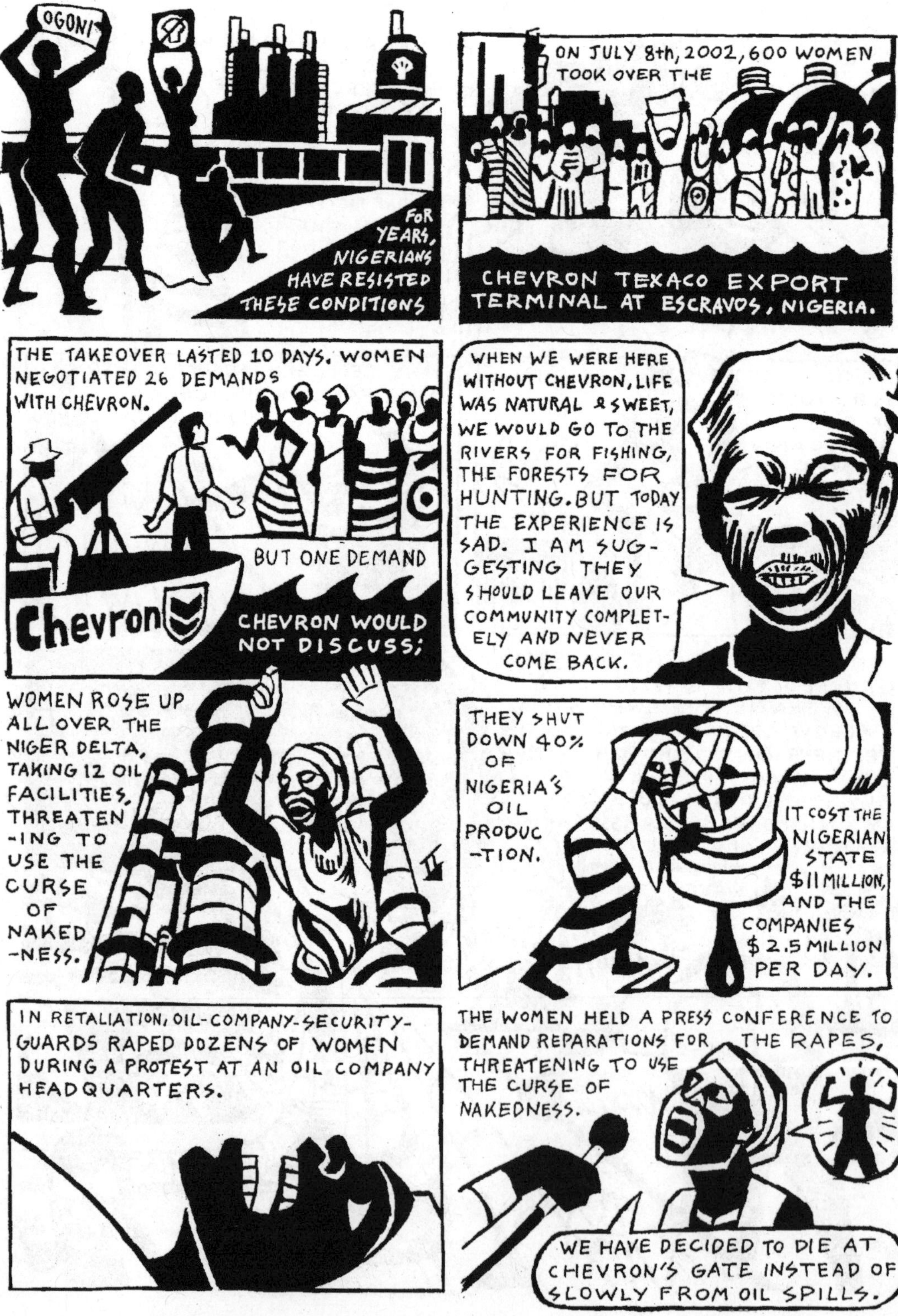
OGONI
FOR YEARS, NIGERIANS HAVE RESISTED THESE CONDITIONS
ON JULY 8th, 2002, 600 WOMEN TOOK OVER THE
CHEVRON TEXACO EXPORT TERMINAL AT ESCRAVOS, NIGERIA.
THE TAKEOVER LASTED 10 DAYS. WOMEN NEGOTIATED 26 DEMANDS WITH CHEVRON.
BUT ONE DEMAND
Chevron
CHEVRON WOULD NOT DISCUSS;
WHEN WE WERE HERE WITHOUT CHEVRON, LIFE WAS NATURAL & SWEET, WE WOULD GO TO THE RIVERS FOR FISHING, THE FORESTS FOR HUNTING. BUT TODAY THE EXPERIENCE IS SAD. I AM SUG-GESTING THEY SHOULD LEAVE OUR COMMUNITY COMPLET-ELY AND NEVER COME BACK.
WOMEN ROSE UP ALL OVER THE NIGER DELTA, TAKING 12 OIL FACILITIES, THREATEN-ING TO USE THE CURSE OF NAKED-NESS.
THEY SHUT DOWN 40% OF NIGERIA'S OIL PRODUC-TION.
IT COST THE NIGERIAN STATE $11 MILLION, AND THE COMPANIES $2.5 MILLION PER DAY.
IN RETALIATION, OIL-COMPANY-SECURITY-GUARDS RAPED DOZENS OF WOMEN DURING A PROTEST AT AN OIL COMPANY HEADQUARTERS.
THE WOMEN HELD A PRESS CONFERENCE TO DEMAND REPARATIONS FOR THE RAPES, THREATENING TO USE THE CURSE OF NAKEDNESS.
WE HAVE DECIDED TO DIE AT CHEVRON'S GATE INSTEAD OF SLOWLY FROM OIL SPILLS.

SOME WOMEN IN THE U.S. & EUROPE HEARD ABOUT THE NIGERIAN WOMEN.

THEY SAW:

THAT THE SAME OIL COMPANIES THAT WERE POLLUTING NIGERIA WERE POLLUTING THE WHOLE WORLD.

THEY SAW THAT AN OIL MAN WAS TAKING AMERICA TO WAR IN IRAQ.

THEY ORGANIZED A

CHEVRON TEXACO

BOYCOTT

BUT THEY DID MORE:

FROM SAN FRANCISO TO SOUTH AMERICA, WOMEN TOOK OFF THEIR CLOTHES TO PROTEST AGAINST THE COMING WAR IN IRAQ, PAINTING SYMBOLS OF PEACE ON THE HILLSIDES WITH THEIR BODIES.

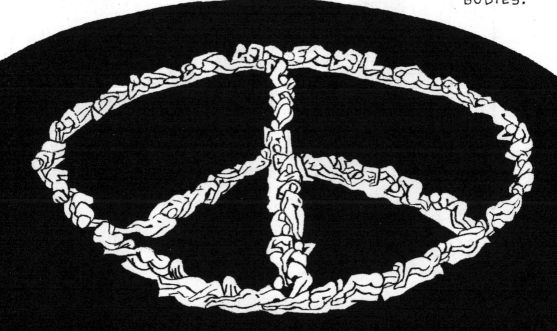

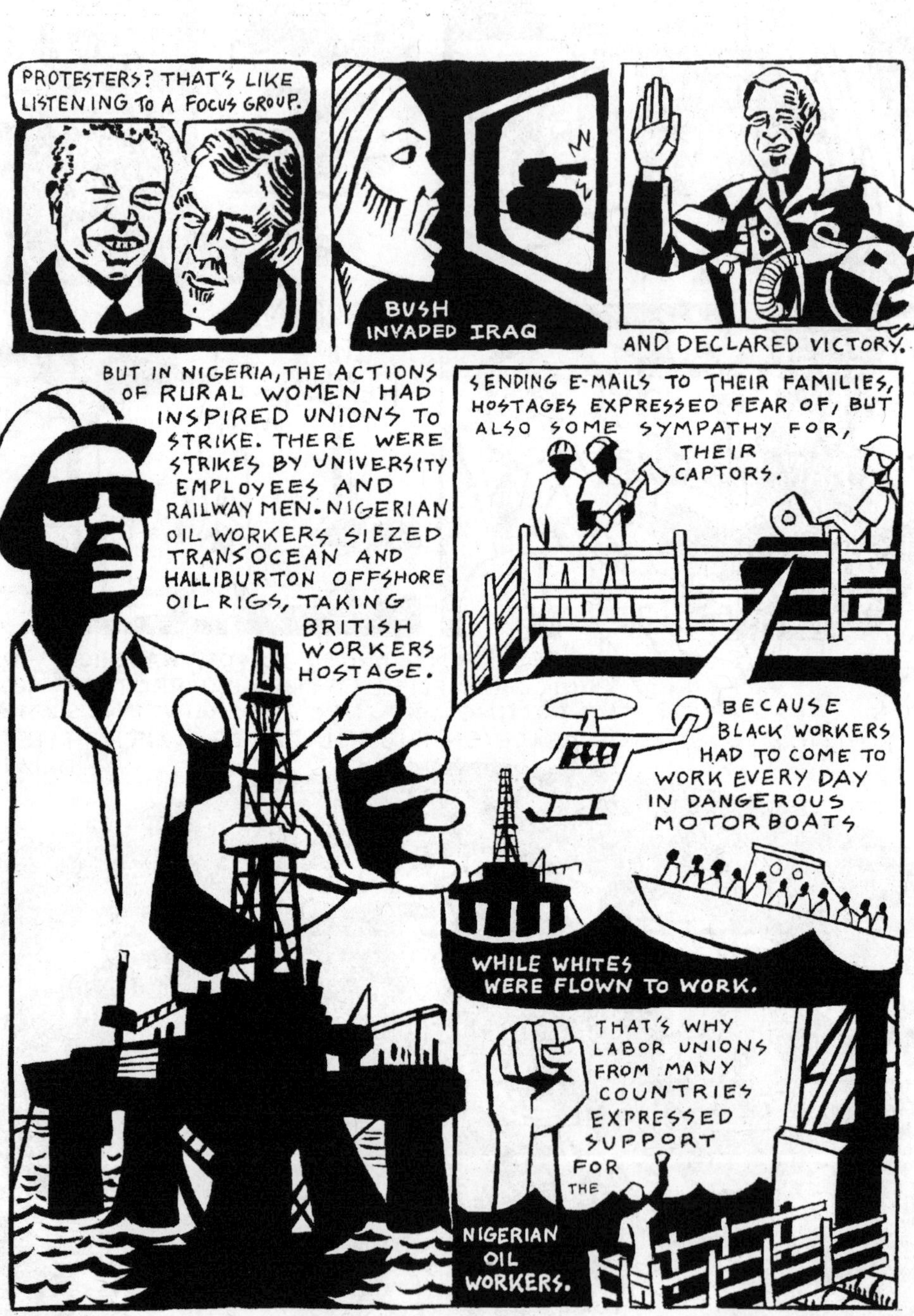
PROTESTERS? THAT'S LIKE LISTENING TO A FOCUS GROUP.
BUSH INVADED IRAQ
AND DECLARED VICTORY.
BUT IN NIGERIA, THE ACTIONS OF RURAL WOMEN HAD INSPIRED UNIONS TO STRIKE. THERE WERE STRIKES BY UNIVERSITY EMPLOYEES AND RAILWAY MEN. NIGERIAN OIL WORKERS SIEZED TRANSOCEAN AND HALLIBURTON OFFSHORE OIL RIGS, TAKING BRITISH WORKERS HOSTAGE.
SENDING E-MAILS TO THEIR FAMILIES, HOSTAGES EXPRESSED FEAR OF, BUT ALSO SOME SYMPATHY FOR, THEIR CAPTORS.
BECAUSE BLACK WORKERS HAD TO COME TO WORK EVERY DAY IN DANGEROUS MOTOR BOATS
WHILE WHITES WERE FLOWN TO WORK.
THAT'S WHY LABOR UNIONS FROM MANY COUNTRIES EXPRESSED SUPPORT FOR THE
NIGERIAN OIL WORKERS.

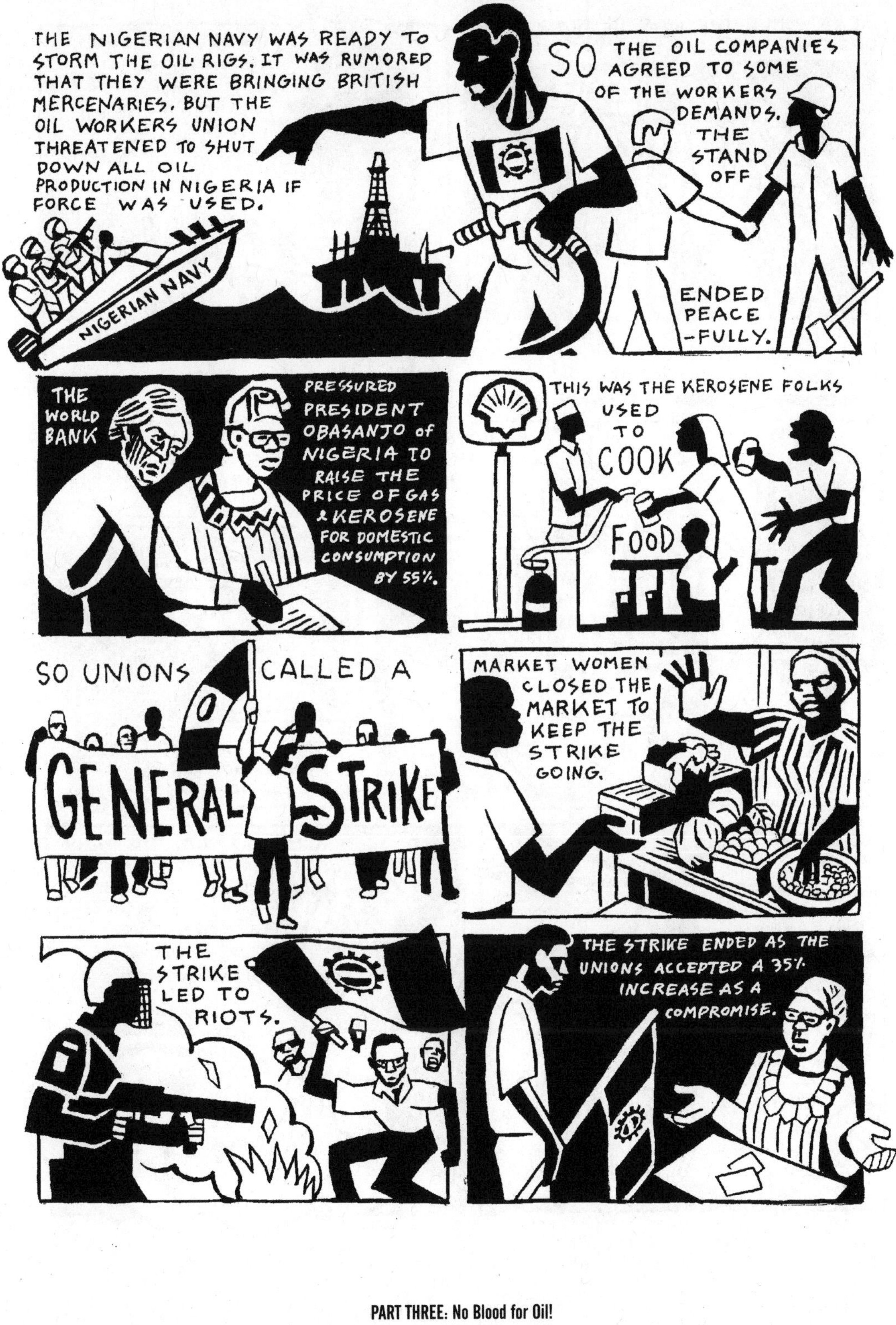

THE NIGERIAN NAVY WAS READY TO STORM THE OIL RIGS. IT WAS RUMORED THAT THEY WERE BRINGING BRITISH MERCENARIES. BUT THE OIL WORKERS UNION THREATENED TO SHUT DOWN ALL OIL PRODUCTION IN NIGERIA IF FORCE WAS USED.
NIGERIAN NAVY
SO THE OIL COMPANIES AGREED TO SOME OF THE WORKERS DEMANDS. THE STAND OFF
ENDED PEACE-FULLY.
THE WORLD BANK
PRESSURED PRESIDENT OBASANJO of NIGERIA TO RAISE THE PRICE OF GAS & KEROSENE FOR DOMESTIC CONSUMPTION BY 55%.
THIS WAS THE KEROSENE FOLKS USED TO COOK
FOOD
SO UNIONS CALLED A
GENERAL STRIKE
MARKET WOMEN CLOSED THE MARKET TO KEEP THE STRIKE GOING.
THE STRIKE LED TO RIOTS.
THE STRIKE ENDED AS THE UNIONS ACCEPTED A 35% INCREASE AS A COMPROMISE.

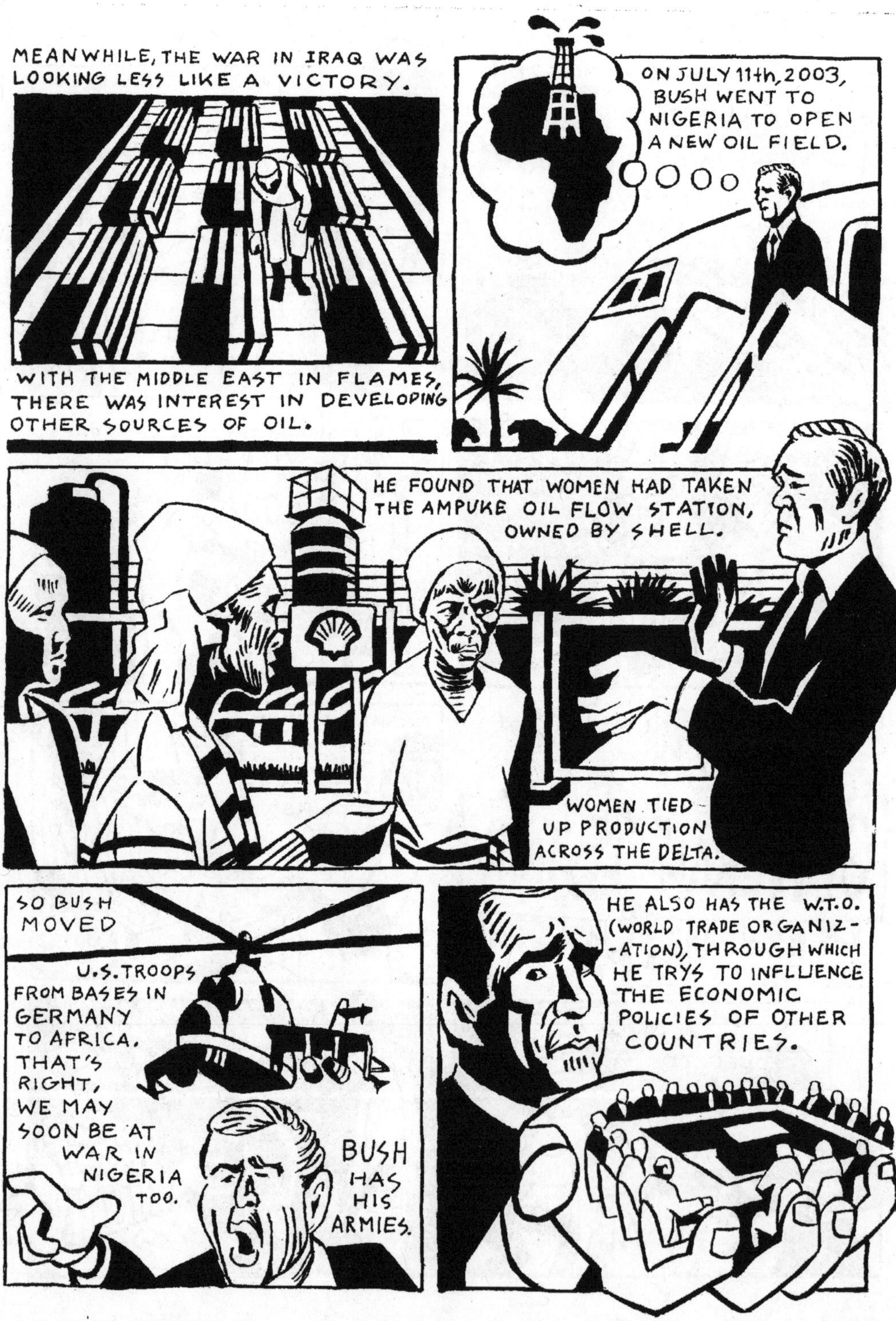
MEANWHILE, THE WAR IN IRAQ WAS LOOKING LESS LIKE A VICTORY.
WITH THE MIDDLE EAST IN FLAMES, THERE WAS INTEREST IN DEVELOPING OTHER SOURCES OF OIL.
ON JULY 11th, 2003, BUSH WENT TO NIGERIA TO OPEN A NEW OIL FIELD.
HE FOUND THAT WOMEN HAD TAKEN THE AMPUKE OIL FLOW STATION, OWNED BY SHELL.
WOMEN TIED UP PRODUCTION ACROSS THE DELTA.
SO BUSH MOVED
U.S. TROOPS FROM BASES IN GERMANY TO AFRICA.
THAT'S RIGHT, WE MAY SOON BE AT WAR IN NIGERIA TOO.
BUSH HAS HIS ARMIES.
HE ALSO HAS THE W.T.O. (WORLD TRADE ORGANIZ- -ATION), THROUGH WHICH HE TRYS TO INFLUENCE THE ECONOMIC POLICIES OF OTHER COUNTRIES.

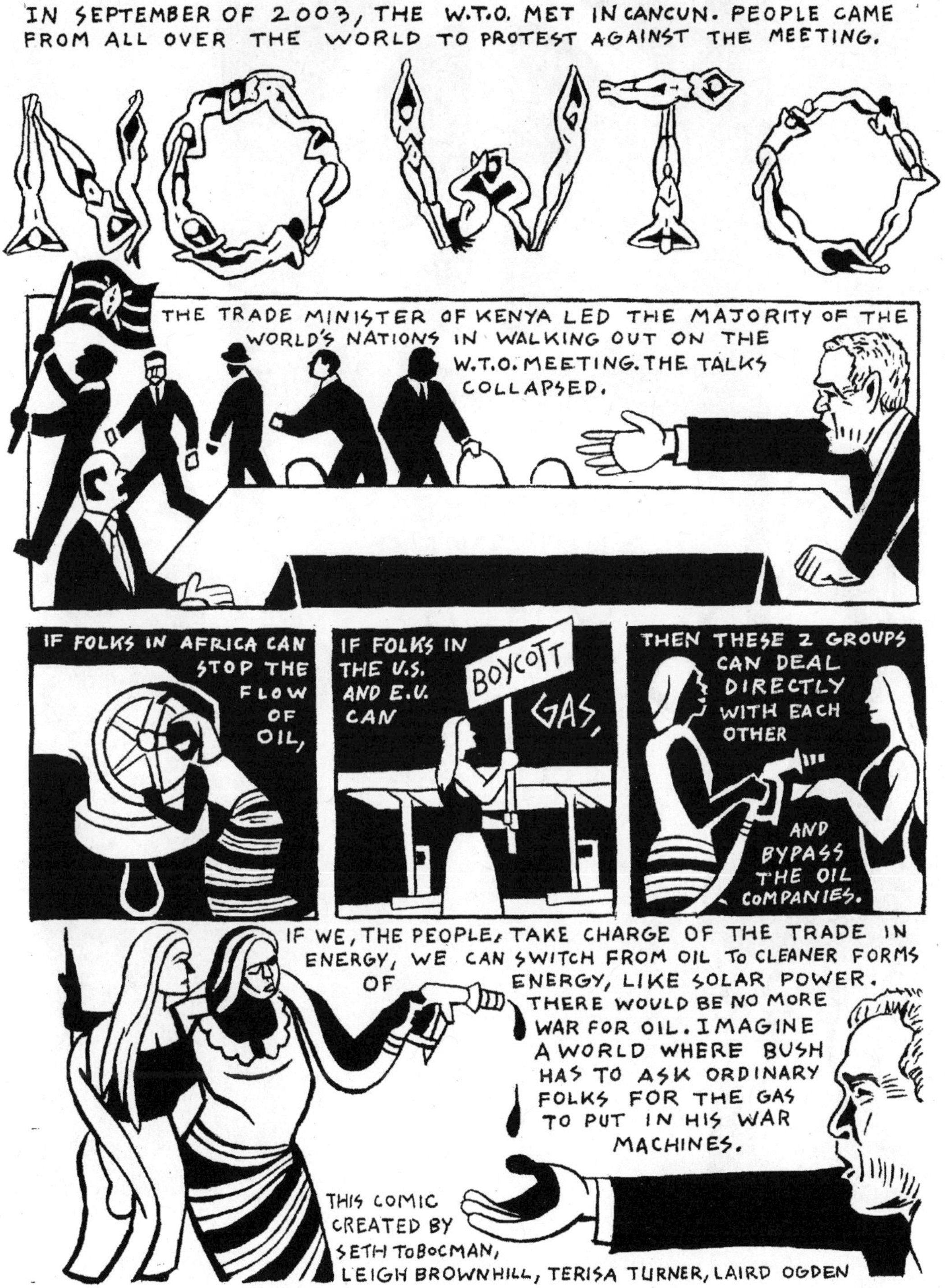

IN SEPTEMBER OF 2003, THE W.T.O. MET IN CANCUN. PEOPLE CAME FROM ALL OVER THE WORLD TO PROTEST AGAINST THE MEETING.
NO WTO
THE TRADE MINISTER OF KENYA LED THE MAJORITY OF THE WORLD'S NATIONS IN WALKING OUT ON THE W.T.O. MEETING. THE TALKS COLLAPSED.
IF FOLKS IN AFRICA CAN STOP THE FLOW OF OIL,
IF FOLKS IN THE U.S. AND E.U. CAN
BOYCOTT
GAS,
THEN THESE 2 GROUPS CAN DEAL DIRECTLY WITH EACH OTHER
AND BYPASS THE OIL COMPANIES.
IF WE, THE PEOPLE, TAKE CHARGE OF THE TRADE IN ENERGY, WE CAN SWITCH FROM OIL TO CLEANER FORMS OF ENERGY, LIKE SOLAR POWER. THERE WOULD BE NO MORE WAR FOR OIL. IMAGINE A WORLD WHERE BUSH HAS TO ASK ORDINARY FOLKS FOR THE GAS TO PUT IN HIS WAR MACHINES.
THIS COMIC CREATED BY SETH TOBOCMAN, LEIGH BROWNHILL, TERISA TURNER, LAIRD OGDEN

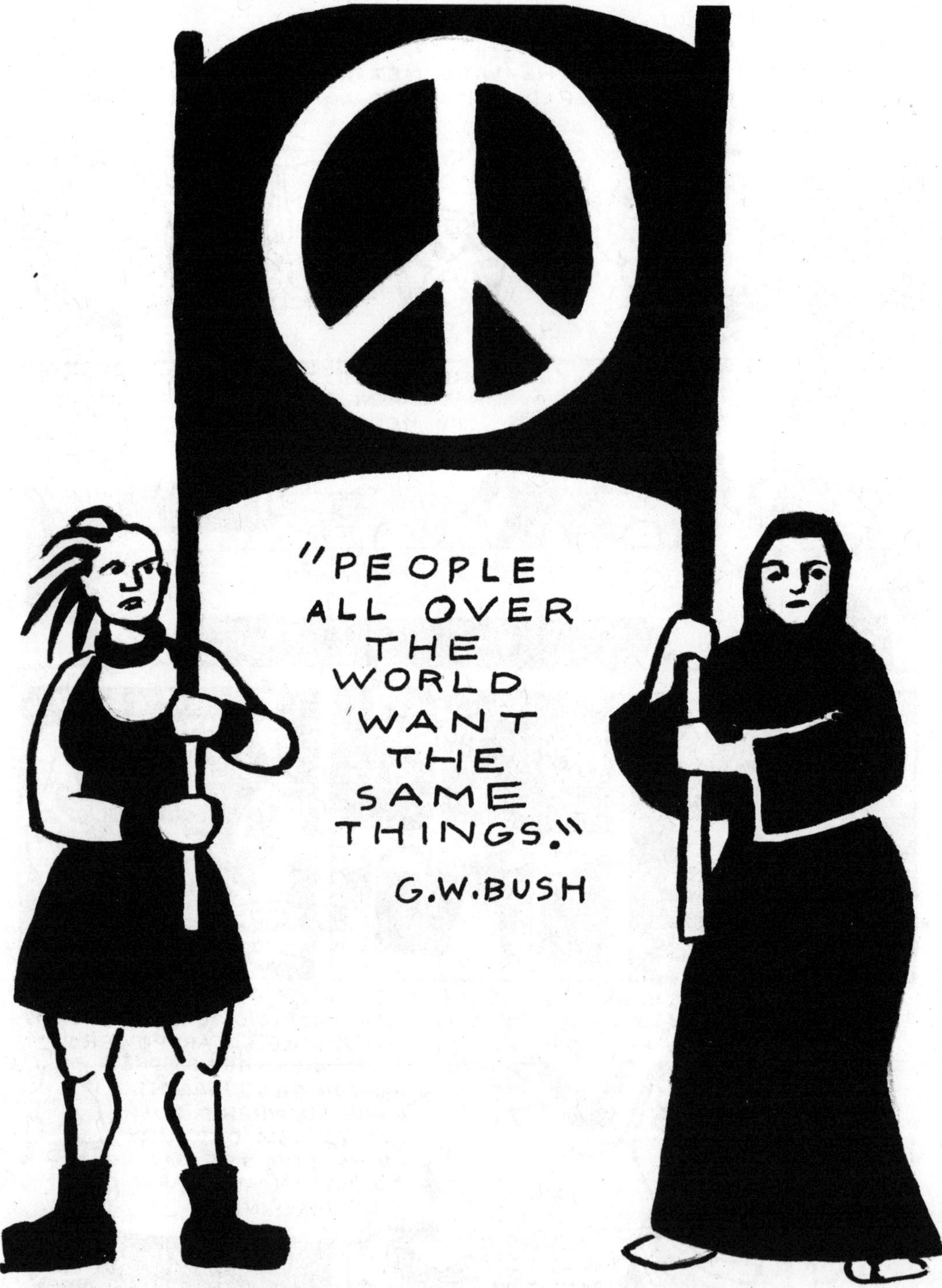
"PEOPLE ALL OVER THE WORLD WANT THE SAME THINGS."
G.W. BUSH

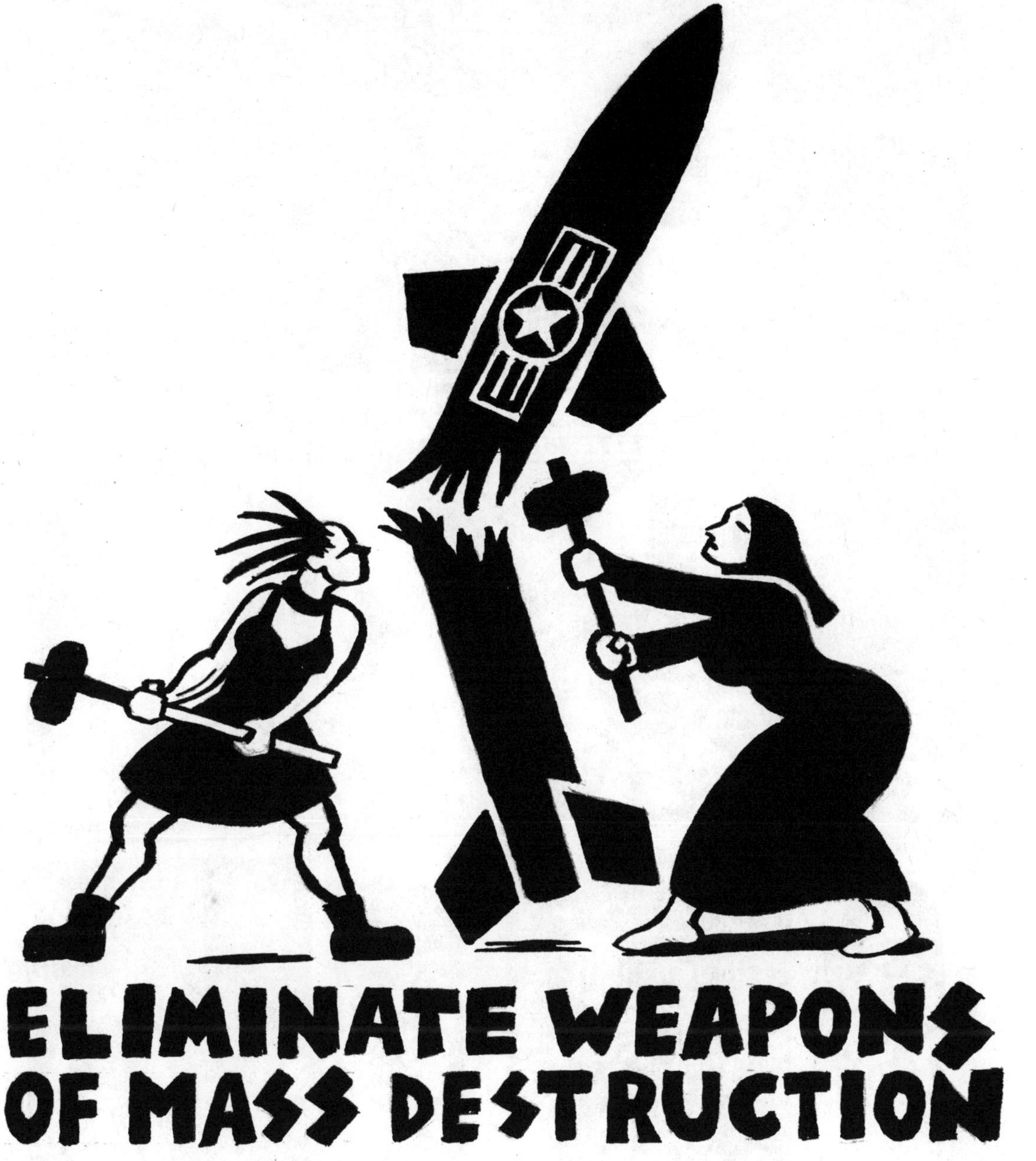
ELIMINATE WEAPONS
OF MASS DESTRUCTION

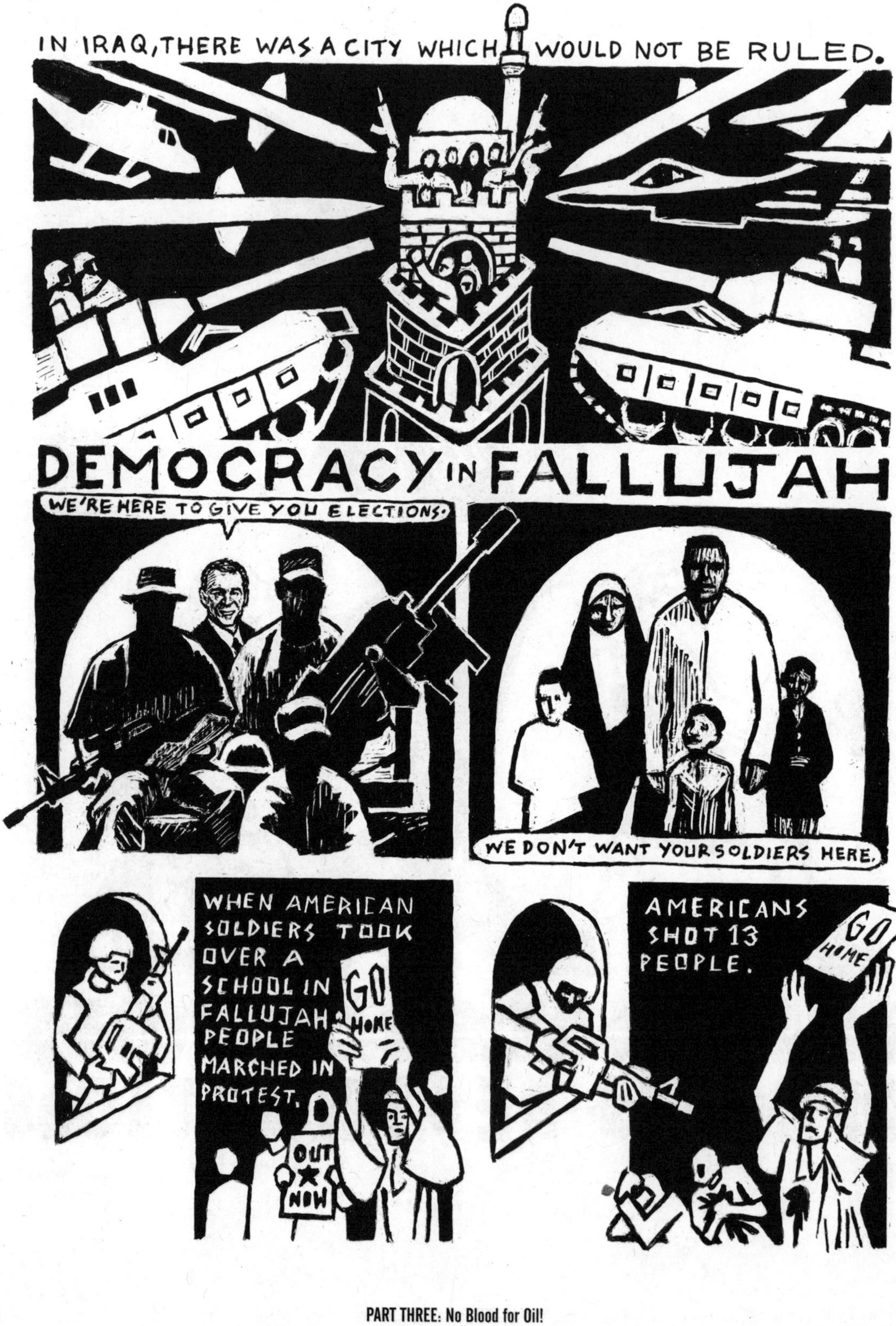
IN IRAQ, THERE WAS A CITY WHICH WOULD NOT BE RULED.
DEMOCRACY IN FALLUJAH
WE'RE HERE TO GIVE YOU ELECTIONS.
WE DON'T WANT YOUR SOLDIERS HERE.
WHEN AMERICAN SOLDIERS TOOK OVER A SCHOOL IN FALLUJAH PEOPLE MARCHED IN PROTEST.
GO HOME
OUT ★ NOW
AMERICANS SHOT 13 PEOPLE.
GO HOME

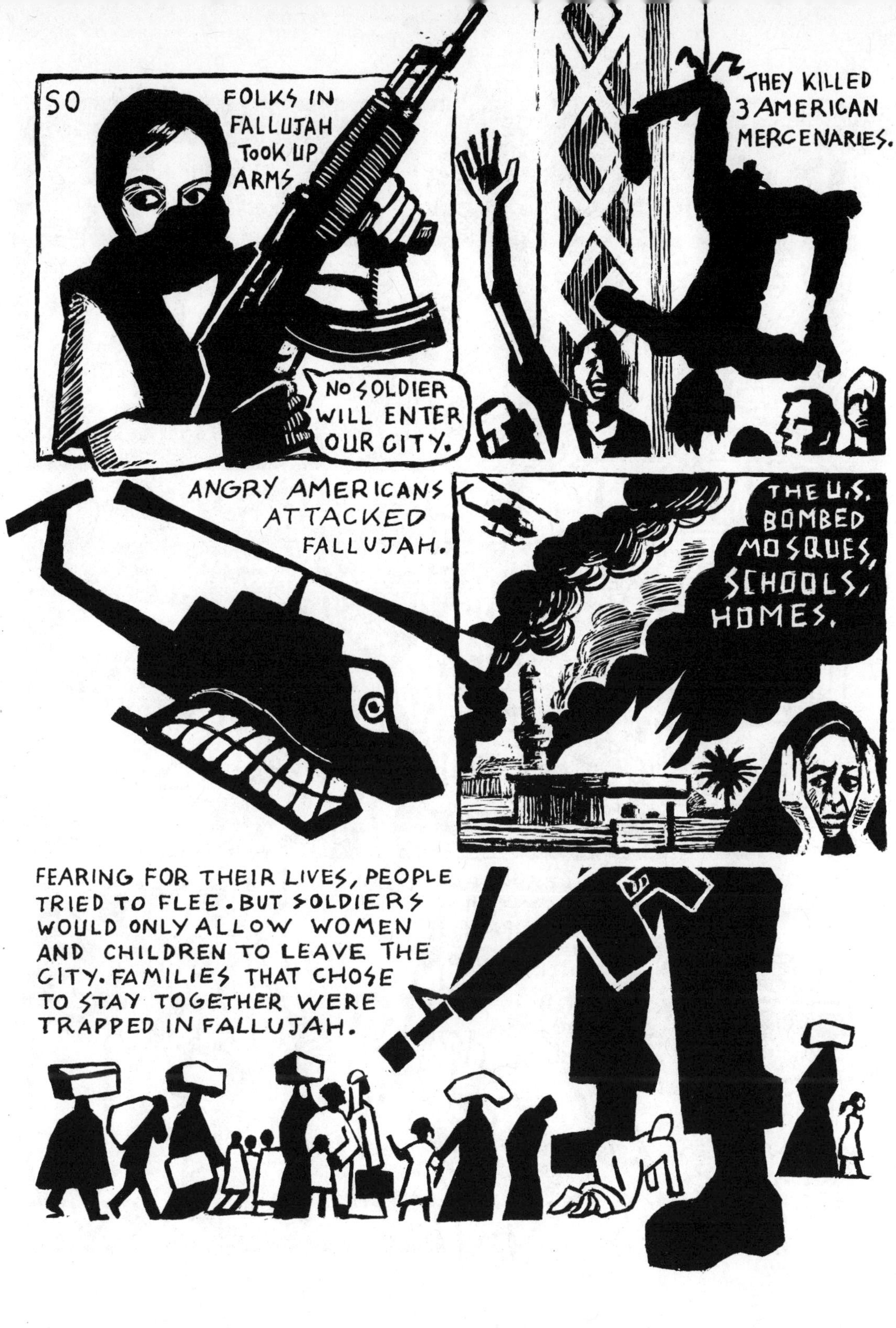
SO
FOLKS IN FALLUJAH TOOK UP ARMS
NO SOLDIER WILL ENTER OUR CITY.
THEY KILLED 3 AMERICAN MERCENARIES.
ANGRY AMERICANS ATTACKED FALLUJAH.
THE U.S. BOMBED MOSQUES, SCHOOLS, HOMES.
FEARING FOR THEIR LIVES, PEOPLE TRIED TO FLEE. BUT SOLDIERS WOULD ONLY ALLOW WOMEN AND CHILDREN TO LEAVE THE CITY. FAMILIES THAT CHOSE TO STAY TOGETHER WERE TRAPPED IN FALLUJAH.

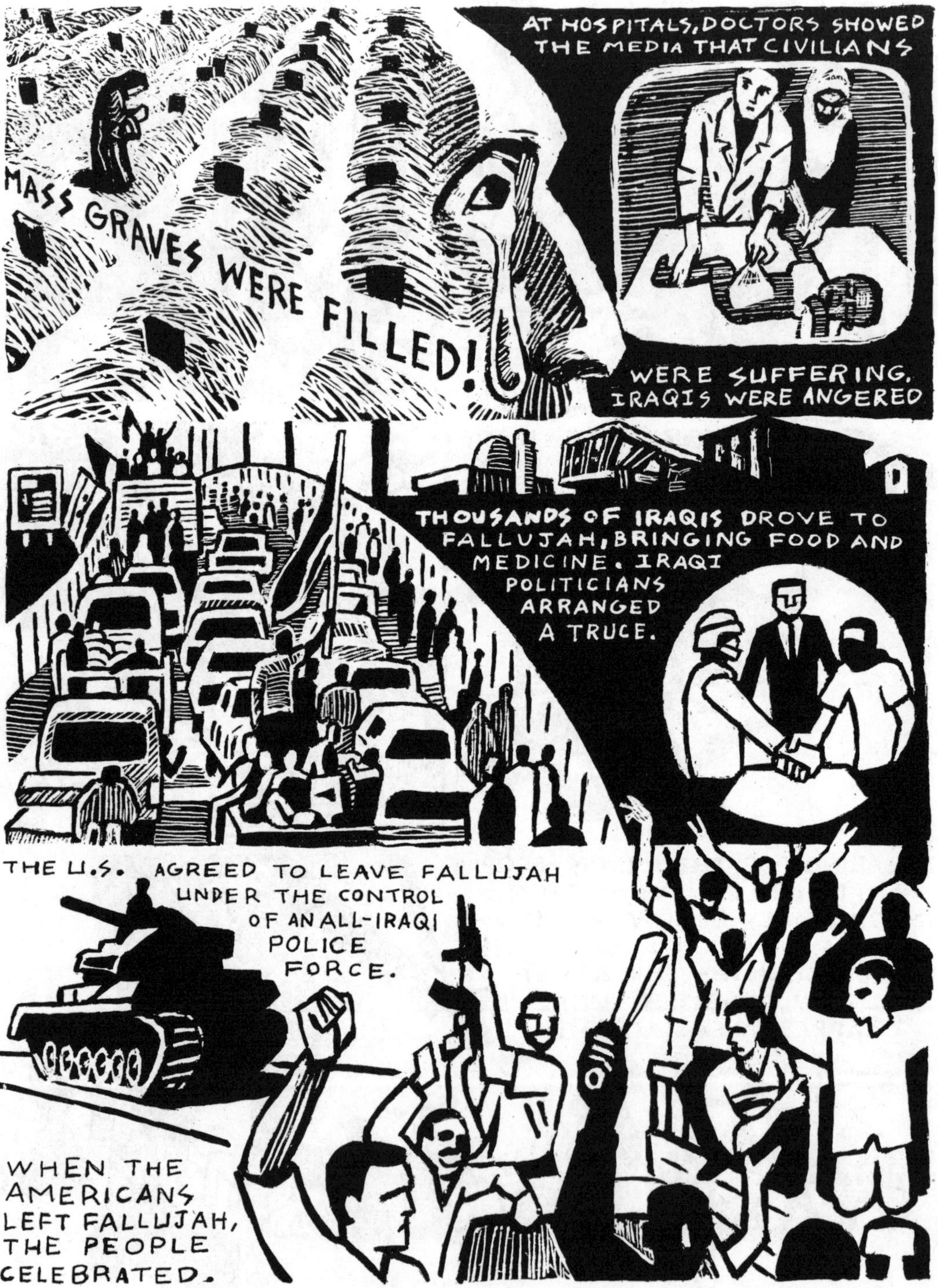
MASS GRAVES WERE FILLED!
AT HOSPITALS, DOCTORS SHOWED THE MEDIA THAT CIVILIANS
WERE SUFFERING. IRAQIS WERE ANGERED
THOUSANDS OF IRAQIS DROVE TO FALLUJAH, BRINGING FOOD AND MEDICINE. IRAQI POLITICIANS ARRANGED A TRUCE.
THE U.S. AGREED TO LEAVE FALLUJAH UNDER THE CONTROL OF AN ALL-IRAQI POLICE FORCE.
WHEN THE AMERICANS LEFT FALLUJAH, THE PEOPLE CELEBRATED.

THE TRUCE HELPED BUSH.

WE'RE MAKING PROGRESS IN IRAQ. REELECT ME & I'LL FINISH THE JOB.

ONCE THE AMERICAN ELECTION WAS OVER IT WAS TIME TO ATTACK FALLUJAH AGAIN.

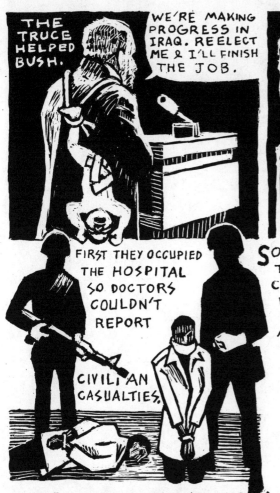

FIRST THEY OCCUPIED THE HOSPITAL SO DOCTORS COULDN'T REPORT

CIVILIAN CASUALTIES.

SOON THEY HAD TAKEN THE CITY AND IT WAS TIME TO SWEEP AWAY THE CORPSES

AND HOLD ELECTIONS.

BY ELECTION TIME, FALLUJAH WAS A GHOST TOWN. ROUGHLY 2% OF THE ORIGINAL POPULATION VOTED.

SETH '05

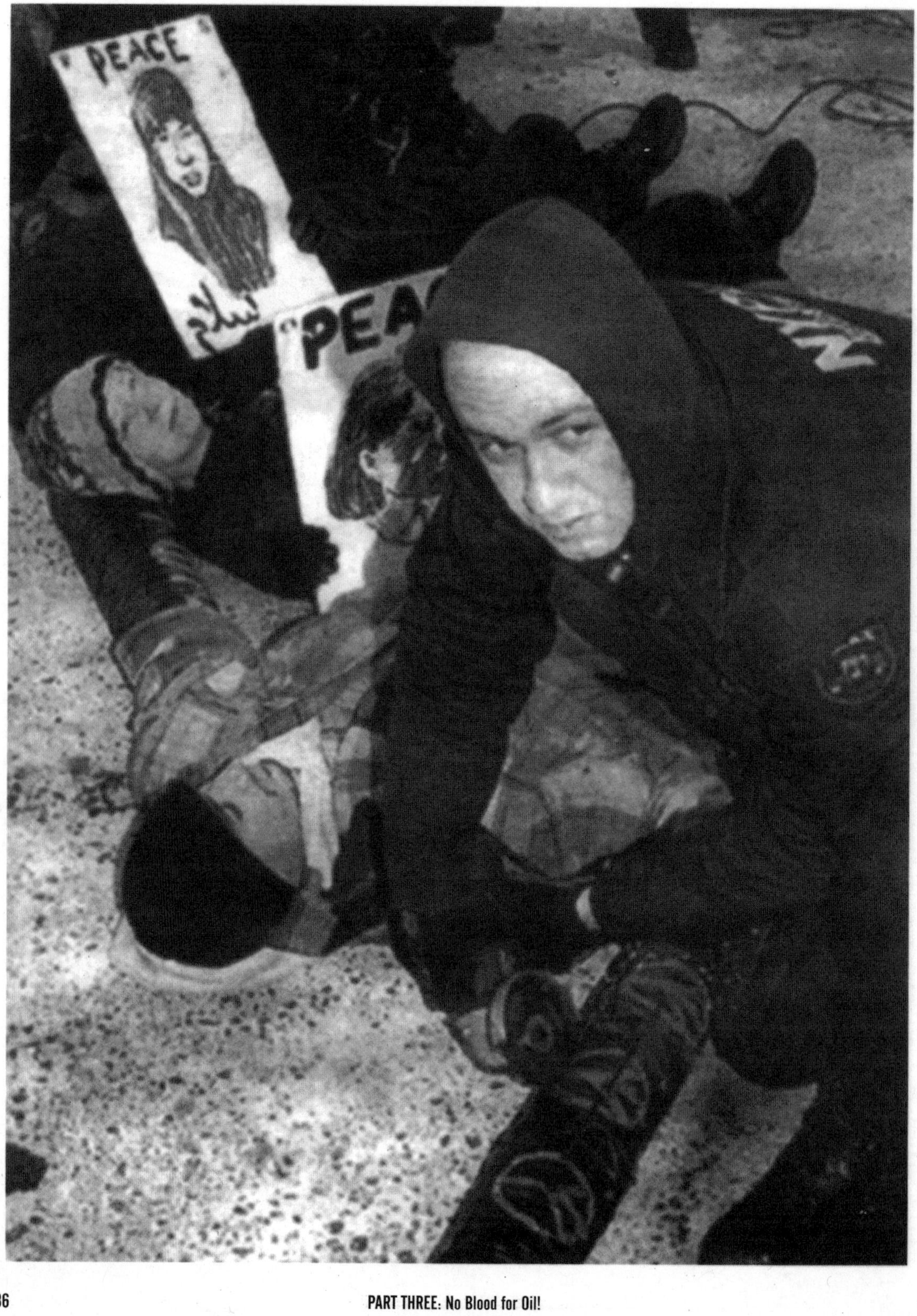
PEACE
PEA

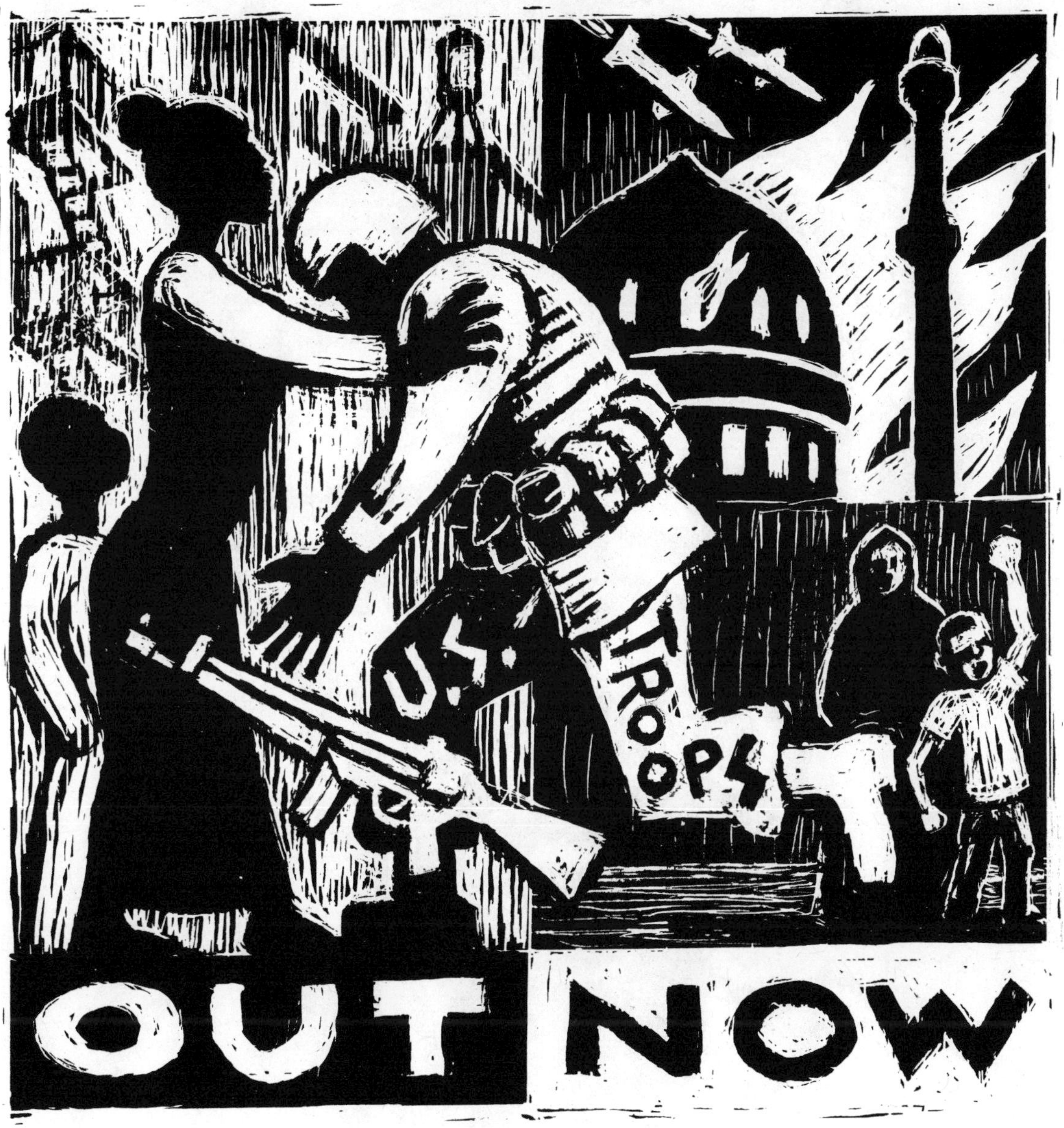
U.S.
TROOPS
OUT NOW

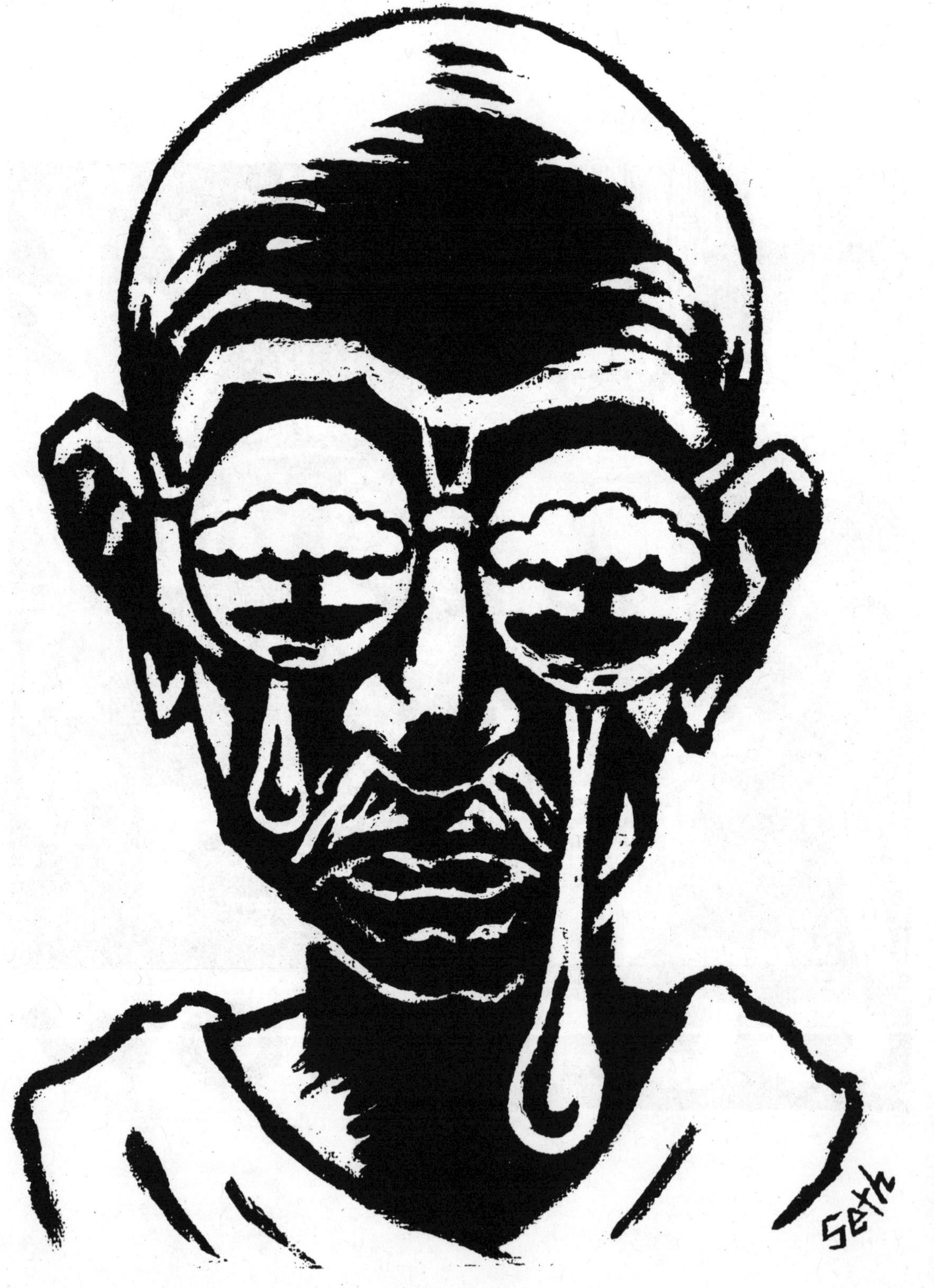
Seth

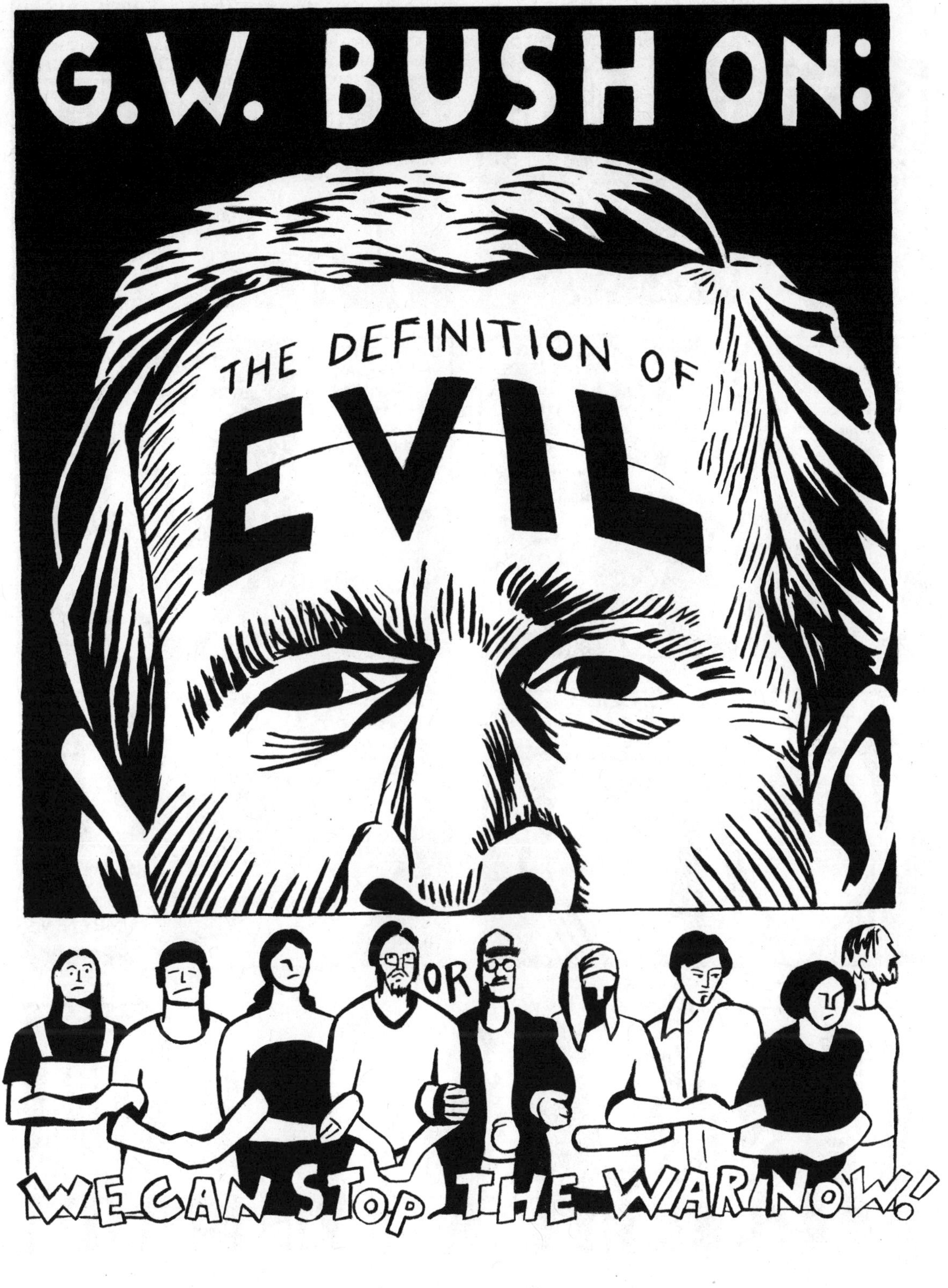
G.W. BUSH ON:
THE DEFINITION OF
EVIL
OR
WE CAN STOP THE WAR NOW!

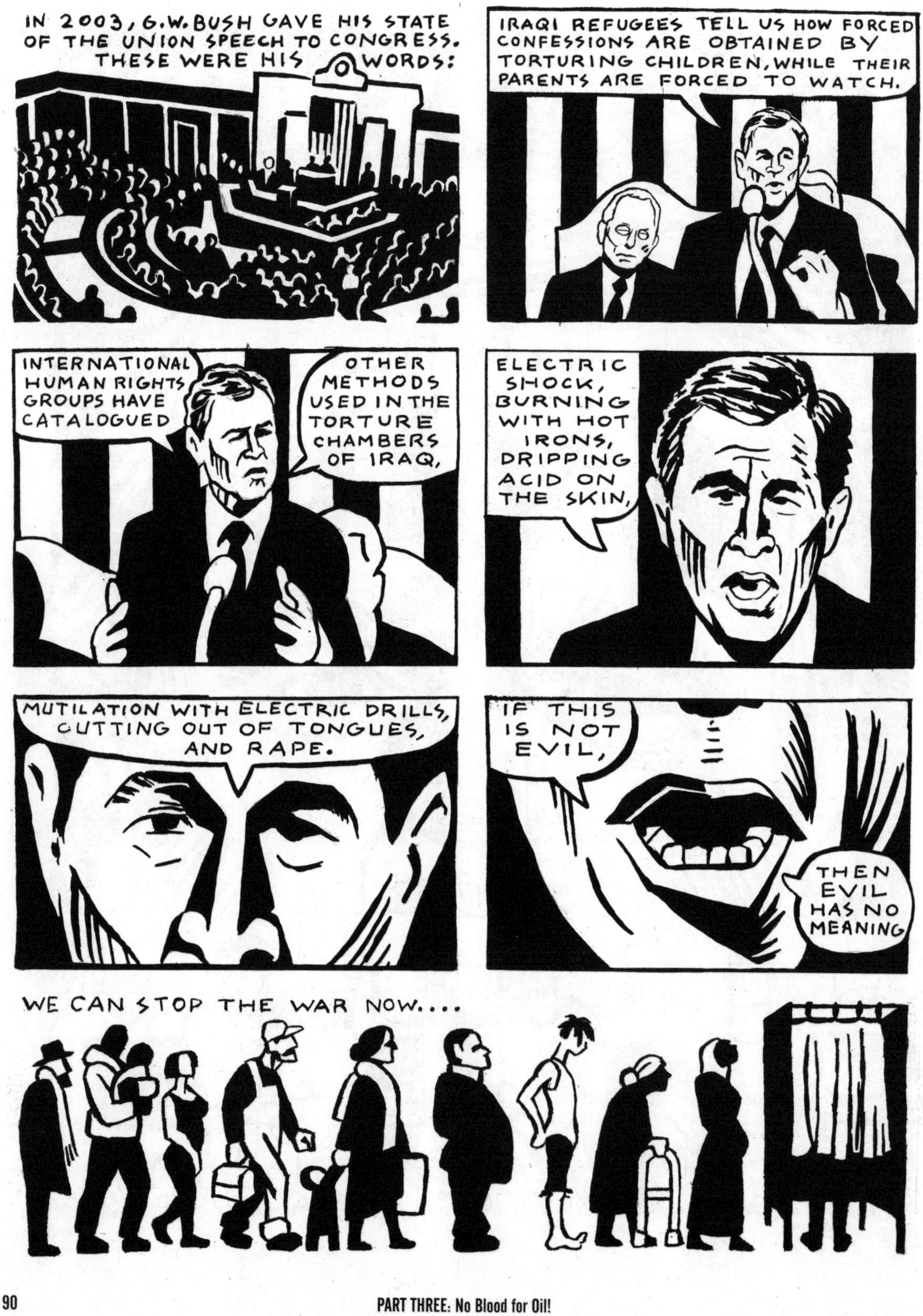
IN 2003, G.W. BUSH GAVE HIS STATE OF THE UNION SPEECH TO CONGRESS. THESE WERE HIS WORDS:
IRAQI REFUGEES TELL US HOW FORCED CONFESSIONS ARE OBTAINED BY TORTURING CHILDREN, WHILE THEIR PARENTS ARE FORCED TO WATCH.
INTERNATIONAL HUMAN RIGHTS GROUPS HAVE CATALOGUED
OTHER METHODS USED IN THE TORTURE CHAMBERS OF IRAQ,
ELECTRIC SHOCK, BURNING WITH HOT IRONS, DRIPPING ACID ON THE SKIN,
MUTILATION WITH ELECTRIC DRILLS, CUTTING OUT OF TONGUES, AND RAPE.
IF THIS IS NOT EVIL,
THEN EVIL HAS NO MEANING
WE CAN STOP THE WAR NOW....

PHOTOS TAKEN BY AMERICAN G.I.S IN IRAQ SHOW US
PERFECT.
HOW FORCED CONFESSIONS
ARE OBTAINED
BY IMPRISONING CHILDREN ALONG WITH THEIR PARENTS.
BY TERRORIZING PEOPLE WITH ATTACK DOGS.
AND RAPE.
SMILE FOR THE CAMERA
AND MURDER.
WE CAN STOP THE WAR NOW....

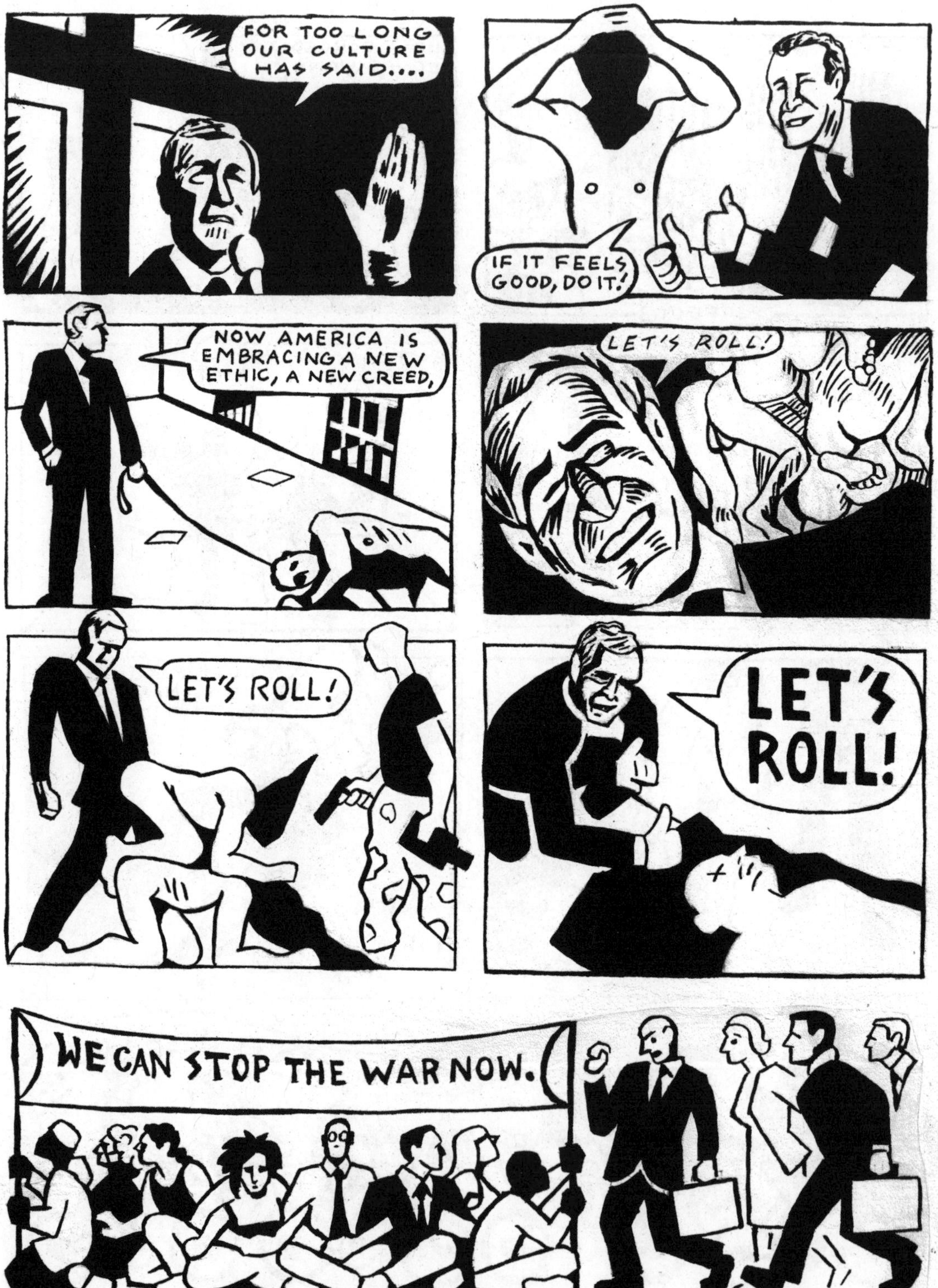
FOR TOO LONG OUR CULTURE HAS SAID....
IF IT FEELS GOOD, DO IT!
NOW AMERICA IS EMBRACING A NEW ETHIC, A NEW CREED,
LET'S ROLL!
LET'S ROLL!
LET'S ROLL!
WE CAN STOP THE WAR NOW.

Part Four:

The Not So Holy Land

THE NOT SO HOLY LAND

In 2000, I was sitting in a New York pizzeria with my friend, a producer of underground films. I drew his attention to the front page of the newspaper, to a picture of a Palestinian kid and his father who were shot for no apparent reason. I suggested that we, as two socially conscious Jewish artists, really ought to have something to say about this.

"You can't say anything about that!" he replied. "It's too controversial."

I was shocked. My friend had made films about gay people in New York and Anarchists in Europe, but an Arab kid in East Jerusalem was off limits.

I don't want walls and checkpoints built around my brain, so, in 2002 and 2003, I traveled to the Middle East to see things for myself, and to try to arrive at my own position about this issue.

Coming back, I found out why my friend was so hesitant to speak out. My work on the Israel/Palestine question is treated differently than anything else I do. A slideshow in Chicago was heckled by Right-wingers in black hats.

My name now appears on an online "Shit List" (one letter shy of a felony) posted by followers of Meir Kahane. My work was also attacked by some sections of the pro-Palestinian Left in the United States.

In such a toxic atmosphere, it is not surprising that honest, rational, and compassionate voices fall silent, leaving the debate to the ultra-nationalists and political hustlers.

So I can't expect that all of you who read the next twenty pages will agree with what I have to say. Instead, I ask those of you who disagree to take this moment as an opportunity to examine your own strongly-held convictions. How did you arrive at those beliefs? Were your sources of information objective? How many Israelis, and how many Palestinians, do you know personally?

Above: Sketch of the checkpoint outside the city of Qalqiliya.

2002, 3 ISRAELI SOLDIERS ARE SHOT ON THE EGYPTIAN BORDER.

THESE SOLDIERS ARE NOT JEWS.

THEY ARE BEDOUIN.

BEDOUIN ARE A RACIALLY DIVERSE ETHNIC GROUP. THEY CAN BE DARK OR LIGHT.

THEY ARE UNITED BY A COMMON CULTURE.

BEDOUIN BLUES

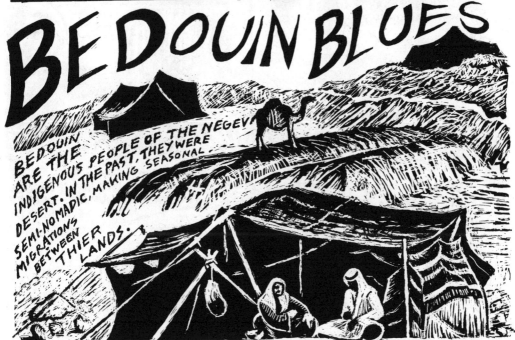

BEDOUIN ARE THE INDIGENOUS PEOPLE OF THE NEGEV DESERT. IN THE PAST, THEY WERE SEMI-NOMADIC, MAKING SEASONAL MIGRATIONS BETWEEN THIER LANDS.

BY SETH TOBOCMAN, WRITTEN WITH THE HELP OF DEVORAH BROUS

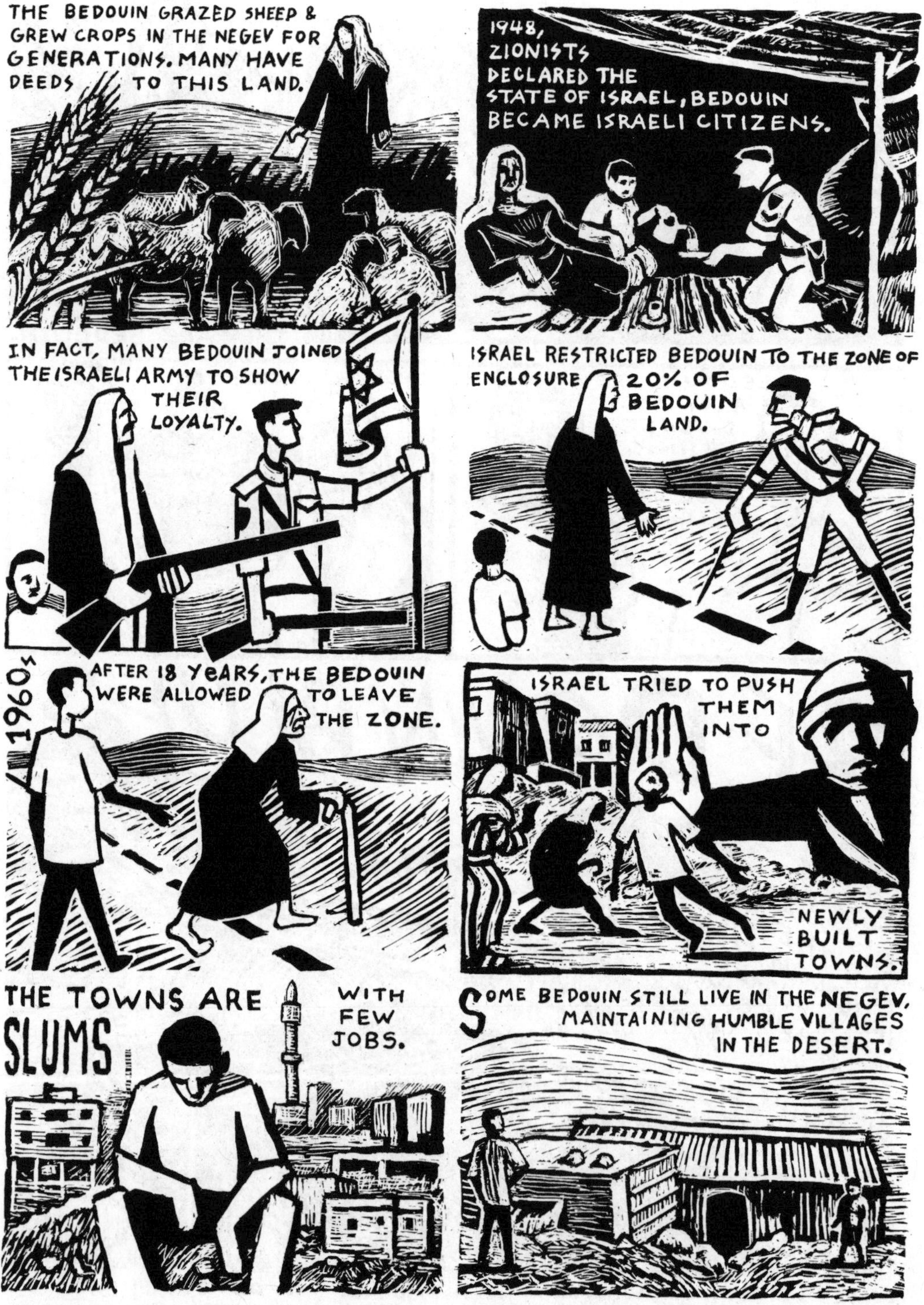
THE BEDOUIN GRAZED SHEEP & GREW CROPS IN THE NEGEV FOR GENERATIONS. MANY HAVE DEEDS TO THIS LAND.
1948, ZIONISTS DECLARED THE STATE OF ISRAEL, BEDOUIN BECAME ISRAELI CITIZENS.
IN FACT, MANY BEDOUIN JOINED THE ISRAELI ARMY TO SHOW THEIR LOYALTY.
ISRAEL RESTRICTED BEDOUIN TO THE ZONE OF ENCLOSURE 20% OF BEDOUIN LAND.
1960s
AFTER 18 YEARS, THE BEDOUIN WERE ALLOWED TO LEAVE THE ZONE.
ISRAEL TRIED TO PUSH THEM INTO
NEWLY BUILT TOWNS.
THE TOWNS ARE SLUMS
WITH FEW JOBS.
SOME BEDOUIN STILL LIVE IN THE NEGEV, MAINTAINING HUMBLE VILLAGES IN THE DESERT.

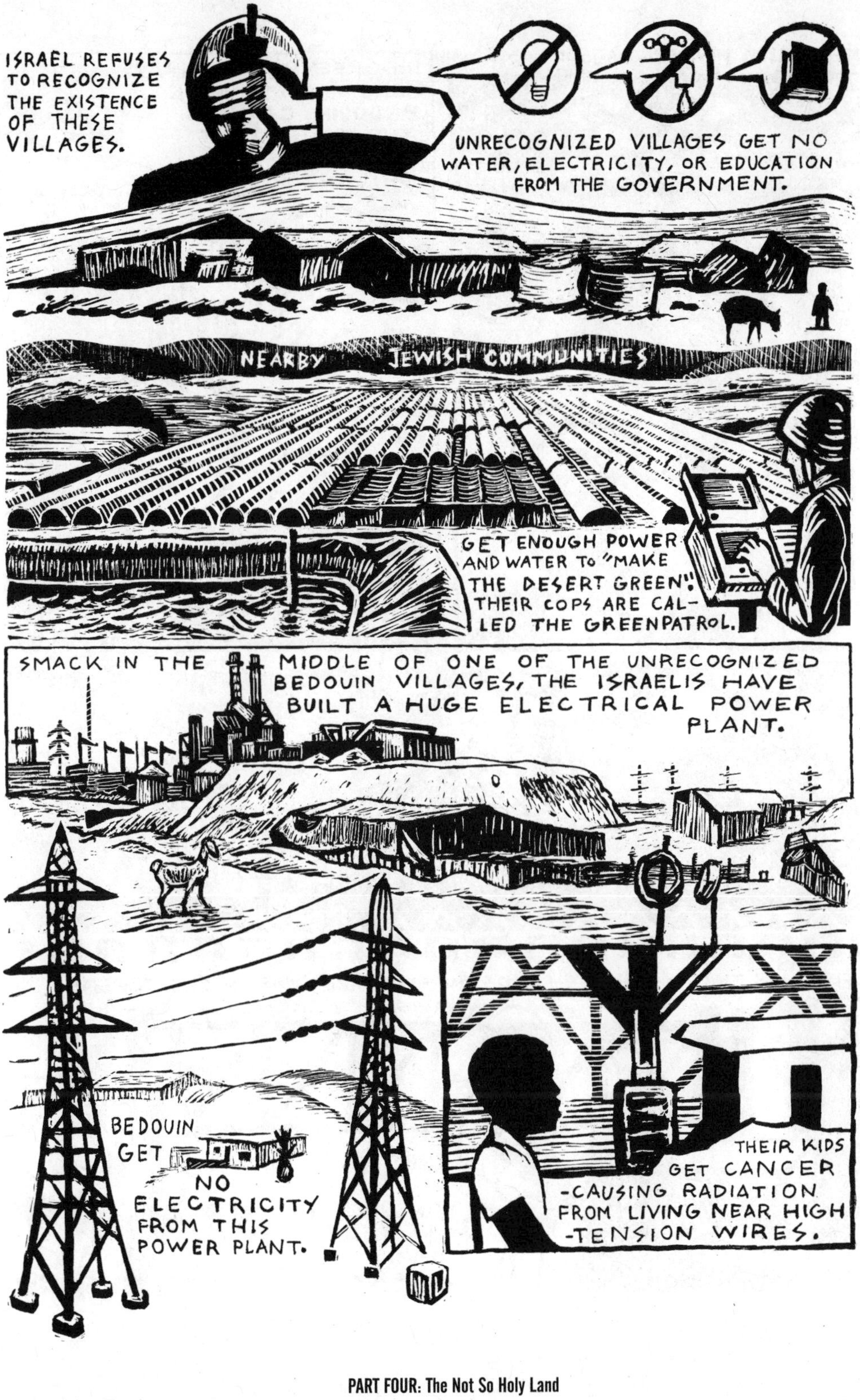
ISRAEL REFUSES TO RECOGNIZE THE EXISTENCE OF THESE VILLAGES.
UNRECOGNIZED VILLAGES GET NO WATER, ELECTRICITY, OR EDUCATION FROM THE GOVERNMENT.
NEARBY JEWISH COMMUNITIES
GET ENOUGH POWER AND WATER TO "MAKE THE DESERT GREEN". THEIR COPS ARE CALLED THE GREENPATROL.
SMACK IN THE MIDDLE OF ONE OF THE UNRECOGNIZED BEDOUIN VILLAGES, THE ISRAELIS HAVE BUILT A HUGE ELECTRICAL POWER PLANT.
BEDOUIN GET NO ELECTRICITY FROM THIS POWER PLANT.
THEIR KIDS GET CANCER-CAUSING RADIATION FROM LIVING NEAR HIGH-TENSION WIRES.

NEARBY, ISRAELIS HAVE BUILT A TOXIC WASTE DUMP.

THE GREEN PATROL SPRAYS HERBICIDES TO KILL BEDOUIN CROPS. THE GAS ALSO CHOKES BEDOUIN CHILDREN.

IN SPITE OF ALL OF THIS, BEDOUIN REFUSE TO LEAVE THEIR LAND IN THE NEGEV.

SO THE ISRAELI GREEN PATROL BULLDOZES BEDOUIN HOMES.

THE LAND IS CLEARED AND GIVEN TO THE JEWISH NATIONAL FUND WHO "MAKE THE DESERT GREEN".

THIS NEW GREEN LAND IS THEN USED TO BUILD HOUSING FOR ISRAEL'S GROWING JEWISH POPULATON.

ISRAEL CLAIMS THAT ITS HUMAN-RIGHTS VIOLATIONS ARE DONE IN SELF DEFENSE AGAINST TERRORISM.

BUT WHAT ACTS OF VIOLENCE DO THE BEDOUIN COMMIT AGAINST ISRAEL?

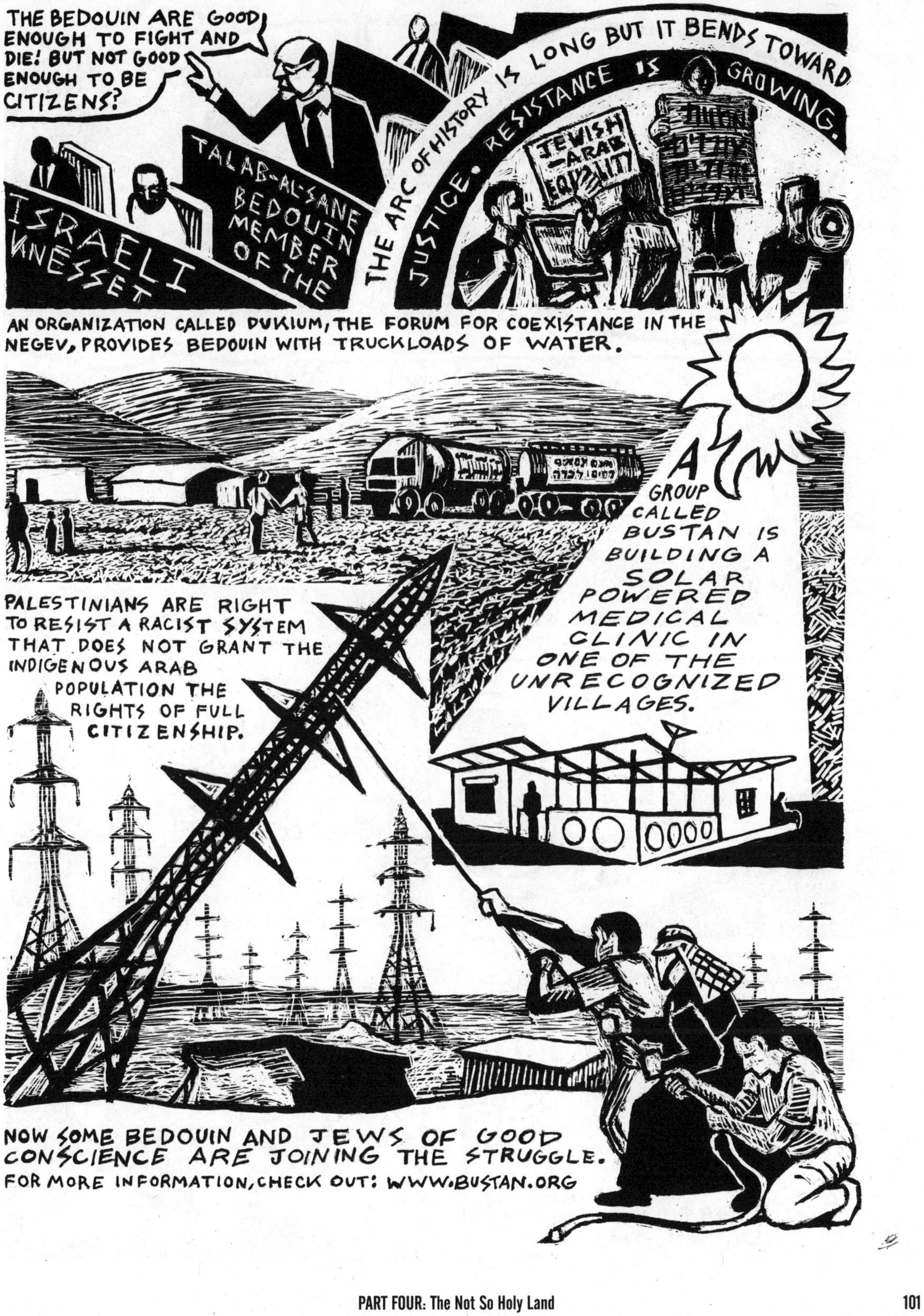
THE BEDOUIN ARE GOOD ENOUGH TO FIGHT AND DIE! BUT NOT GOOD ENOUGH TO BE CITIZENS?
TALAB-AL-SANE BEDOUIN MEMBER OF THE ISRAELI KNESSET
THE ARC OF HISTORY IS LONG BUT IT BENDS TOWARD JUSTICE. RESISTANCE IS GROWING.
JEWISH-ARAB EQUALITY
AN ORGANIZATION CALLED DUKIUM, THE FORUM FOR COEXISTANCE IN THE NEGEV, PROVIDES BEDOUIN WITH TRUCKLOADS OF WATER.
A GROUP CALLED BUSTAN IS BUILDING A SOLAR POWERED MEDICAL CLINIC IN ONE OF THE UNRECOGNIZED VILLAGES.
PALESTINIANS ARE RIGHT TO RESIST A RACIST SYSTEM THAT DOES NOT GRANT THE INDIGENOUS ARAB POPULATION THE RIGHTS OF FULL CITIZENSHIP.
NOW SOME BEDOUIN AND JEWS OF GOOD CONSCIENCE ARE JOINING THE STRUGGLE.
FOR MORE INFORMATION, CHECK OUT: WWW.BUSTAN.ORG

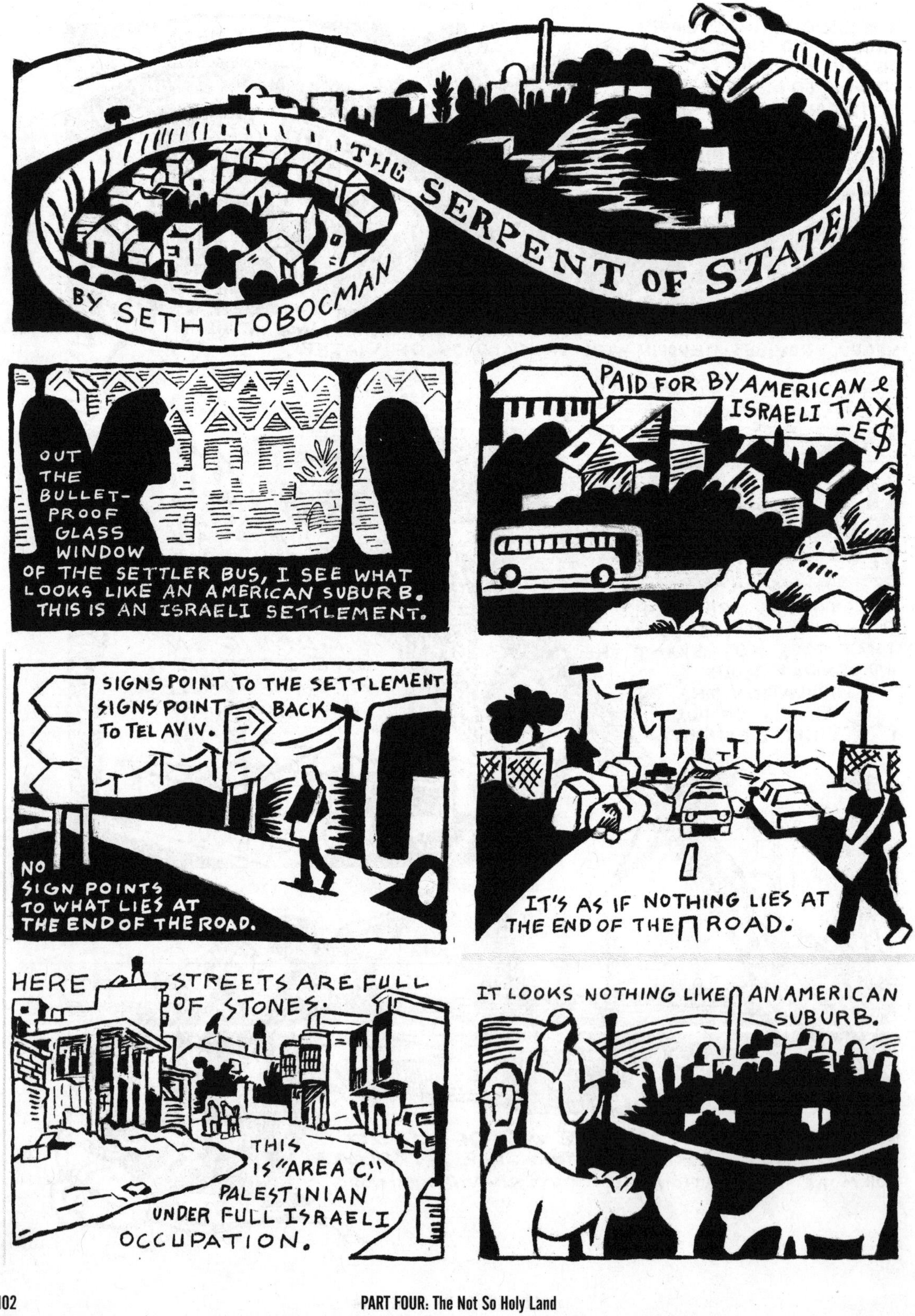
THE SERPENT OF STATE
BY SETH TOBOCMAN
OUT THE BULLET-PROOF GLASS WINDOW OF THE SETTLER BUS, I SEE WHAT LOOKS LIKE AN AMERICAN SUBURB. THIS IS AN ISRAELI SETTLEMENT.
PAID FOR BY AMERICAN & ISRAELI TAX-E$
SIGNS POINT TO THE SETTLEMENT
SIGNS POINT BACK TO TEL AVIV.
NO SIGN POINTS TO WHAT LIES AT THE END OF THE ROAD.
IT'S AS IF NOTHING LIES AT THE END OF THE ROAD.
HERE STREETS ARE FULL OF STONES.
THIS IS "AREA C," PALESTINIAN UNDER FULL ISRAELI OCCUPATION.
IT LOOKS NOTHING LIKE AN AMERICAN SUBURB.

BUT WAIT, THERE IS NEW CONSTRUCTION GOING ON IN THIS VILLAGE.

AT FIRST IT APPEARS THE ISRAELIS ARE BUILDING....

...A LONG HIGHWAY WITH A DEEP DITCH NEXT TO IT.

BARBED WIRE IS ADDED. THE ROAD BECOMES A FENCE.

THEN, IN PLACES, CEMENT AND GUARD TOWERS ARE ADDED. THE ISRAELIS ARE BUILDING A WALL IN PALESTINE.

THEY SAY THIS WALL IS FOR THE
SECURITY OF ISRAEL.

BUT THE WALL DOES NOT FOLLOW THE GREEN LINE, THE INTERNATIONALLY RECOGNIZED BORDER OF ISRAEL.

INSTEAD, IT SNAKES AROUND THE LARGER SETTLEMENTS.

THE WALL WILL SEPARATE PALESTINIAN FARMERS FROM THEIR LAND.

IN OTHER PLACES THE WALL WILL LOCK PALESTINIANS INTO A NO-MAN'S LAND WHERE THEY WILL BE NEITHER ISRAELI NOR PALESTINIAN CITIZENS, AND SO HAVE NO LEGAL RIGHTS.

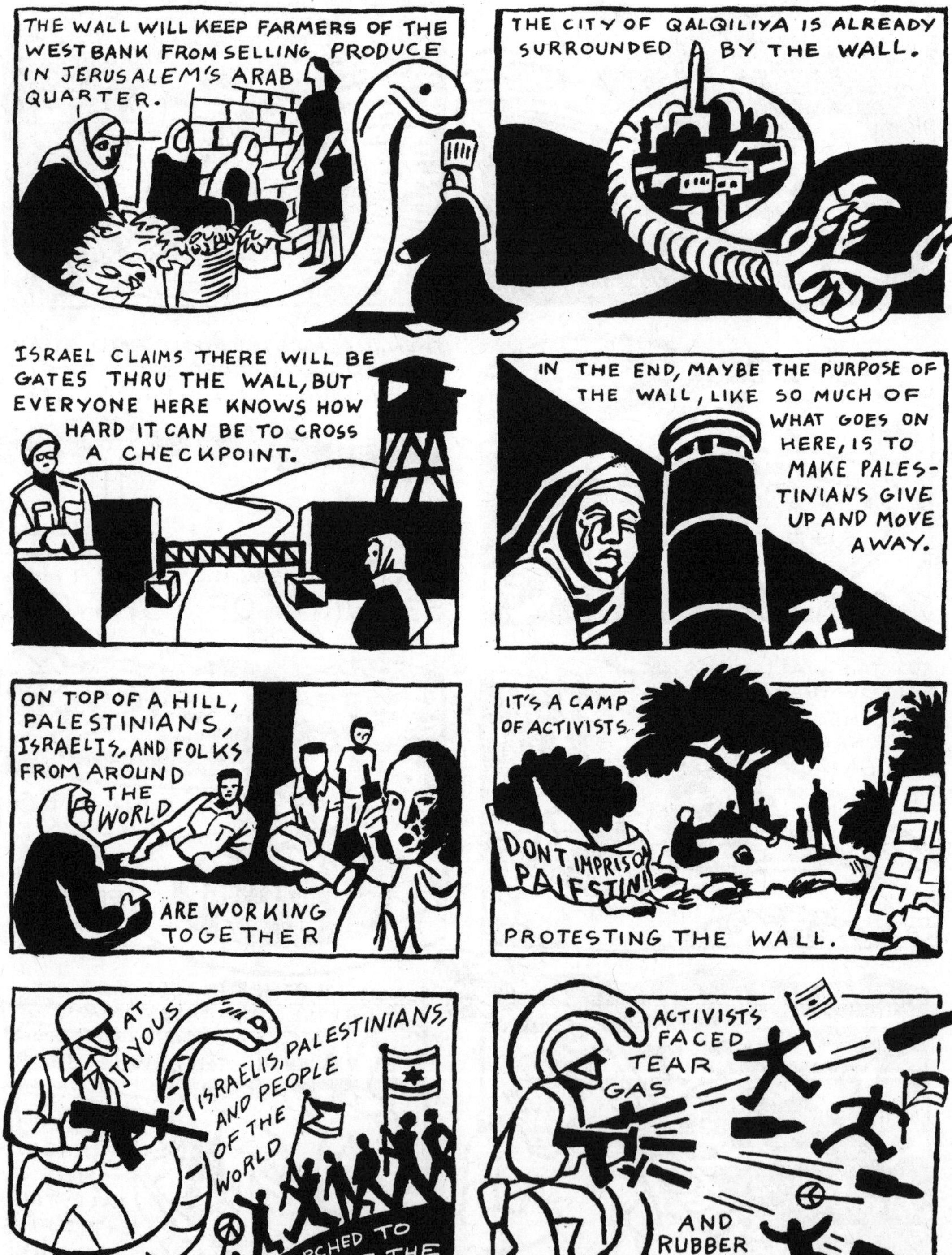
THE WALL WILL KEEP FARMERS OF THE WESTBANK FROM SELLING PRODUCE IN JERUSALEM'S ARAB QUARTER.
THE CITY OF QALQILIYA IS ALREADY SURROUNDED BY THE WALL.
ISRAEL CLAIMS THERE WILL BE GATES THRU THE WALL, BUT EVERYONE HERE KNOWS HOW HARD IT CAN BE TO CROSS A CHECKPOINT.
IN THE END, MAYBE THE PURPOSE OF THE WALL, LIKE SO MUCH OF WHAT GOES ON HERE, IS TO MAKE PALESTINIANS GIVE UP AND MOVE AWAY.
ON TOP OF A HILL, PALESTINIANS, ISRAELIS, AND FOLKS FROM AROUND THE WORLD
ARE WORKING TOGETHER
IT'S A CAMP OF ACTIVISTS
DONT IMPRISO
PALESTINI
PROTESTING THE WALL.
AT JAYOUS
ISRAELIS, PALESTINIANS, AND PEOPLE OF THE WORLD
MARCHED TO STOP THE WALL.
ACTIVISTS FACED TEAR GAS
AND RUBBER BULLETS.

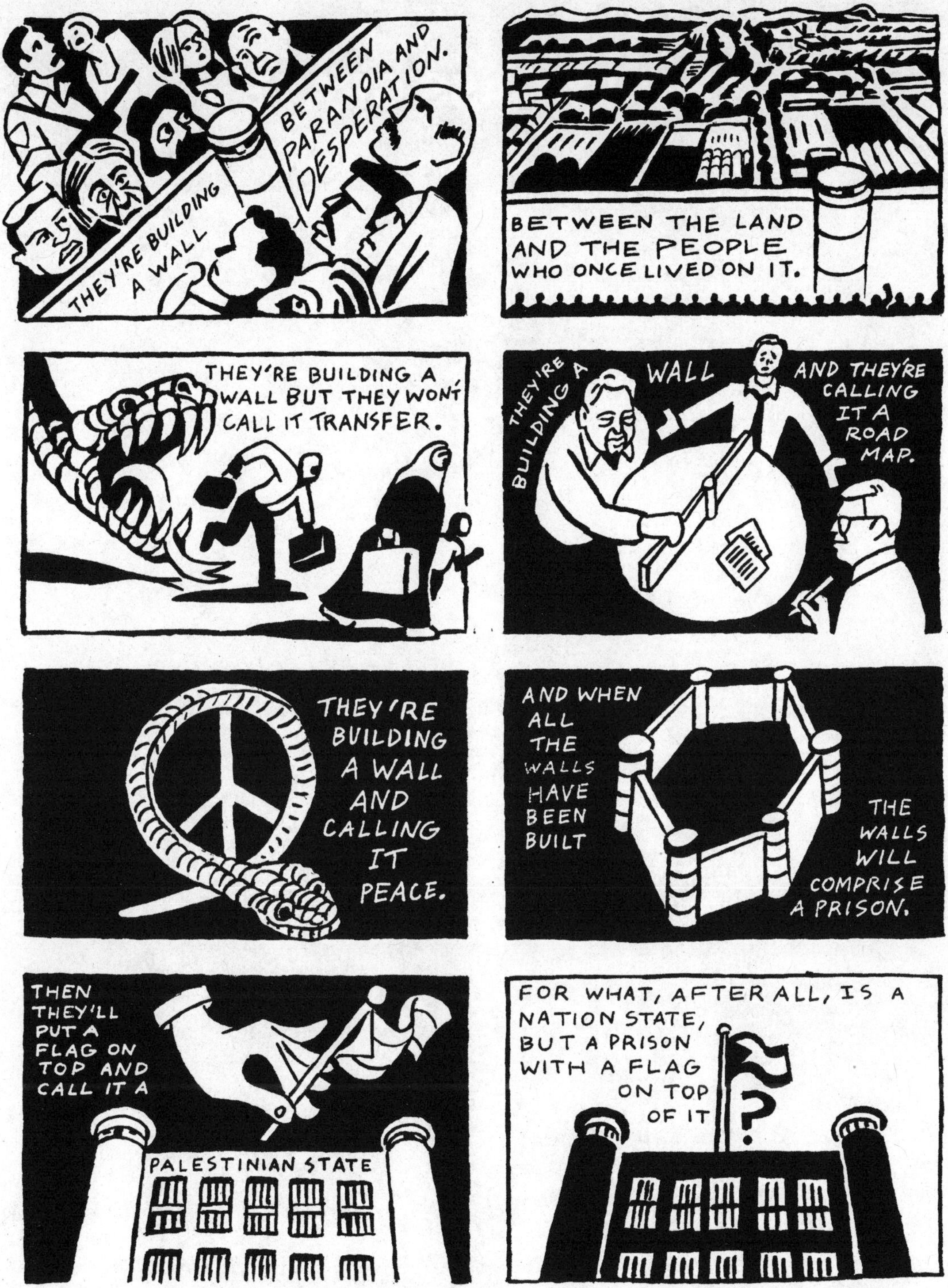
THEY'RE BUILDING A WALL
BETWEEN PARANOIA AND DESPERATION.
BETWEEN THE LAND AND THE PEOPLE WHO ONCE LIVED ON IT.
THEY'RE BUILDING A WALL BUT THEY WON'T CALL IT TRANSFER.
THEY'RE BUILDING A WALL
AND THEY'RE CALLING IT A ROAD MAP.
THEY'RE BUILDING A WALL AND CALLING IT PEACE.
AND WHEN ALL THE WALLS HAVE BEEN BUILT
THE WALLS WILL COMPRISE A PRISON.
THEN THEY'LL PUT A FLAG ON TOP AND CALL IT A
PALESTINIAN STATE
FOR WHAT, AFTER ALL, IS A NATION STATE, BUT A PRISON WITH A FLAG ON TOP OF IT
?

BROTHERLY MASS GRAVE

A song by the Israeli hardcore band DIR -YASSIN
(slightly re written by Seth Tobocman)

There's been a bombing
and only quiet songs will play.
There's been a bombing-
and only pretty songs will play.
The voices of multitudes,
of all the many Aric Einstiens. ← FRANK SINATRAS

There's been a bombing, no doubt,
and like 30 people died.

← 3000

Voices of survivors provide the descriptions.
There's been a bombing, and they'll broadcast
the wounded as entertainment.
No one has anything intelligent to say
and they're all gonna say it at once.

There's been a bombing- so collective punishments
and starvation have been imposed on them.
There's been a bombing and so martial law has
been declared on the minds and the thoughts of the
Jews ← AMERICANS

We are all one big consensus
We are all brothers
this is not the time for protests
These are the times for tears'
and racist stances
as long as they're directed against Arabs.

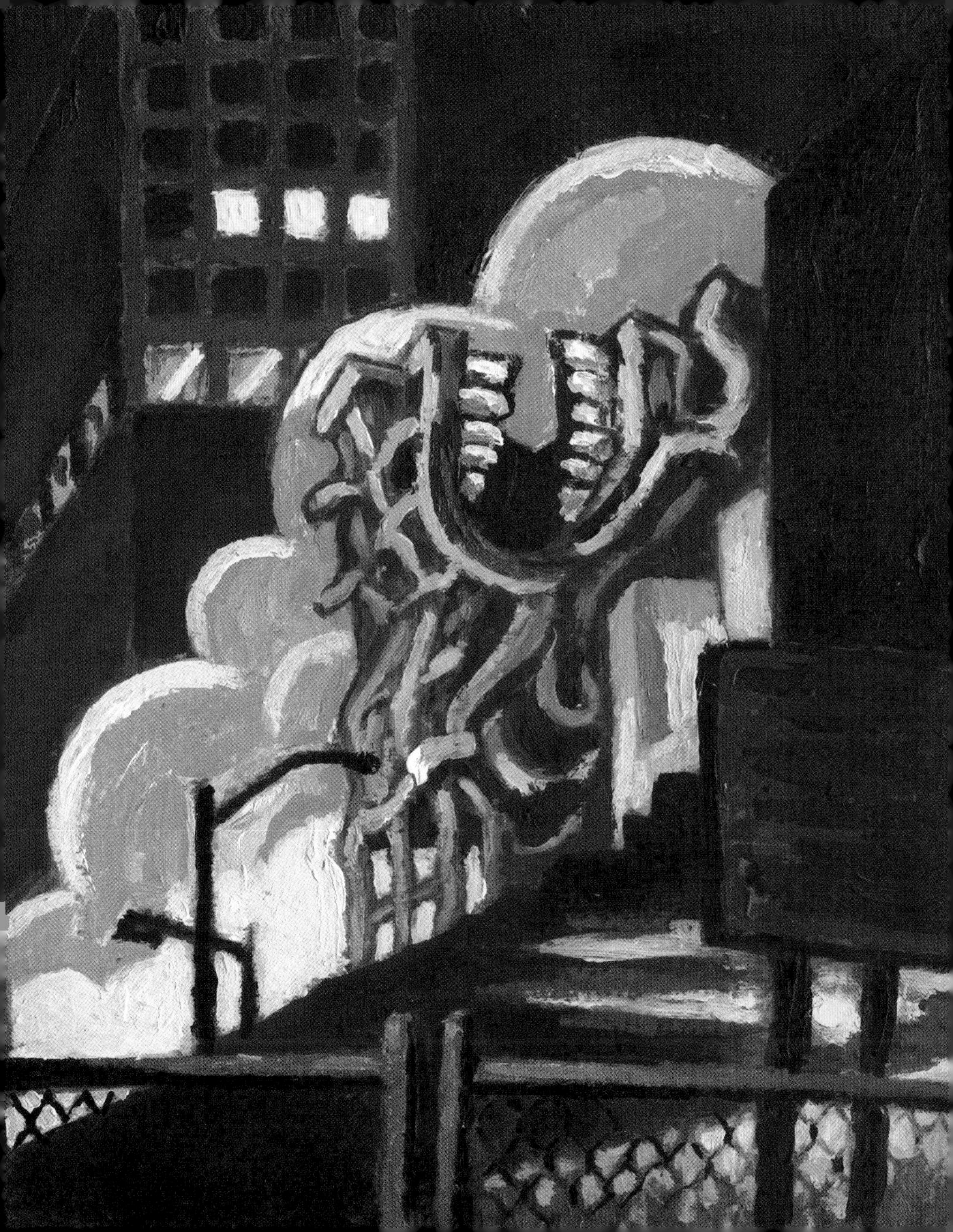

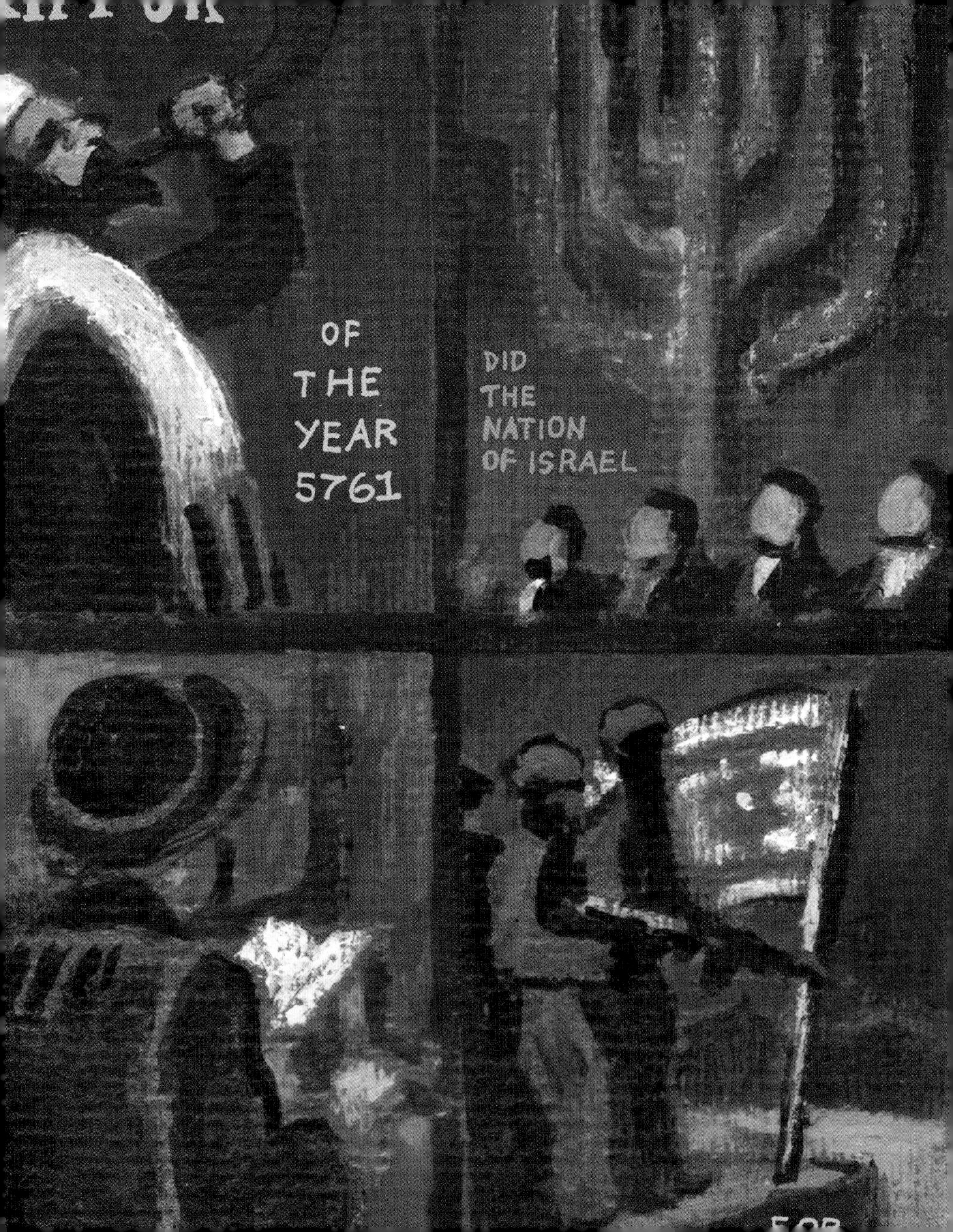
OF
THE
YEAR
5761
DID
THE
NATION
OF ISRAEL

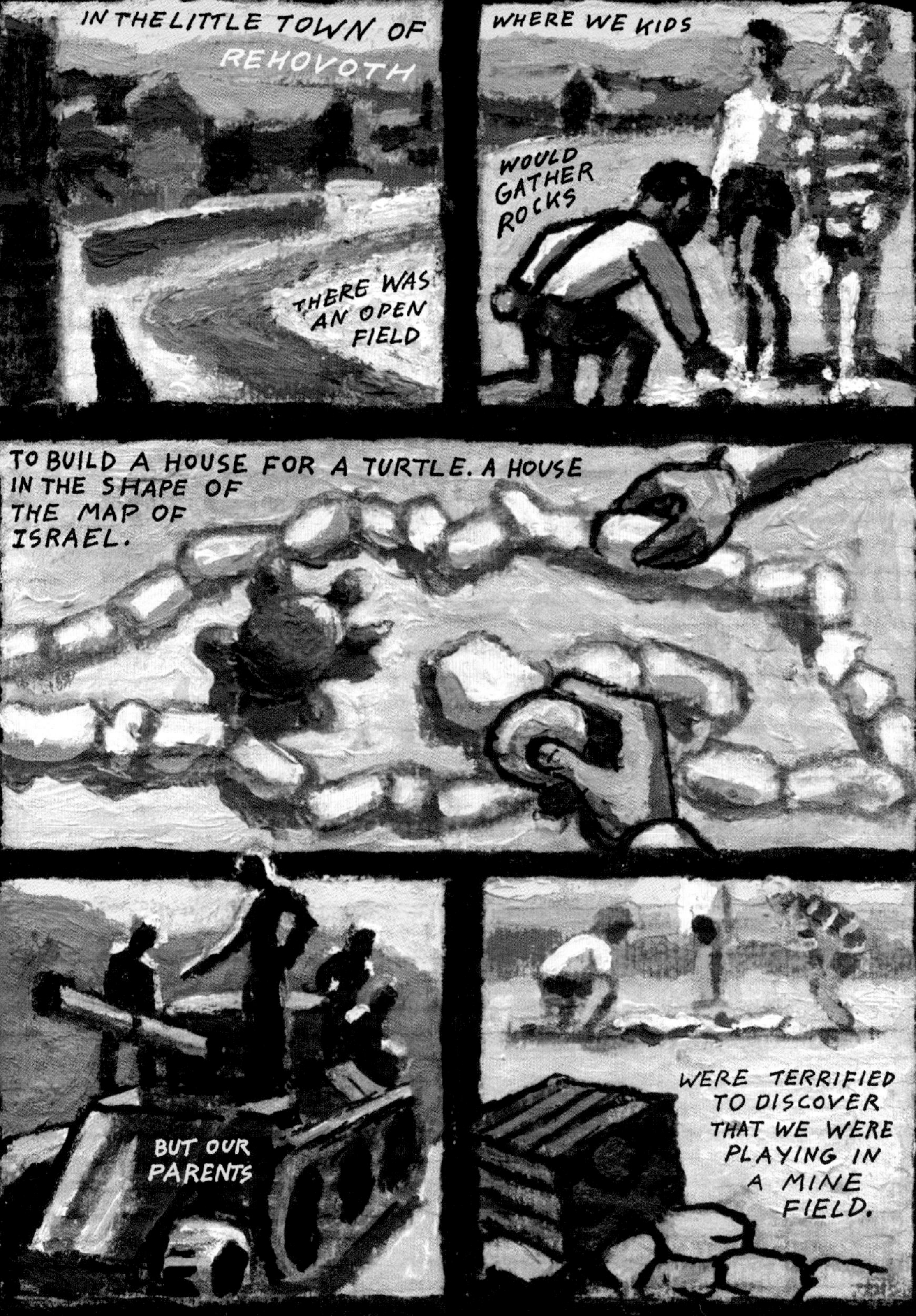
IN THE LITTLE TOWN OF
REHOVOTH
THERE WAS AN OPEN FIELD
WHERE WE KIDS
WOULD GATHER ROCKS
TO BUILD A HOUSE FOR A TURTLE. A HOUSE IN THE SHAPE OF THE MAP OF ISRAEL.
BUT OUR PARENTS
WERE TERRIFIED TO DISCOVER THAT WE WERE PLAYING IN A MINE FIELD.

ON YOM
KIPPUR
OF THE
YEAR
5761

DID THE
STATE OF
ISRAEL

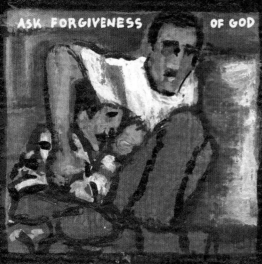

ASK FORGIVENESS OF GOD

FOR THE
SHOOTING
OF A BOY

WHO DIED

IN HIS
FATHER'S
ARMS?

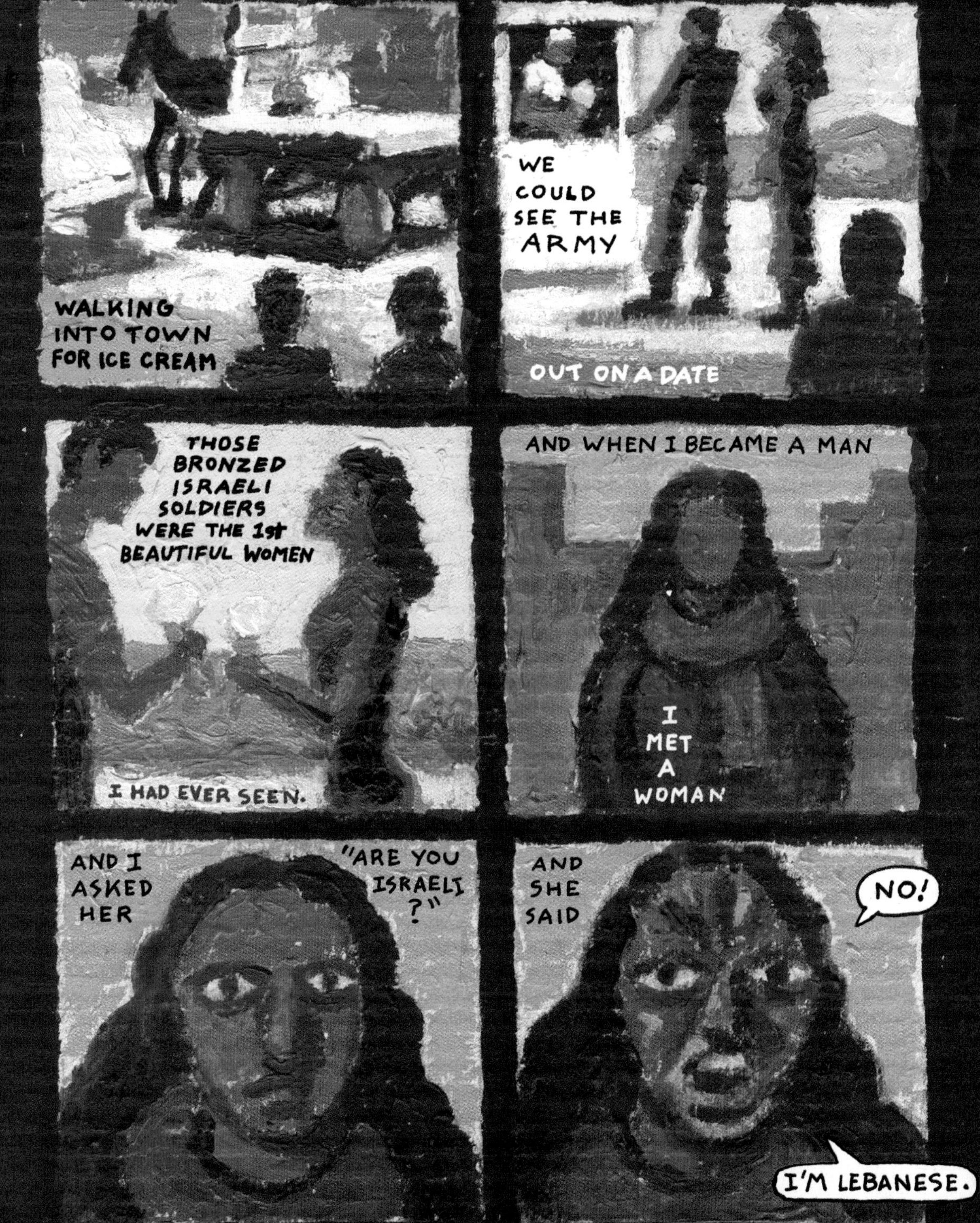

WALKING INTO TOWN FOR ICE CREAM
WE COULD SEE THE ARMY
OUT ON A DATE
THOSE BRONZED ISRAELI SOLDIERS WERE THE 1st BEAUTIFUL WOMEN
I HAD EVER SEEN.
AND WHEN I BECAME A MAN
I MET A WOMAN
AND I ASKED HER
"ARE YOU ISRAELI?"
AND SHE SAID
NO!
I'M LEBANESE.

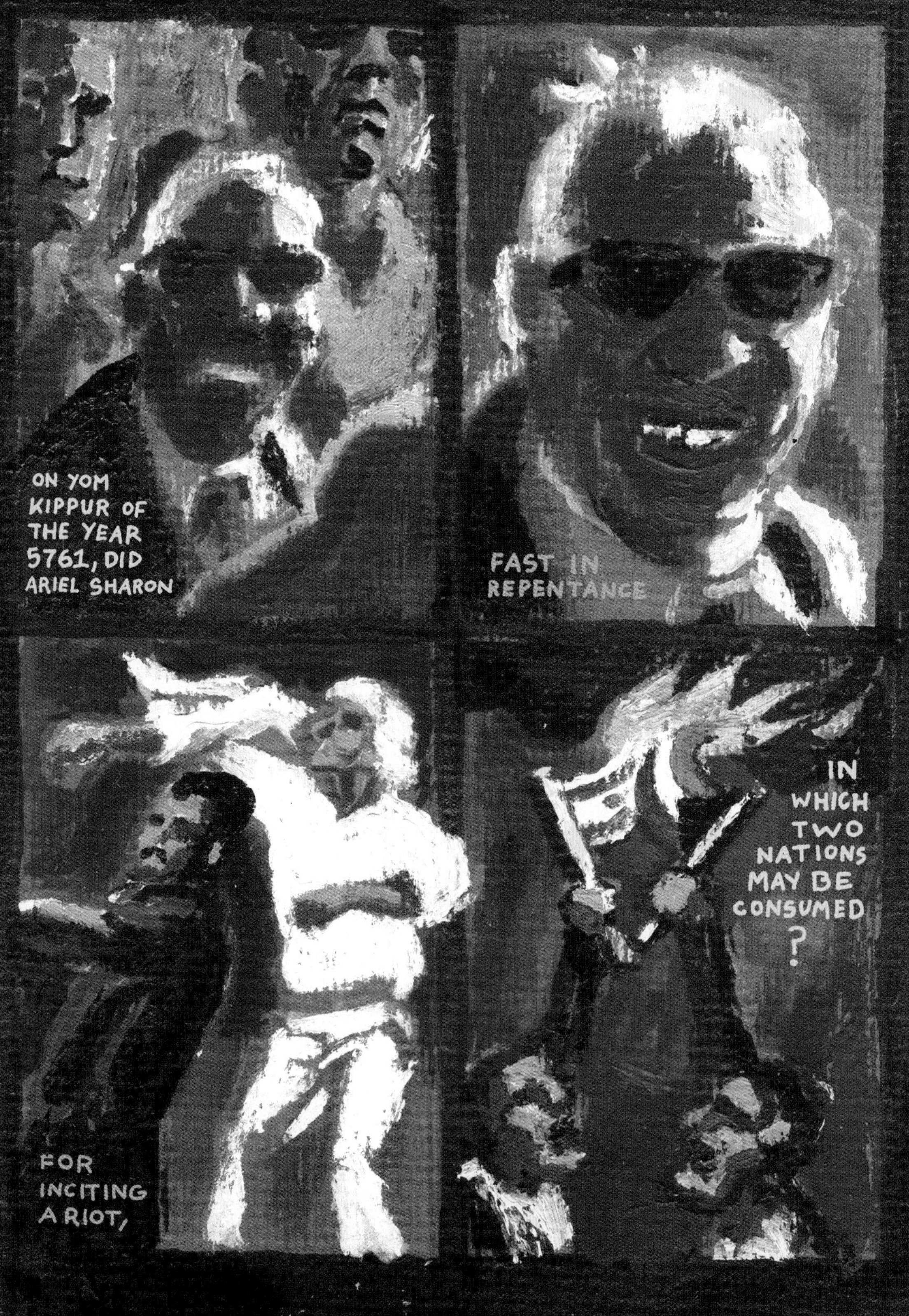
ON YOM KIPPUR OF THE YEAR 5761, DID ARIEL SHARON
FAST IN REPENTANCE
FOR INCITING A RIOT,
IN WHICH TWO NATIONS MAY BE CONSUMED
?

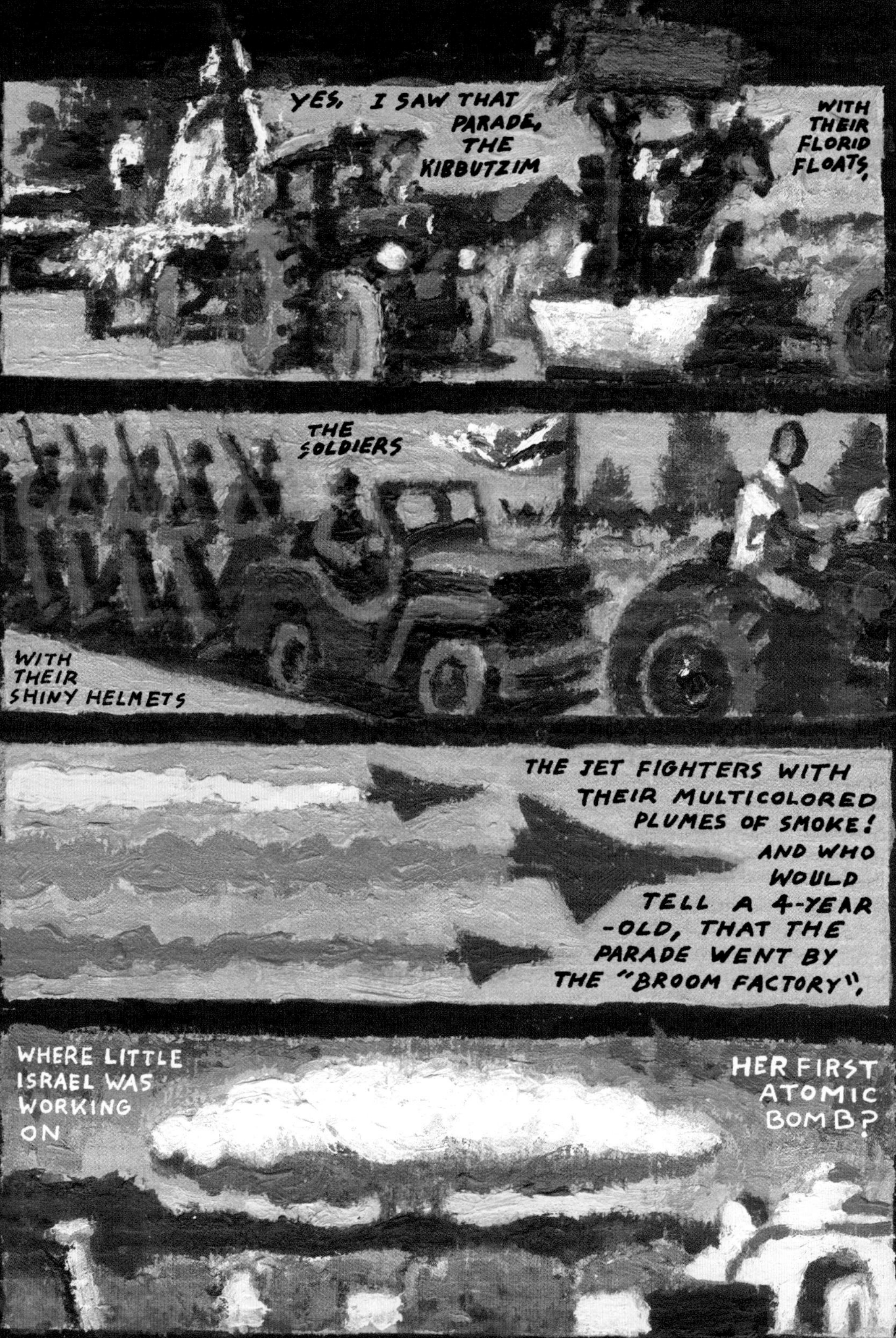
YES, I SAW THAT PARADE, THE KIBBUTZIM
WITH THEIR FLORID FLOATS,
THE SOLDIERS
WITH THEIR SHINY HELMETS
THE JET FIGHTERS WITH THEIR MULTICOLORED PLUMES OF SMOKE!
AND WHO WOULD TELL A 4-YEAR -OLD, THAT THE PARADE WENT BY THE "BROOM FACTORY",
WHERE LITTLE ISRAEL WAS WORKING ON
HER FIRST ATOMIC BOMB?

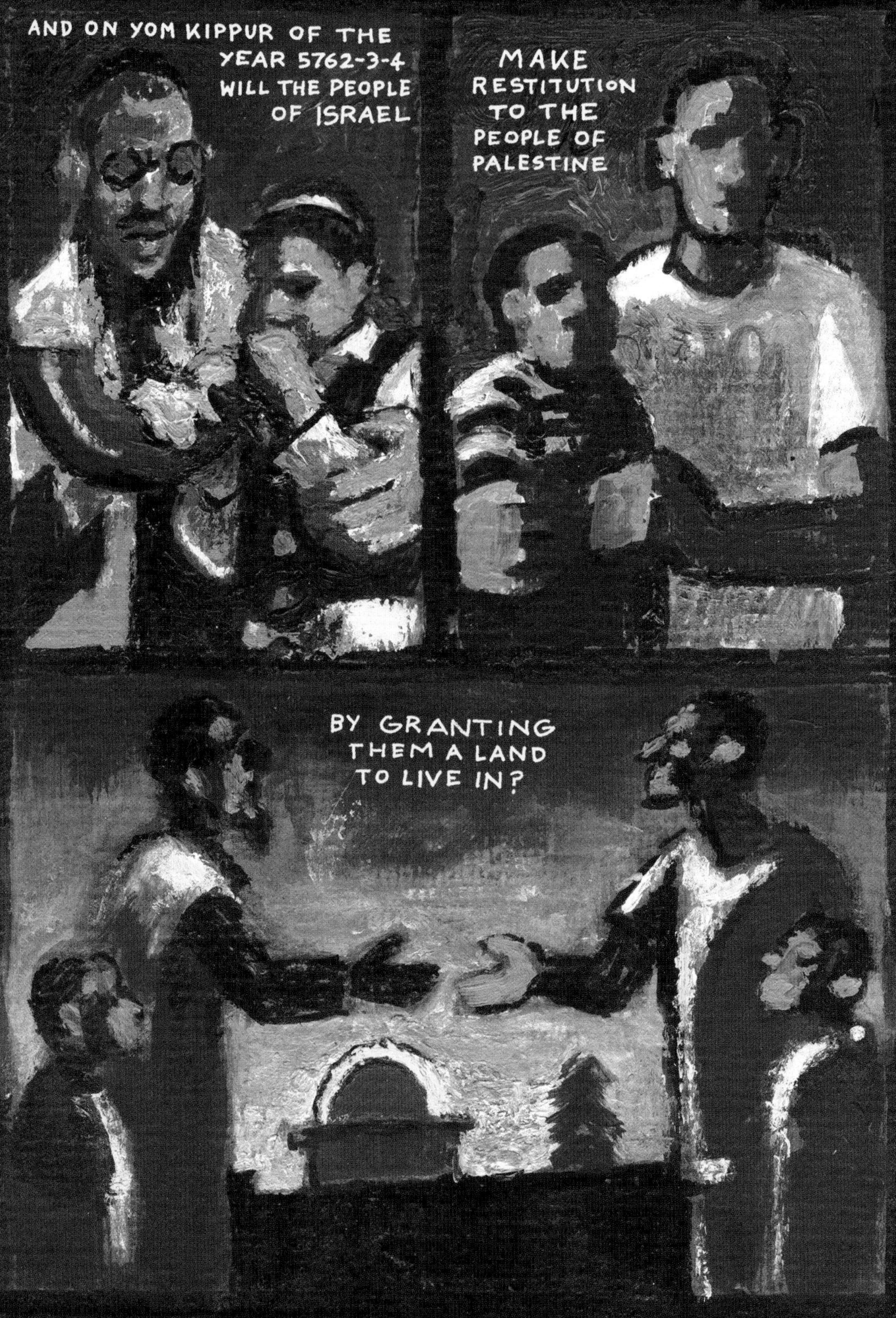

AND ON YOM KIPPUR OF THE YEAR 5762-3-4 WILL THE PEOPLE OF ISRAEL
MAKE RESTITUTION TO THE PEOPLE OF PALESTINE
BY GRANTING THEM A LAND TO LIVE IN?

Part Five:

After the Flood

AFTER THE FLOOD

In September 2005, a friend of mine called and told me that she was going to try to get into New Orleans with two trucks of medical supplies. As it turned out, only the truck driven by whites was allowed past the checkpoints. That truck arrived at the home of a local activist named Malik Rahim, and, together, they set up a clinic that grew into the relief effort known as Common Ground.

I was teaching at two universities at the time and could not get to New Orleans until January. What I saw when I got there was impressive. Volunteers had built several powerful organizations that were rebuilding people's homes and providing other services.

By contrast, the government was doing very little, and what they were doing was often counterproductive.

This shouldn't be surprising. Scientists had been warning us for years that global warming was going to cause floods and hurricanes, but nothing was done about it. The government knew that the levees were inadequate, but next to nothing was done to improve them. Then when people were stuck in the flooded city, little or nothing was done to rescue them. So the failure to rebuild New Orleans is not an aberration, but part of a consistent pattern and practice. A whole history of doing nothing.

One has to wonder about the government's motivations in this situation. A rapper's controversial remark that "George Bush doesn't give a fuck about black people" is, in fact, rather charitable, because it implies that this was only a matter of negligence—not malicious intent.

I claim no inside information on the decisions made by politicians. As an artist I can show you what I see and tell you how I feel. This is how it looks and feels to me: I believe that this situation was allowed to happen because there are powerful interests that want to change the demographics of the area.

In fact, there is a disturbing pattern in the world with regard to the politics of disaster relief. In the wake of the Asian Tsunami, the government of Indonesia withheld aid from the rebellious province of Aceh to break the resistance there.

Above: Sketch of the Lower 9th Ward.
Opposite: Poster for Common Ground.

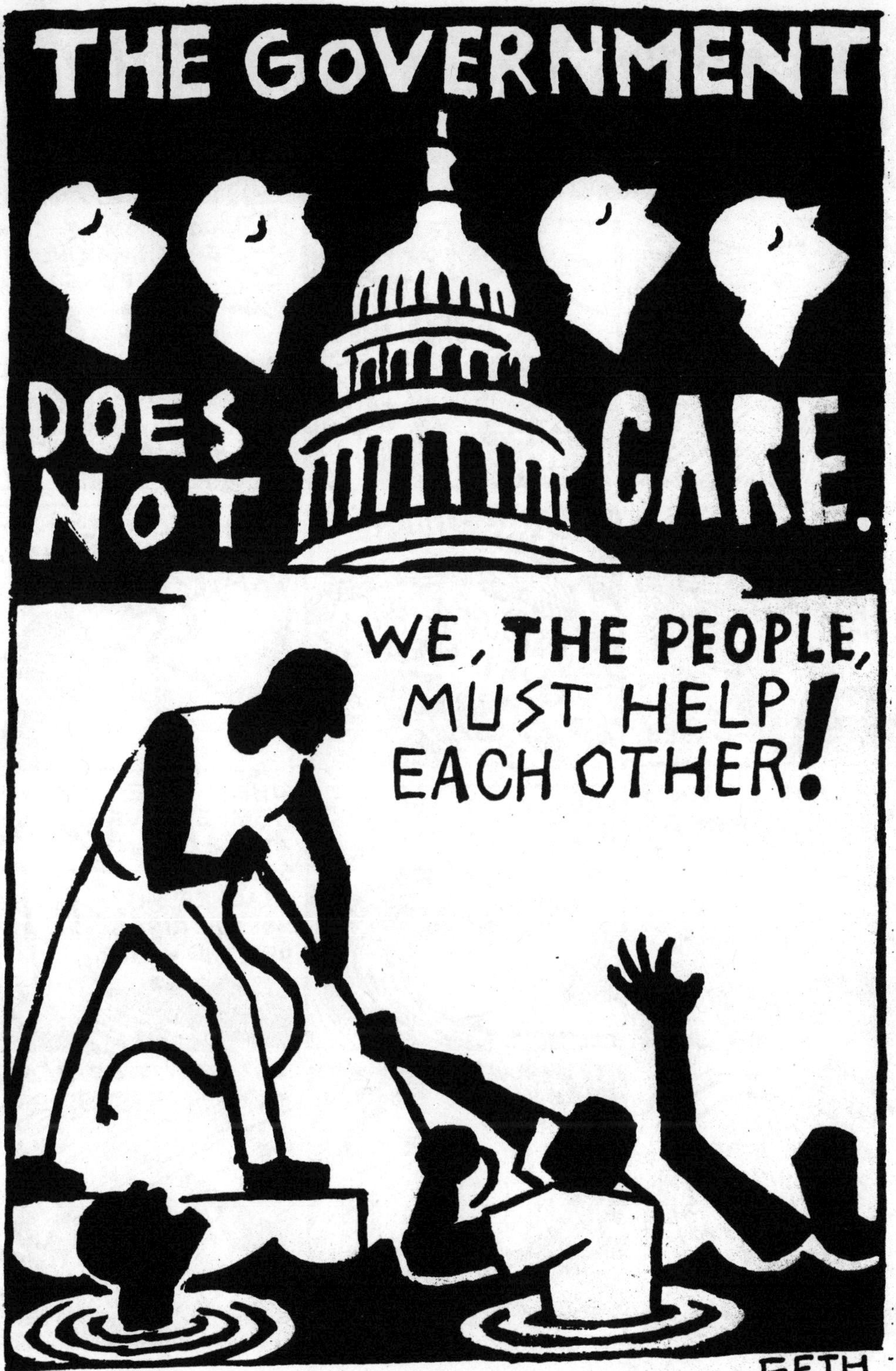
THE GOVERNMENT
DOES NOT CARE.
WE, THE PEOPLE, MUST HELP EACH OTHER!
SETH

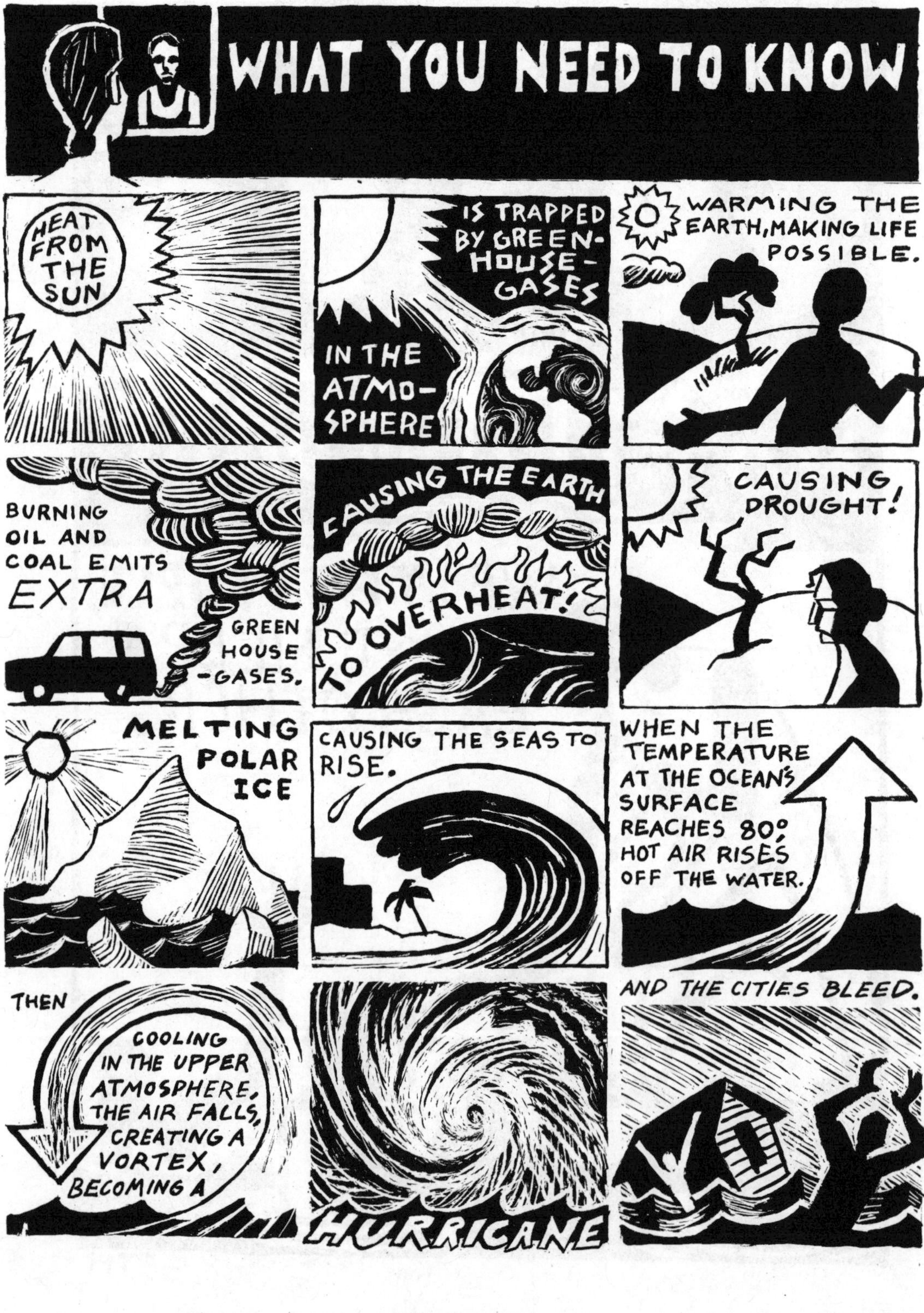
WHAT YOU NEED TO KNOW
HEAT FROM THE SUN
IS TRAPPED BY GREEN-HOUSE-GASES
IN THE ATMO-SPHERE
WARMING THE EARTH, MAKING LIFE POSSIBLE.
BURNING OIL AND COAL EMITS EXTRA
GREEN HOUSE -GASES.
CAUSING THE EARTH
TO OVERHEAT!
CAUSING DROUGHT!
MELTING POLAR ICE
CAUSING THE SEAS TO RISE.
WHEN THE TEMPERATURE AT THE OCEAN'S SURFACE REACHES 80°, HOT AIR RISES OFF THE WATER.
THEN
COOLING IN THE UPPER ATMOSPHERE, THE AIR FALLS, CREATING A VORTEX, BECOMING A
HURRICANE
AND THE CITIES BLEED.

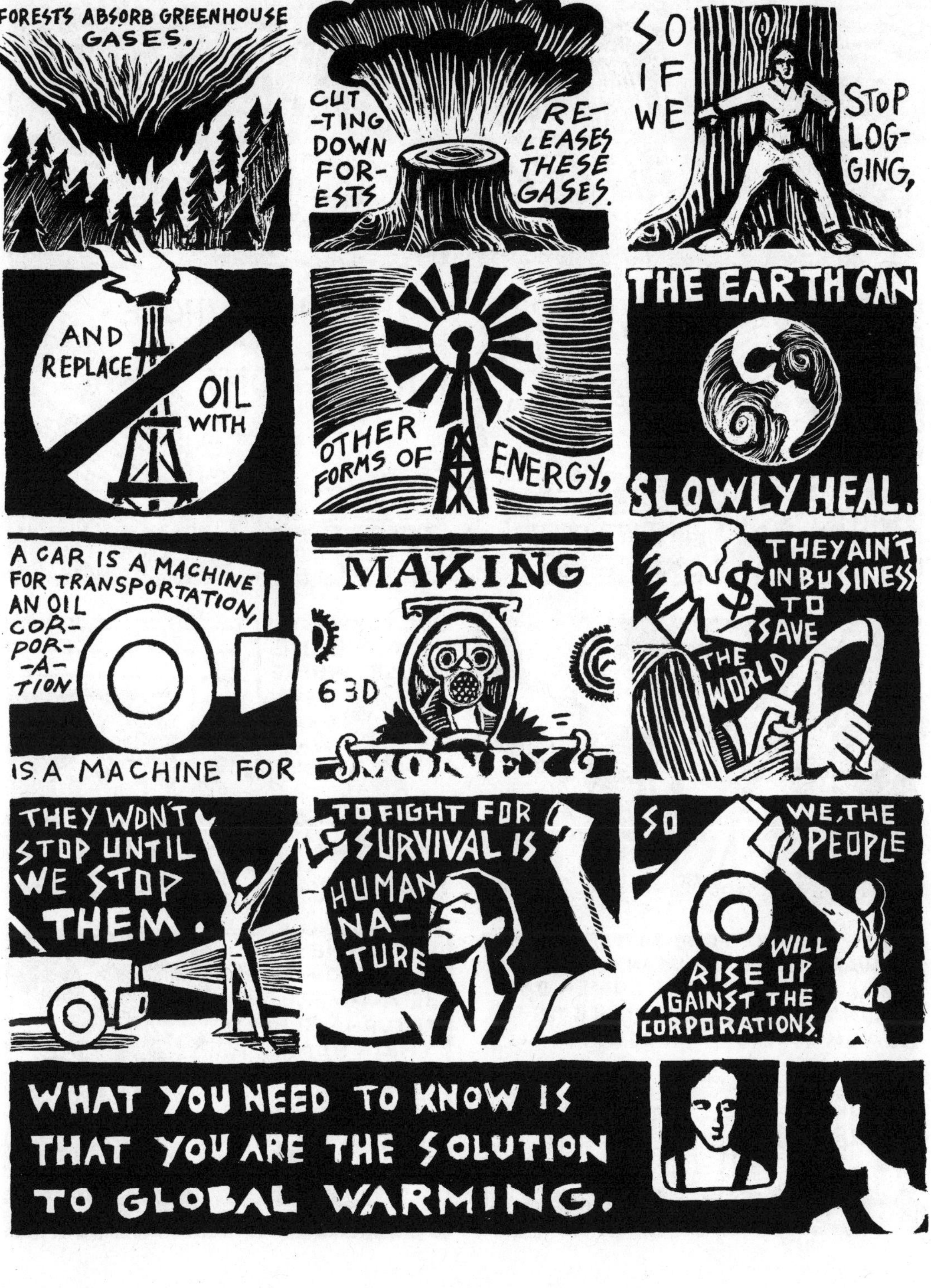
FORESTS ABSORB GREENHOUSE GASES.
CUTTING DOWN FORESTS
RELEASES THESE GASES.
SO IF WE
STOP LOGGING,
AND REPLACE
OIL WITH
OTHER FORMS OF
ENERGY,
THE EARTH CAN
SLOWLY HEAL.
A CAR IS A MACHINE FOR TRANSPORTATION,
AN OIL CORPORATION
IS A MACHINE FOR
MAKING
MONEY
THEY AIN'T IN BUSINESS TO SAVE THE WORLD
THEY WON'T STOP UNTIL WE STOP THEM.
TO FIGHT FOR SURVIVAL IS HUMAN NATURE
SO
WE, THE PEOPLE
WILL RISE UP AGAINST THE CORPORATIONS.
WHAT YOU NEED TO KNOW IS THAT YOU ARE THE SOLUTION TO GLOBAL WARMING.

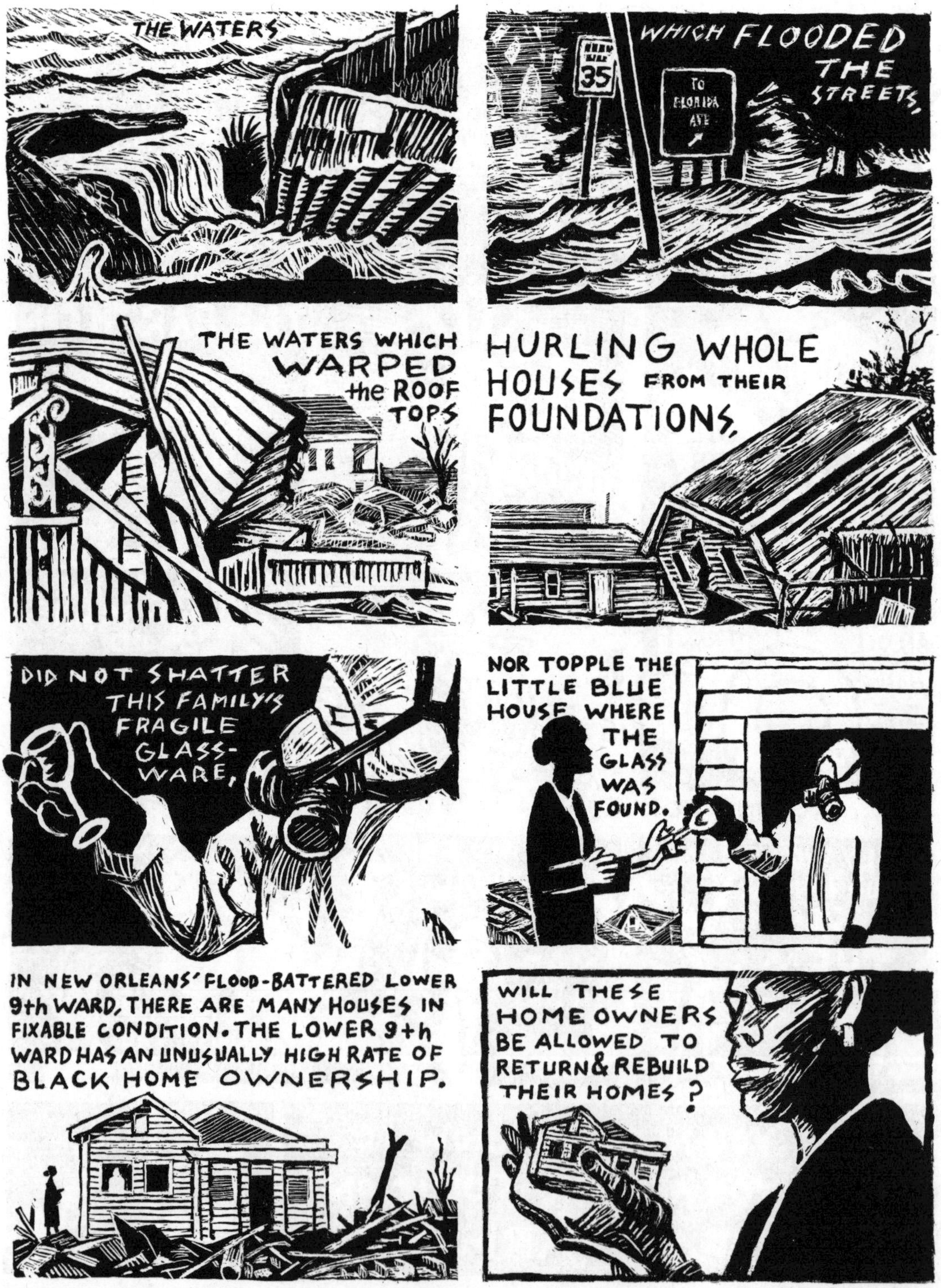
THE WATERS
WHICH FLOODED THE STREETS,
35
TO FLORIDA AVE
THE WATERS WHICH WARPED the ROOF TOPS
HURLING WHOLE HOUSES FROM THEIR FOUNDATIONS,
DID NOT SHATTER THIS FAMILY'S FRAGILE GLASS-WARE,
NOR TOPPLE THE LITTLE BLUE HOUSE WHERE THE GLASS WAS FOUND.
IN NEW ORLEANS' FLOOD-BATTERED LOWER 9th WARD, THERE ARE MANY HOUSES IN FIXABLE CONDITION. THE LOWER 9th WARD HAS AN UNUSUALLY HIGH RATE OF BLACK HOME OWNERSHIP.
WILL THESE HOME OWNERS BE ALLOWED TO RETURN & REBUILD THEIR HOMES?

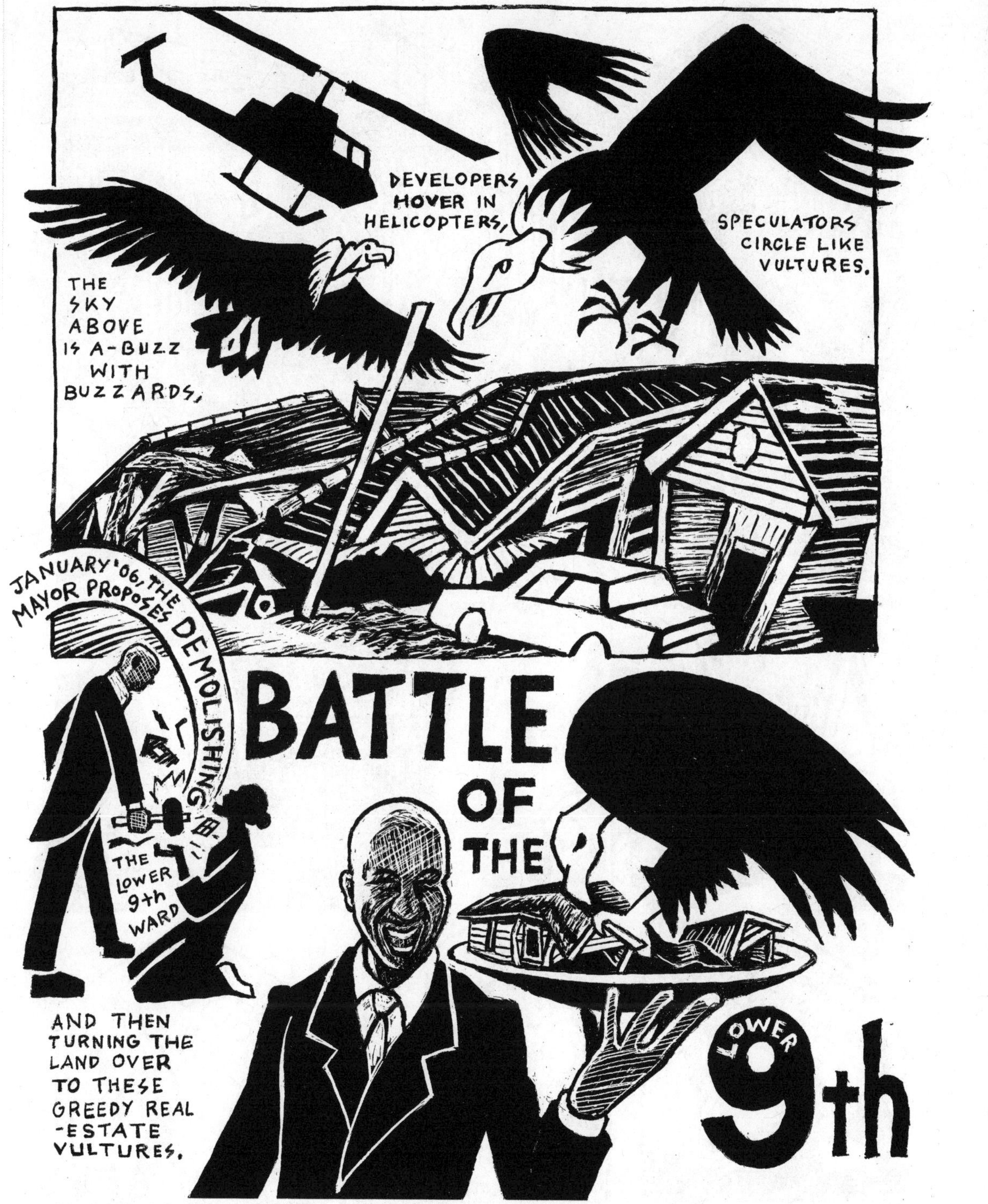
DEVELOPERS HOVER IN HELICOPTERS,
SPECULATORS CIRCLE LIKE VULTURES.
THE SKY ABOVE IS A-BUZZ WITH BUZZARDS.
JANUARY '06, THE MAYOR PROPOSES DEMOLISHING
THE LOWER 9th WARD
AND THEN TURNING THE LAND OVER TO THESE GREEDY REAL-ESTATE VULTURES.
BATTLE OF THE LOWER 9th

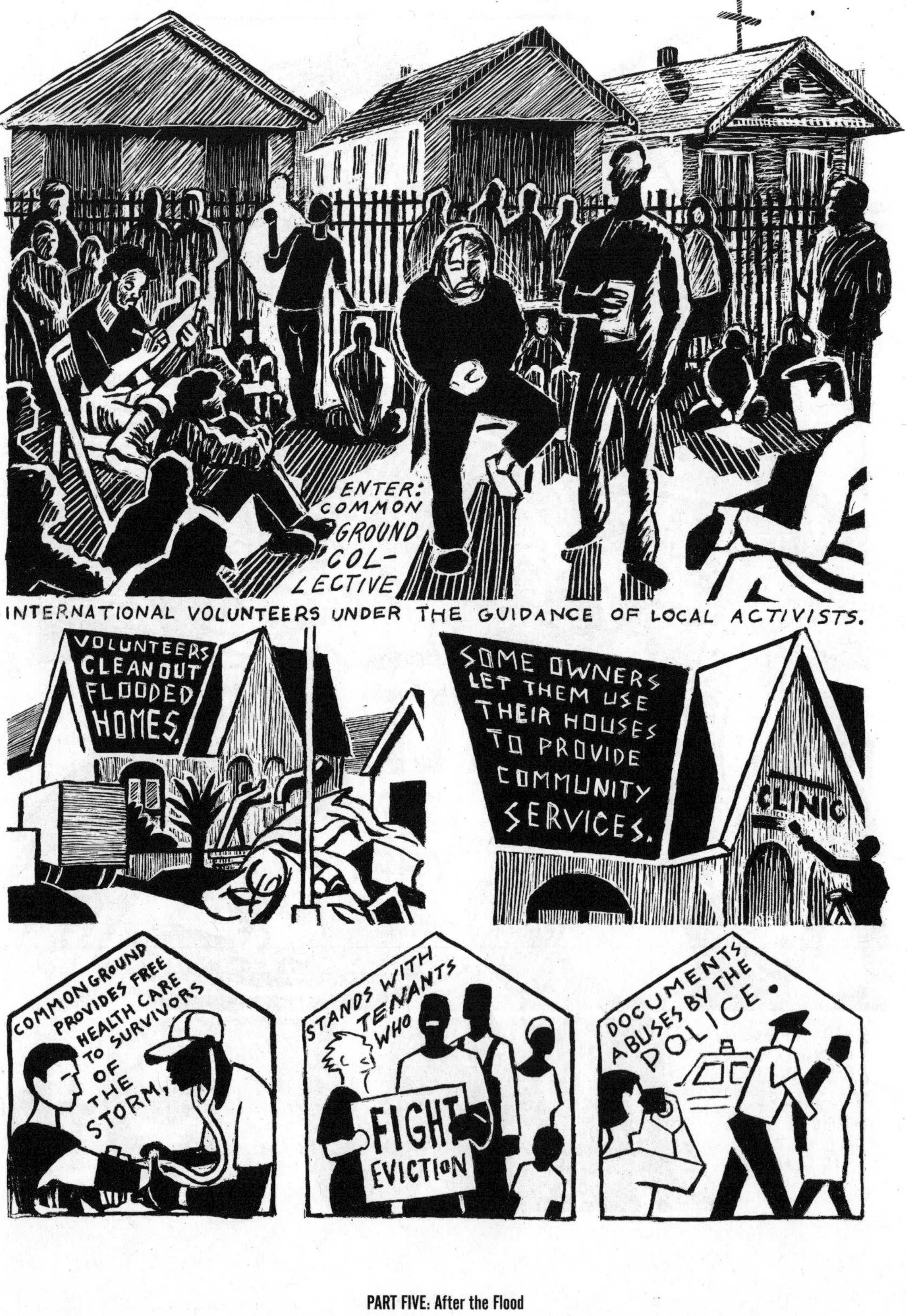
ENTER: COMMON GROUND COL- LECTIVE
INTERNATIONAL VOLUNTEERS UNDER THE GUIDANCE OF LOCAL ACTIVISTS.
VOLUNTEERS CLEAN OUT FLOODED HOMES.
SOME OWNERS LET THEM USE THEIR HOUSES TO PROVIDE COMMUNITY SERVICES.
CLINIC
COMMONGROUND PROVIDES FREE HEALTH CARE TO SURVIVORS OF THE STORM,
STANDS WITH TENANTS WHO
FIGHT EVICTION
DOCUMENTS ABUSES BY THE POLICE.

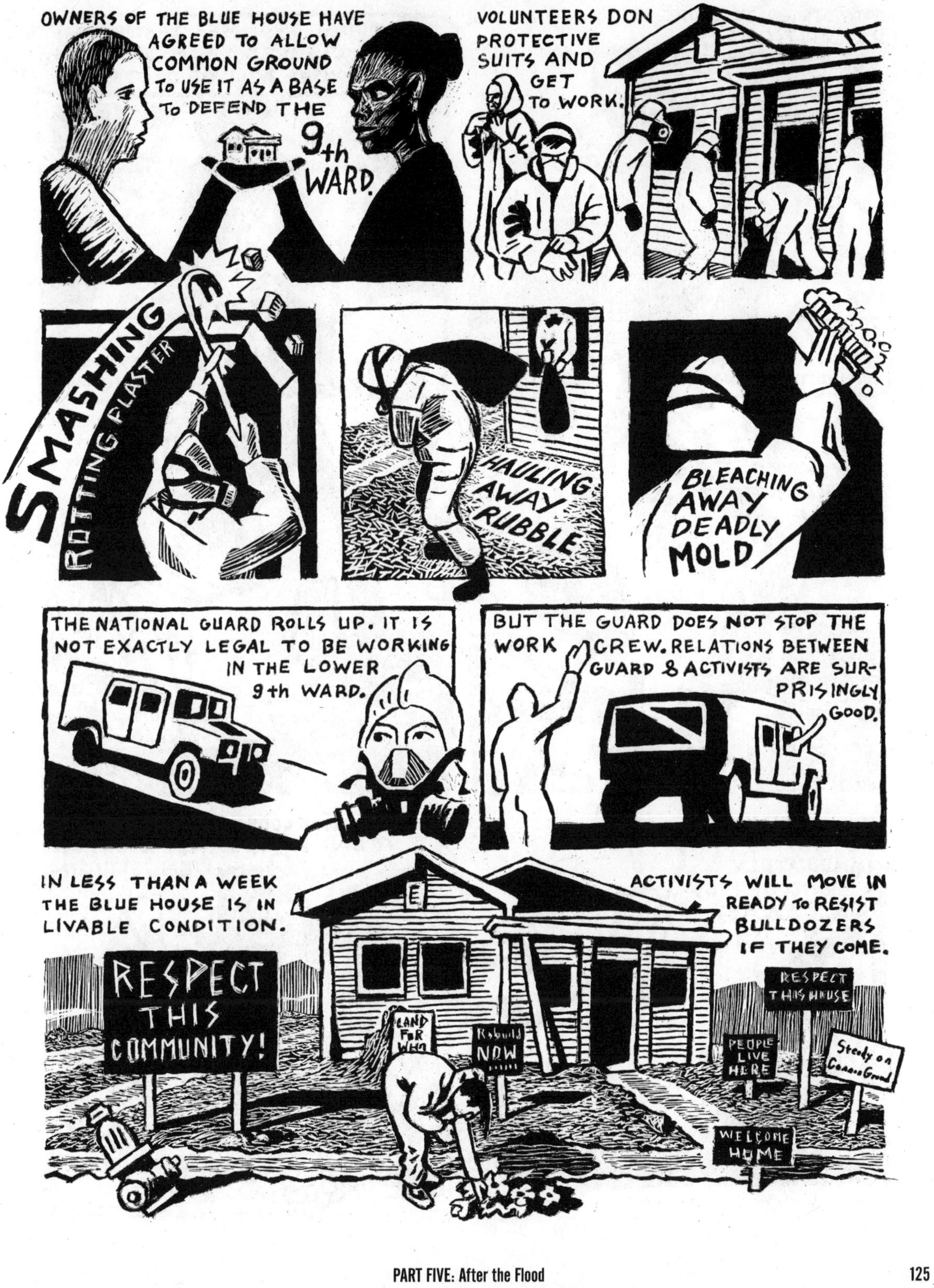
OWNERS OF THE BLUE HOUSE HAVE AGREED TO ALLOW COMMON GROUND TO USE IT AS A BASE TO DEFEND THE 9th WARD.
VOLUNTEERS DON PROTECTIVE SUITS AND GET TO WORK.
SMASHING ROTTING PLASTER
HAULING AWAY RUBBLE
BLEACHING AWAY DEADLY MOLD
THE NATIONAL GUARD ROLLS UP. IT IS NOT EXACTLY LEGAL TO BE WORKING IN THE LOWER 9th WARD.
BUT THE GUARD DOES NOT STOP THE WORK CREW. RELATIONS BETWEEN GUARD & ACTIVISTS ARE SURPRISINGLY GOOD.
IN LESS THAN A WEEK THE BLUE HOUSE IS IN LIVABLE CONDITION.
ACTIVISTS WILL MOVE IN READY TO RESIST BULLDOZERS IF THEY COME.
E
RESPECT THIS COMMUNITY!
LAND FOR WHO
Rebuild NOW
RESPECT THIS HOUSE
PEOPLE LIVE HERE
WELCOME HOME

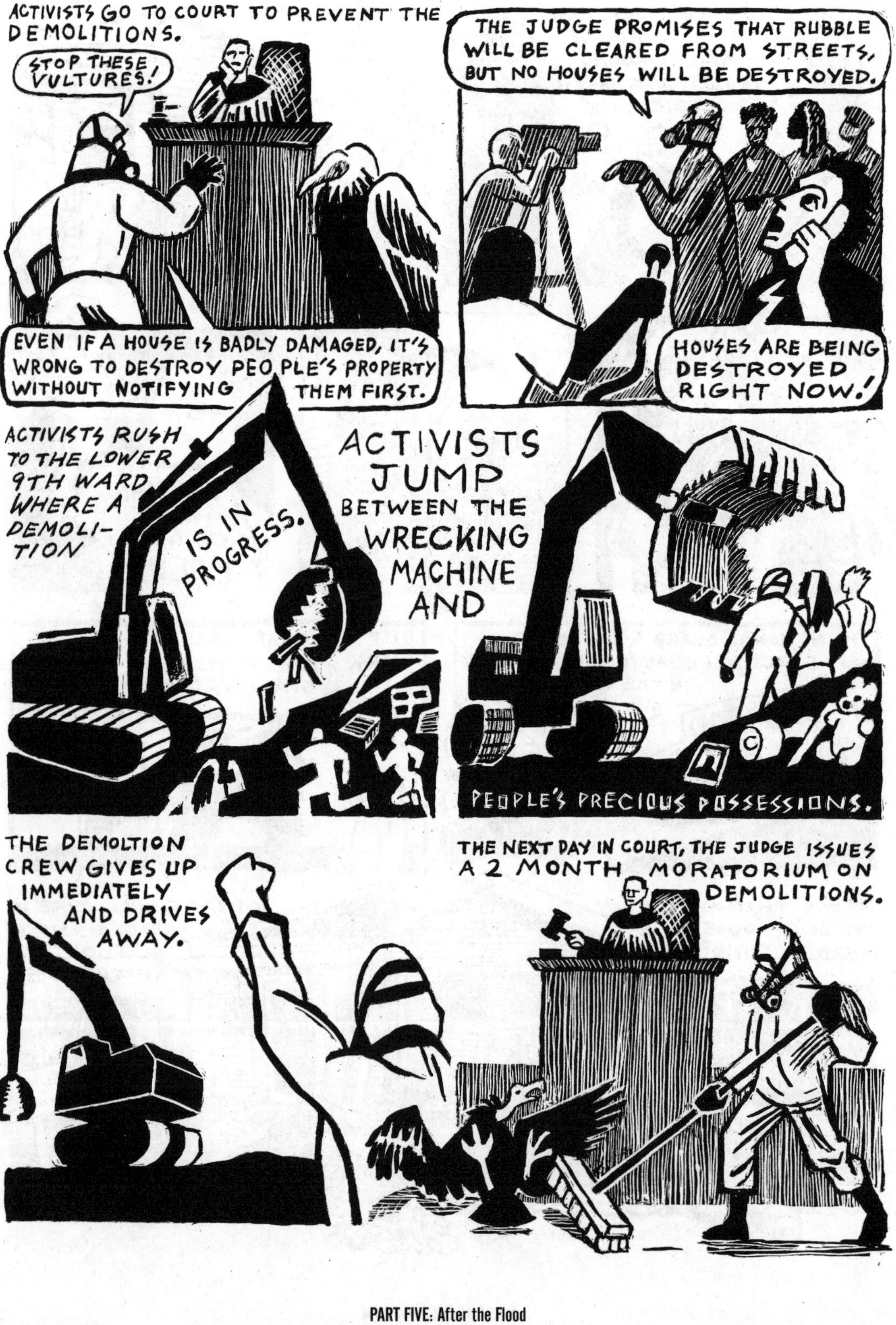

ACTIVISTS GO TO COURT TO PREVENT THE DEMOLITIONS.
STOP THESE VULTURES!
EVEN IF A HOUSE IS BADLY DAMAGED, IT'S WRONG TO DESTROY PEOPLE'S PROPERTY WITHOUT NOTIFYING THEM FIRST.
THE JUDGE PROMISES THAT RUBBLE WILL BE CLEARED FROM STREETS, BUT NO HOUSES WILL BE DESTROYED.
HOUSES ARE BEING DESTROYED RIGHT NOW!
ACTIVISTS RUSH TO THE LOWER 9TH WARD WHERE A DEMOLITION
IS IN PROGRESS.
ACTIVISTS JUMP BETWEEN THE WRECKING MACHINE AND
PEOPLE'S PRECIOUS POSSESSIONS.
THE DEMOLTION CREW GIVES UP IMMEDIATELY AND DRIVES AWAY.
THE NEXT DAY IN COURT, THE JUDGE ISSUES A 2 MONTH MORATORIUM ON DEMOLITIONS.

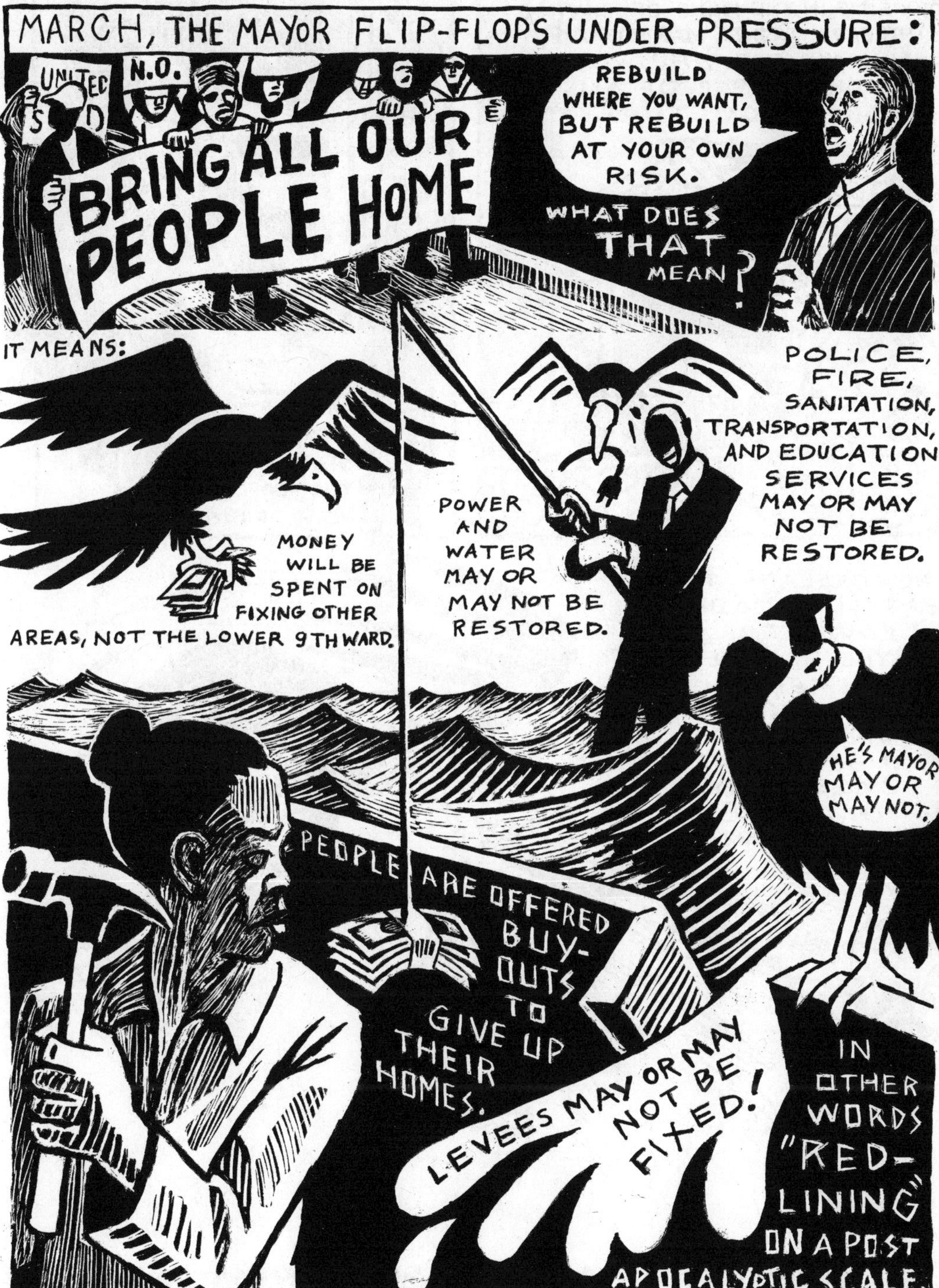
MARCH, THE MAYOR FLIP-FLOPS UNDER PRESSURE:
UNITED
N.O.
BRING ALL OUR PEOPLE HOME
REBUILD WHERE YOU WANT, BUT REBUILD AT YOUR OWN RISK.
WHAT DOES THAT MEAN?
IT MEANS:
MONEY WILL BE SPENT ON FIXING OTHER AREAS, NOT THE LOWER 9TH WARD.
POWER AND WATER MAY OR MAY NOT BE RESTORED.
POLICE, FIRE, SANITATION, TRANSPORTATION, AND EDUCATION SERVICES MAY OR MAY NOT BE RESTORED.
HE'S MAYOR MAY OR MAY NOT.
PEOPLE ARE OFFERED BUY-OUTS TO GIVE UP THEIR HOMES.
LEVEES MAY OR MAY NOT BE FIXED!
IN OTHER WORDS "RED-LINING" ON A POST APOCALYPTIC SCALE.

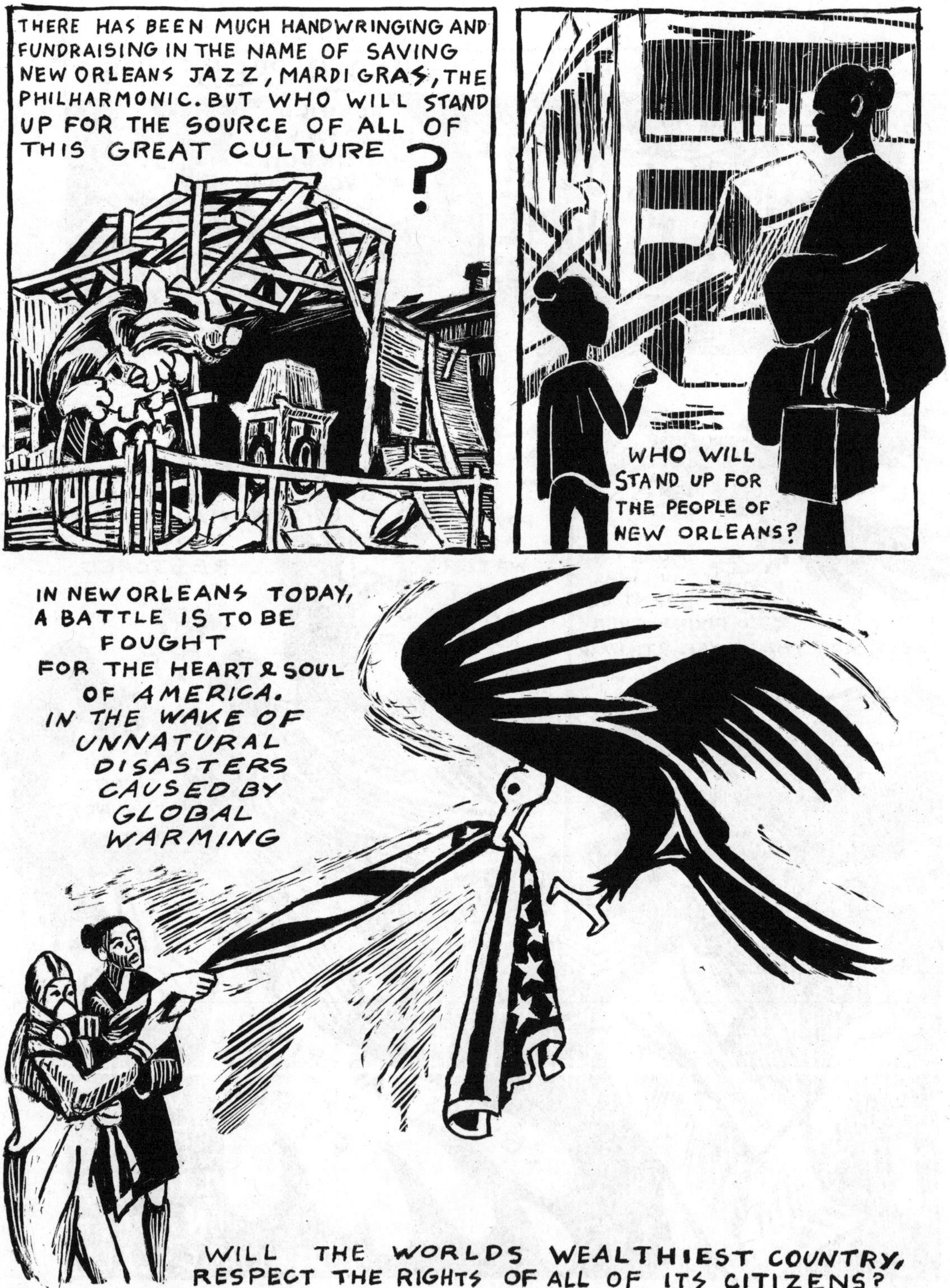
THERE HAS BEEN MUCH HANDWRINGING AND FUNDRAISING IN THE NAME OF SAVING NEW ORLEANS JAZZ, MARDI GRAS, THE PHILHARMONIC. BUT WHO WILL STAND UP FOR THE SOURCE OF ALL OF THIS GREAT CULTURE ?
WHO WILL STAND UP FOR THE PEOPLE OF NEW ORLEANS?
IN NEW ORLEANS TODAY, A BATTLE IS TO BE FOUGHT FOR THE HEART & SOUL OF AMERICA. IN THE WAKE OF UNNATURAL DISASTERS CAUSED BY GLOBAL WARMING
WILL THE WORLDS WEALTHIEST COUNTRY, RESPECT THE RIGHTS OF ALL OF ITS CITIZENS?
SETH '06

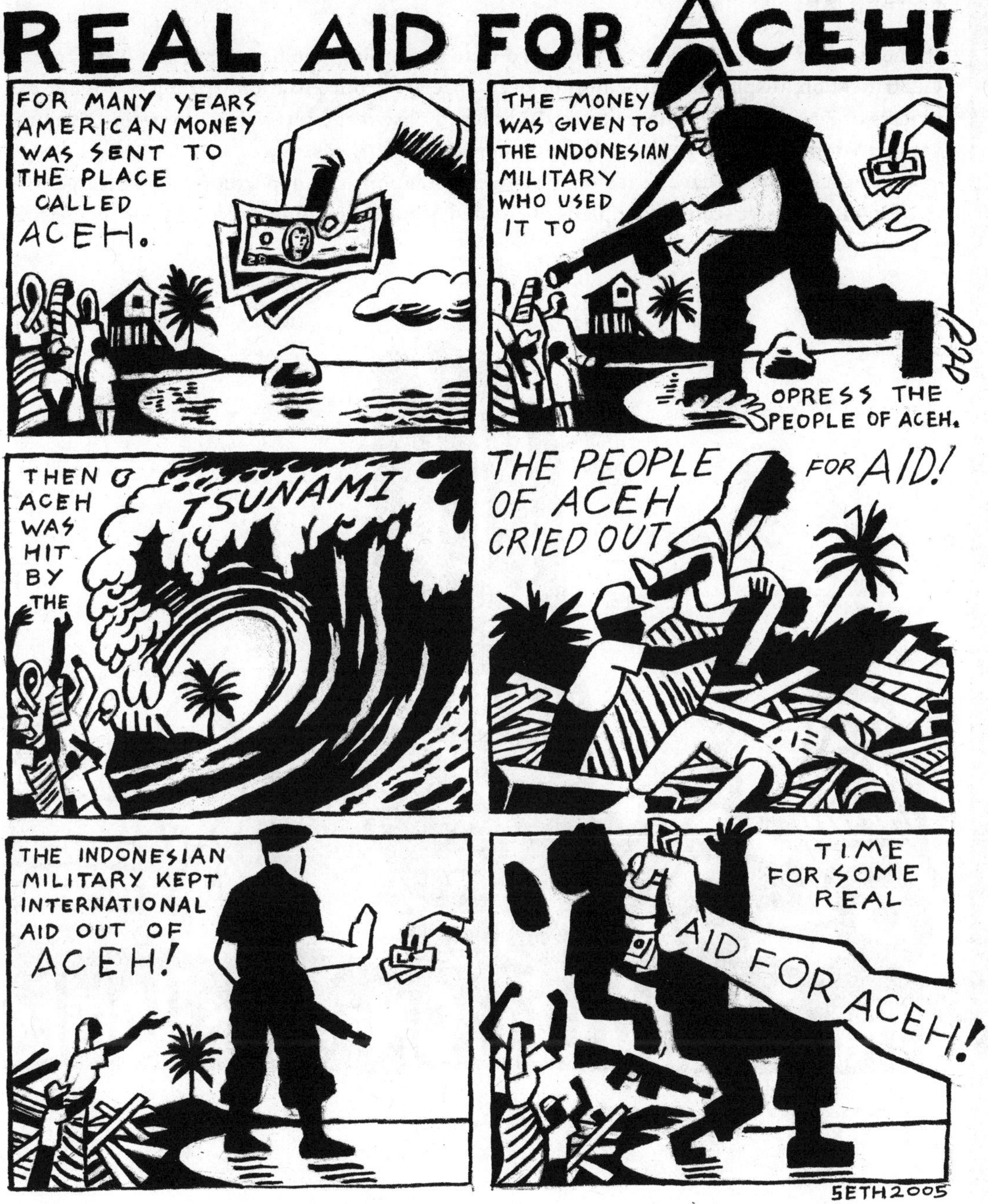

REAL AID FOR ACEH!
FOR MANY YEARS AMERICAN MONEY WAS SENT TO THE PLACE CALLED ACEH.
THE MONEY WAS GIVEN TO THE INDONESIAN MILITARY WHO USED IT TO
OPRESS THE PEOPLE OF ACEH.
THEN ACEH WAS HIT BY THE
TSUNAMI
THE PEOPLE OF ACEH CRIED OUT
FOR AID!
THE INDONESIAN MILITARY KEPT INTERNATIONAL AID OUT OF ACEH!
TIME FOR SOME REAL
AID FOR ACEH!
SETH2005

FENCED OUT

In the ruins of this strange city, I stumbled onto something familiar to me as a New Yorker. Gentrification, displacement, benign neglect, spacial deconcentration. All big words for the process of making the poor leave town. In order to raise real estate values. In order to change voting patterns. In order to break up communities of resistance.

The powers-that-be have seized on the current situation as an opportunity to impose gentrification on a massive scale. Their plans, if enacted, would constitute a second flood, displacing as many people as the hurricane.

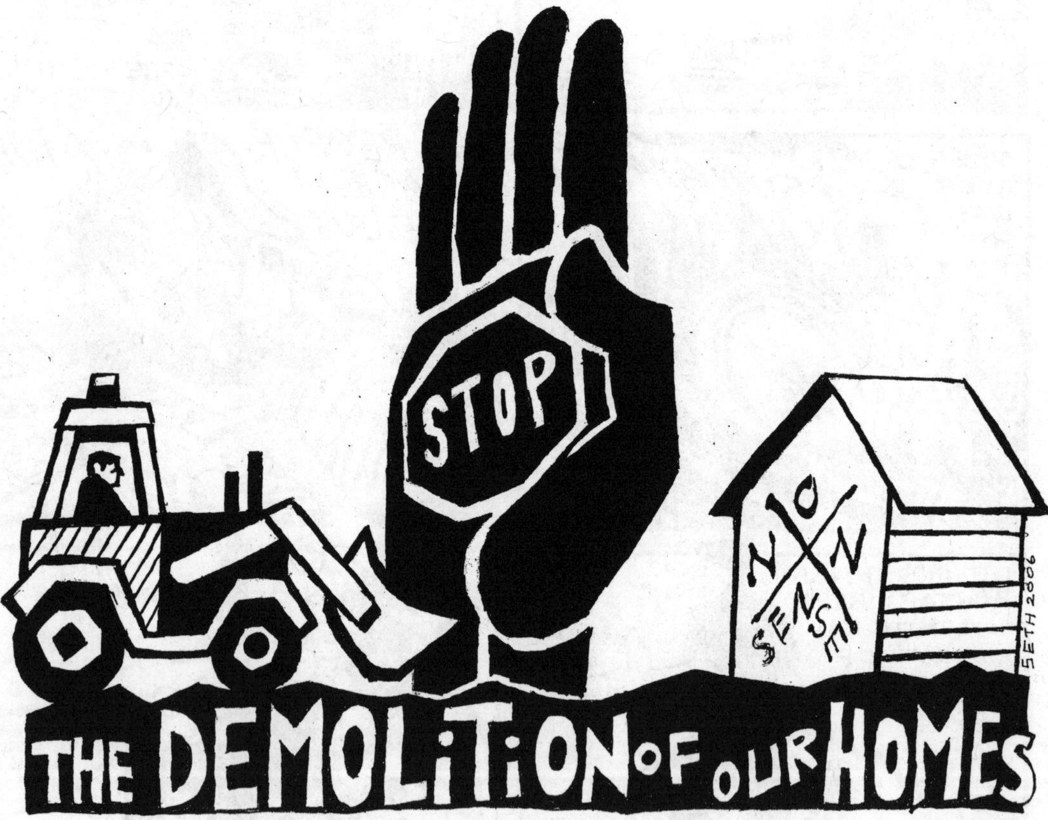
STOP
NON SENSE
SETH 2006
THE DEMOLITION OF OUR HOMES

Above: A poster put out by Common Ground.

FENCED OUT

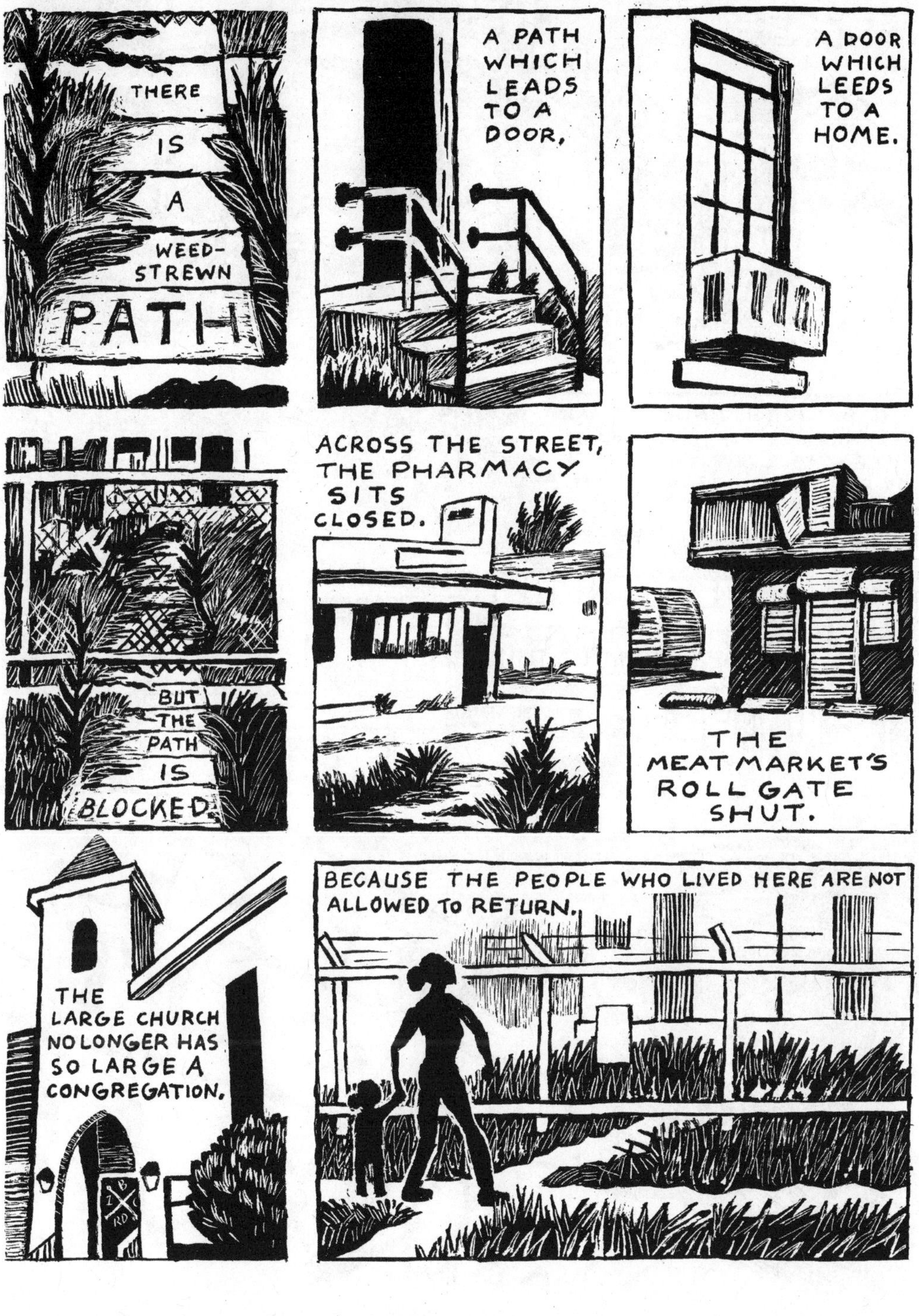
THERE IS A WEED-STREWN PATH
A PATH WHICH LEADS TO A DOOR,
A DOOR WHICH LEEDS TO A HOME.
BUT THE PATH IS BLOCKED.
ACROSS THE STREET, THE PHARMACY SITS CLOSED.
THE MEAT MARKET'S ROLL GATE SHUT.
THE LARGE CHURCH NO LONGER HAS SO LARGE A CONGREGATION.
BECAUSE THE PEOPLE WHO LIVED HERE ARE NOT ALLOWED TO RETURN.

IN A CITY THAT HAS SUSTAINED NEAR APOCALYPTIC DAMAGE,

BURGER ORLEANS

THE BRICK BUILDINGS AT SAINT BERNARD AVENUE HAVE PROVEN TO BE STABLE. BUT THOUSANDS OF RESIDENTS ARE KEPT OUT WITH A FENCE.

BECAUSE THESE BUILDINGS CONSTITUTE SOMETHING AMERICA FEARS MORE THAN A HURRICANE,

THESE BUILDINGS ARE HOUSING PROJECTS.

FENCED OUT

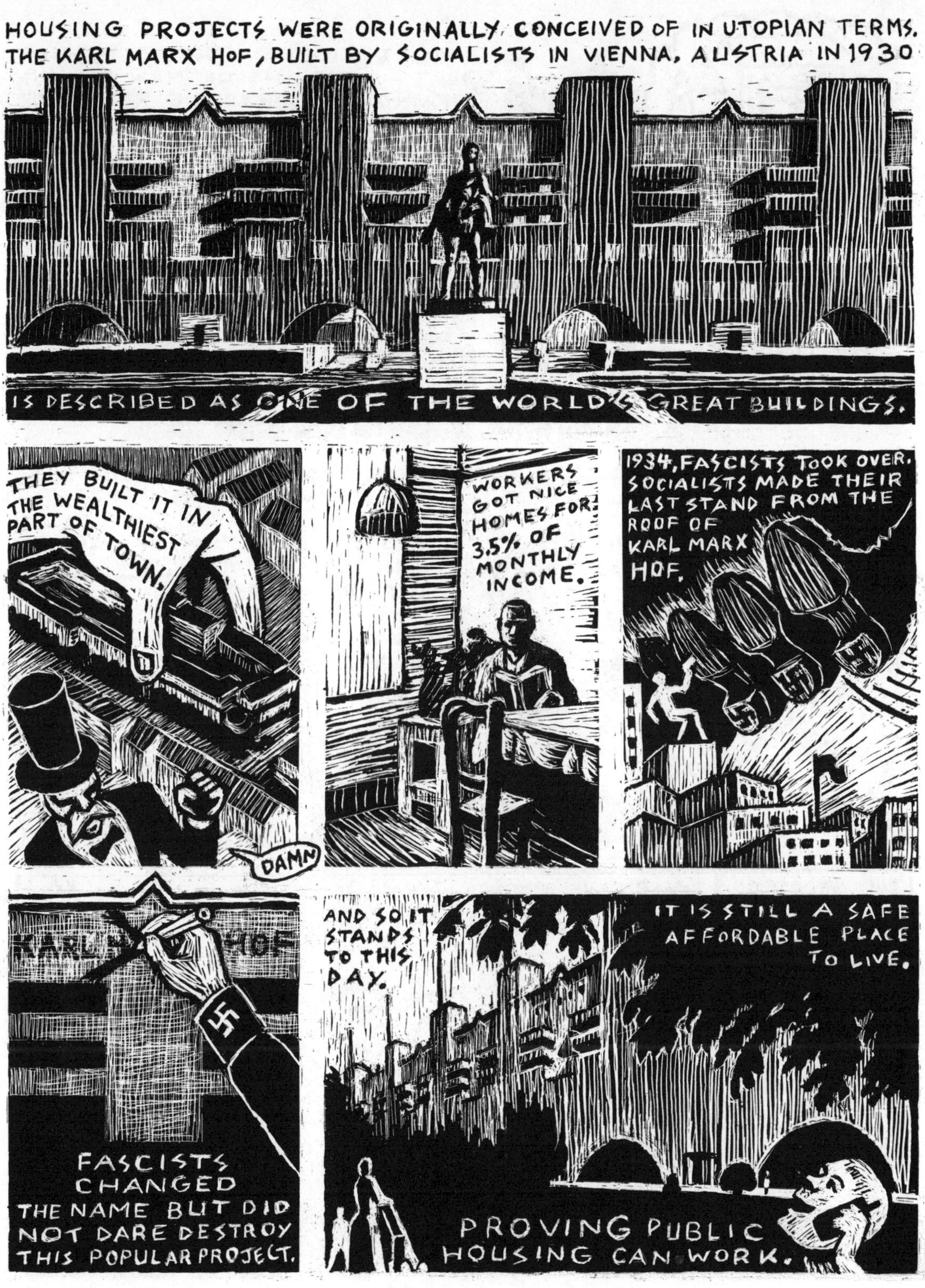
HOUSING PROJECTS WERE ORIGINALLY CONCEIVED OF IN UTOPIAN TERMS. THE KARL MARX HOF, BUILT BY SOCIALISTS IN VIENNA, AUSTRIA IN 1930
IS DESCRIBED AS ONE OF THE WORLD'S GREAT BUILDINGS.
THEY BUILT IT IN THE WEALTHIEST PART OF TOWN.
DAMN
WORKERS GOT NICE HOMES FOR 3.5% OF MONTHLY INCOME.
1934, FASCISTS TOOK OVER. SOCIALISTS MADE THEIR LAST STAND FROM THE ROOF OF KARL MARX HOF.
KARL HOF
FASCISTS CHANGED THE NAME BUT DID NOT DARE DESTROY THIS POPULAR PROJECT.
AND SO IT STANDS TO THIS DAY.
IT IS STILL A SAFE AFFORDABLE PLACE TO LIVE.
PROVING PUBLIC HOUSING CAN WORK.

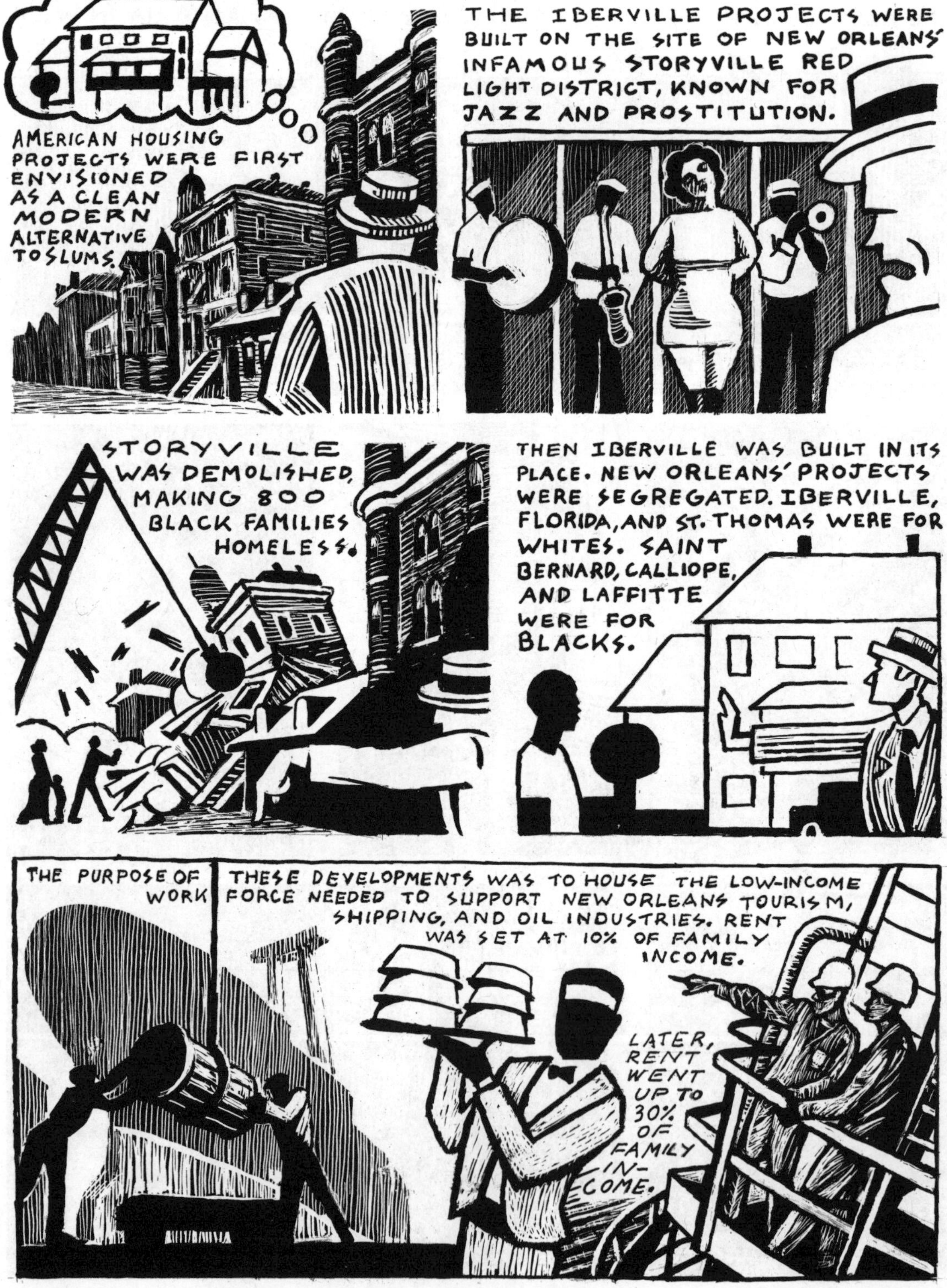
AMERICAN HOUSING PROJECTS WERE FIRST ENVISIONED AS A CLEAN MODERN ALTERNATIVE TO SLUMS.
THE IBERVILLE PROJECTS WERE BUILT ON THE SITE OF NEW ORLEANS' INFAMOUS STORYVILLE RED LIGHT DISTRICT, KNOWN FOR JAZZ AND PROSTITUTION.
STORYVILLE WAS DEMOLISHED, MAKING 800 BLACK FAMILIES HOMELESS.
THEN IBERVILLE WAS BUILT IN ITS PLACE. NEW ORLEANS' PROJECTS WERE SEGREGATED. IBERVILLE, FLORIDA, AND ST. THOMAS WERE FOR WHITES. SAINT BERNARD, CALLIOPE, AND LAFFITTE WERE FOR BLACKS.
THE PURPOSE OF THESE DEVELOPMENTS WAS TO HOUSE THE LOW-INCOME WORK FORCE NEEDED TO SUPPORT NEW ORLEANS TOURISM, SHIPPING, AND OIL INDUSTRIES. RENT WAS SET AT 10% OF FAMILY INCOME.
LATER, RENT WENT UP TO 30% OF FAMILY IN-COME.

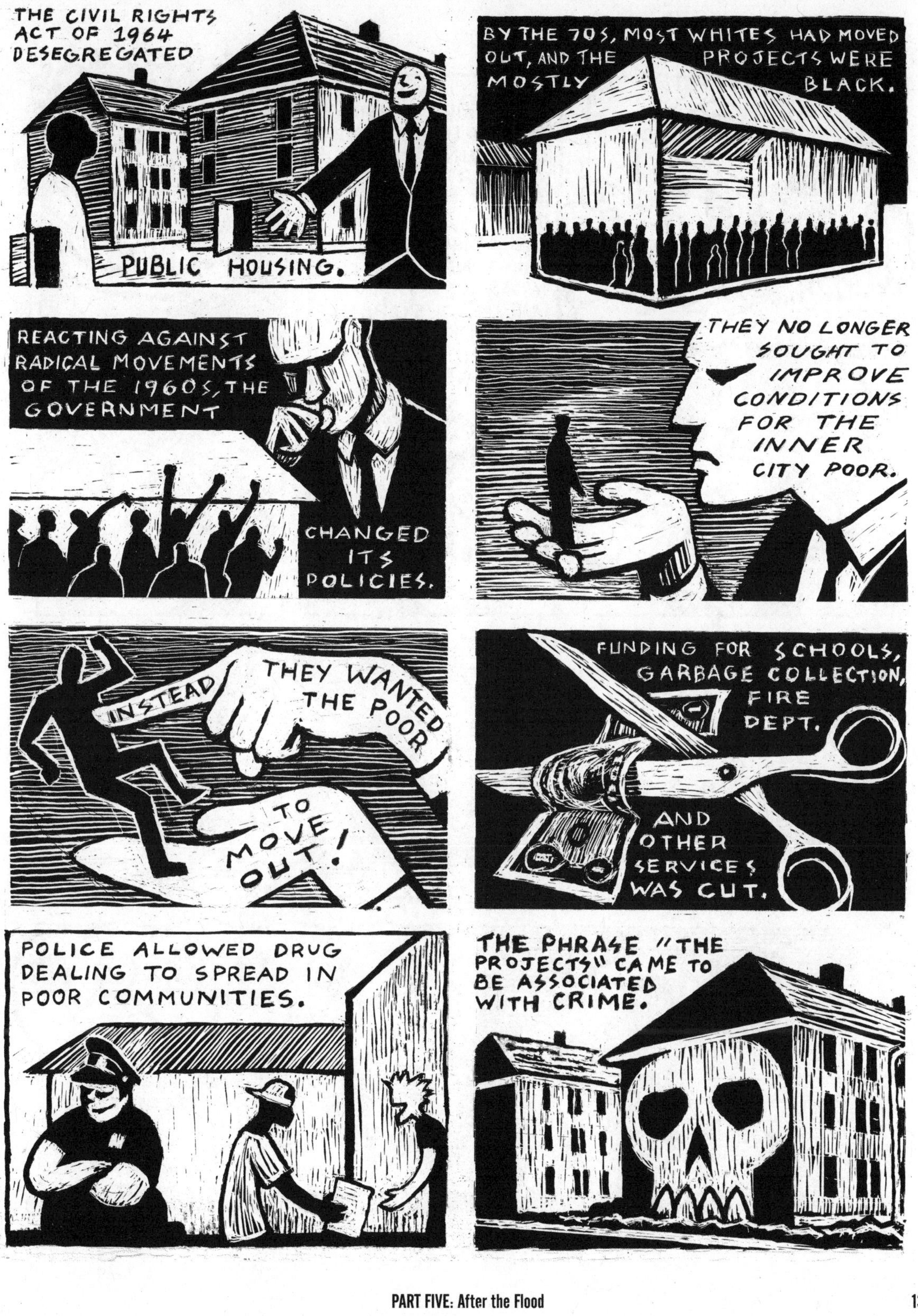
THE CIVIL RIGHTS ACT OF 1964 DESEGREGATED
PUBLIC HOUSING.
BY THE 70S, MOST WHITES HAD MOVED OUT, AND THE PROJECTS WERE MOSTLY BLACK.
REACTING AGAINST RADICAL MOVEMENTS OF THE 1960S, THE GOVERNMENT
CHANGED ITS POLICIES.
THEY NO LONGER SOUGHT TO IMPROVE CONDITIONS FOR THE INNER CITY POOR.
INSTEAD
THEY WANTED THE POOR
TO MOVE OUT!
FUNDING FOR SCHOOLS, GARBAGE COLLECTION, FIRE DEPT.
AND OTHER SERVICES WAS CUT.
POLICE ALLOWED DRUG DEALING TO SPREAD IN POOR COMMUNITIES.
THE PHRASE "THE PROJECTS" CAME TO BE ASSOCIATED WITH CRIME.

IN THE 1990s

PRESIDENT CLINTON CAME UP WITH A PROGRAM CALLED HOPE 6

HOPE 6 INVOLVED DEMOLISHING HOUSING PROJECTS AND THEN REBUILDING THEM SMALLER AS "MIXED INCOME HOUSING." ONLY A FEW OF THE APARTMENTS IN THESE NEW PROJECTS WOULD BE FOR LOW-INCOME PEOPLE. ONLY A FEW OF THE ORIGINAL RESIDENTS WOULD GET INTO THE NEW HOMES.

MOST WOULD BE FORCED TO MOVE. SOME WOULD RECEIVE VOUCHERS TO RENT APART-MENTS ELSEWHERE. SOME WENT TO OTHER PROJECTS.

OTHERS WOULD SIMPLY "DISAPPEAR."

THE ARCHITECTS OF HOPE 6 HAD A THEORY THAT POOR PEOPLE WOULD DO BETTER IN MIDDLE-CLASS NEIGHBORHOODS.

PLANNERS BELIEVED THEY WERE PROTECTING THE POOR FROM CRIME.

IT'S NOT THAT SIMPLE.

UNDER NEW RULES, A WOMAN CAN BE EVICTED JUST BECAUSE HER SON LIVES WITH HER AND HE HAS A CRIMMINAL RECORD.

THIS MAKES BUILDING MANAGERS INTO VIRTUAL DICTATORS, ABLE TO GET RID OF TENANTS THEY DON'T LIKE.

MANY TENANTS ARE AFRAID TO CRITICIZE HOPE 6 POLICIES LEST THEY BE DEEMED UNWORTHY FOR THE NEW SMALLER PROJECTS.

PLANNERS SAID THAT THE PROJECTS TO BE DEMOLISHED WERE IN BAD SHAPE. BUT MANAGEMENT OFTEN LETS BUILDINGS DETERIORATE IN ORDER TO JUSTIFY DEMOLITION. FOR EXAMPLE, AT THE CAPPER PROJECTS IN WASHINGTON D.C. RESIDENTS COMPLAINED FOR MONTHS

THAT A FALLEN TREE HAD PULLED POWER LINES INTO THE PLAYGROUND.

THE WIRES WERE NOT FIXED BUT THE CAPPER PROJECTS WERE EVENTUALLY TORN DOWN.

IN FACT, MOST HOPE 6 DEMOLITION SITES HAVE BEEN ON PRIME REAL ESTATE.

WHERE SPECULATORS ARE INTERESTED IN THE PROPERTY.

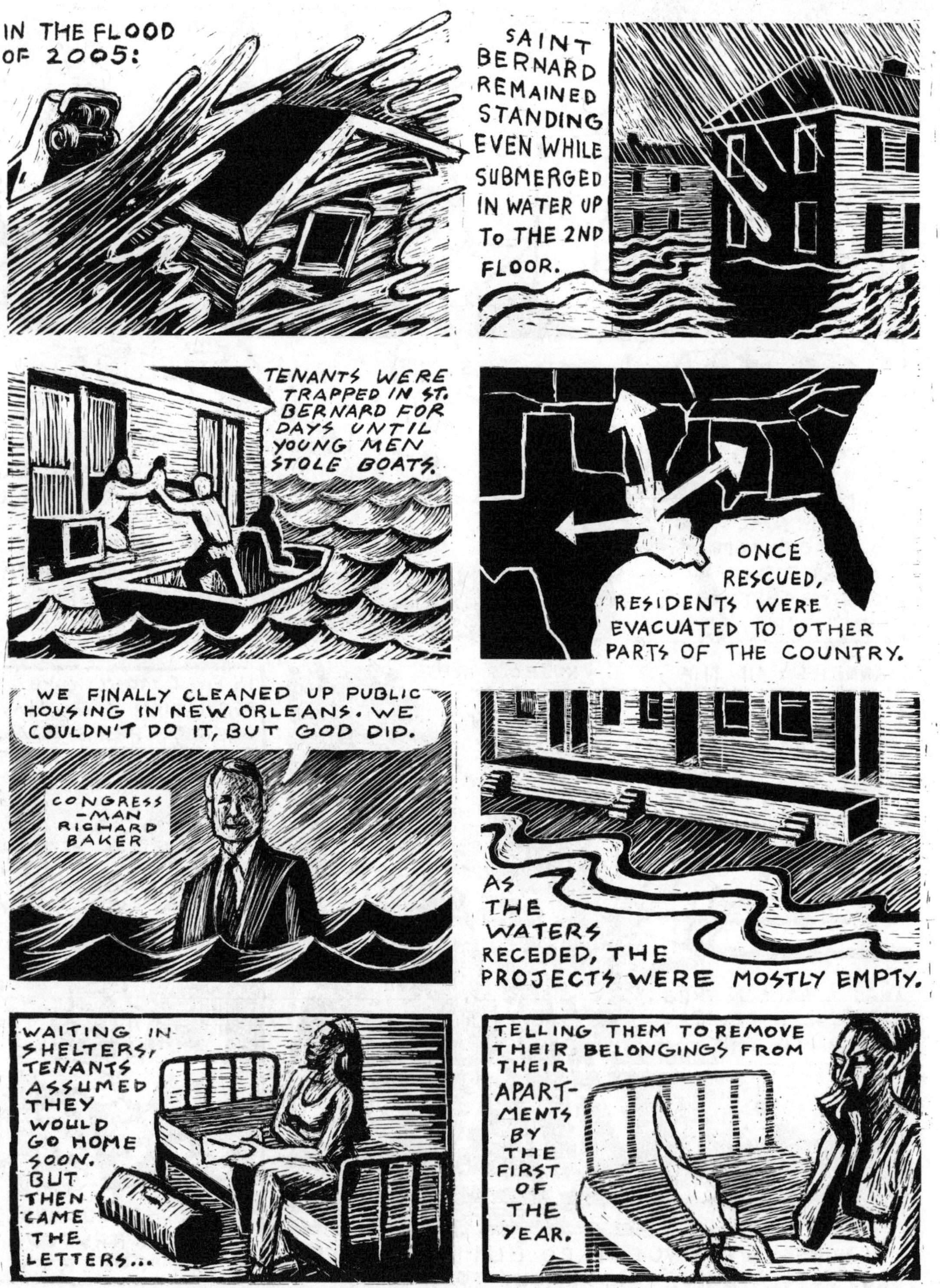
IN THE FLOOD OF 2005:
SAINT BERNARD REMAINED STANDING EVEN WHILE SUBMERGED IN WATER UP TO THE 2ND FLOOR.
TENANTS WERE TRAPPED IN ST. BERNARD FOR DAYS UNTIL YOUNG MEN STOLE BOATS.
ONCE RESCUED, RESIDENTS WERE EVACUATED TO OTHER PARTS OF THE COUNTRY.
WE FINALLY CLEANED UP PUBLIC HOUSING IN NEW ORLEANS. WE COULDN'T DO IT, BUT GOD DID.
CONGRESS-MAN RICHARD BAKER
AS THE WATERS RECEDED, THE PROJECTS WERE MOSTLY EMPTY.
WAITING IN SHELTERS, TENANTS ASSUMED THEY WOULD GO HOME SOON. BUT THEN CAME THE LETTERS...
TELLING THEM TO REMOVE THEIR BELONGINGS FROM THEIR APARTMENTS BY THE FIRST OF THE YEAR.

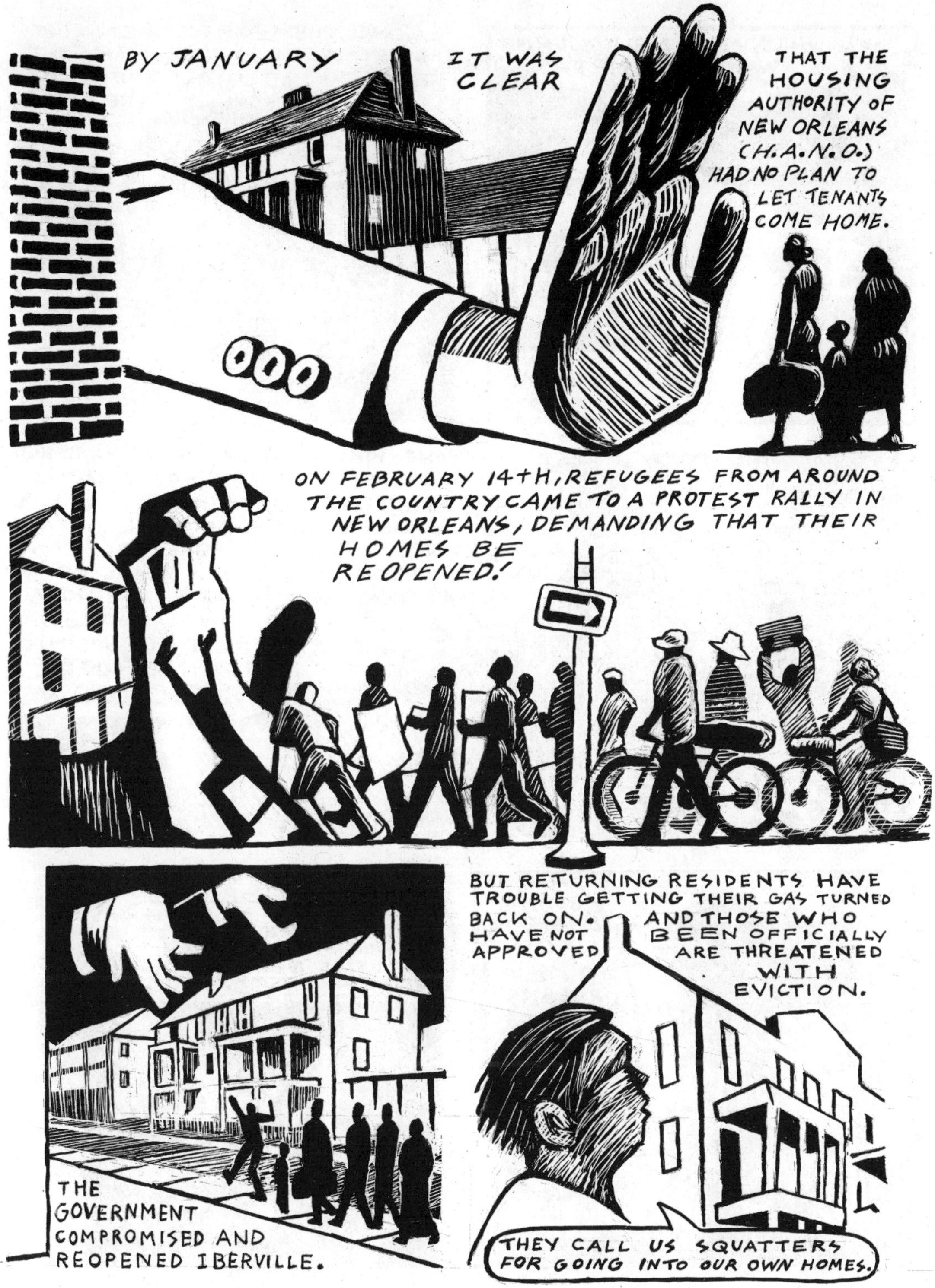
BY JANUARY
IT WAS CLEAR
THAT THE HOUSING AUTHORITY OF NEW ORLEANS (H.A.N.O.) HAD NO PLAN TO LET TENANTS COME HOME.
ON FEBRUARY 14TH, REFUGEES FROM AROUND THE COUNTRY CAME TO A PROTEST RALLY IN NEW ORLEANS, DEMANDING THAT THEIR HOMES BE REOPENED!
THE GOVERNMENT COMPROMISED AND REOPENED IBERVILLE.
BUT RETURNING RESIDENTS HAVE TROUBLE GETTING THEIR GAS TURNED BACK ON. AND THOSE WHO HAVE NOT BEEN OFFICIALLY APPROVED ARE THREATENED WITH EVICTION.
THEY CALL US SQUATTERS FOR GOING INTO OUR OWN HOMES.

MEANWHILE, MOST PUBLIC HOUSING WAS STILL EMPTY.

H.A.N.O. BEGAN BUILDING A FENCE AROUND THE SAINT BERNARD PROJECTS.

FEARING THE WORST, TENANTS RALLIED ACROSS THE STREET. ENDESHA JUKALI SPOKE TO THE CROWD.

EVERYONE WHO LIVED IN ST. BERNARD HAD A LEGAL LEASE! NOBODY HAS GONE TO COURT AND GIVEN YOU A NOTICE OF EVICTION! THERE HAS BEEN NO LEGAL PROCESS START-ED AGAINST YOU. THEREFORE, EACH AND EVERY PERSON WHO HAD A LEASE PRIOR TO KATRINA HAS A LEGAL LEASE NOW! THEREFORE, YOU HAVE A LEGAL RIGHT TO GO INTO YOUR DWELLING UNIT RIGHT NOW!

DON'T COME BACK TO NEW ORLEANS UNLESS YOU'RE READY TO FIGHT!

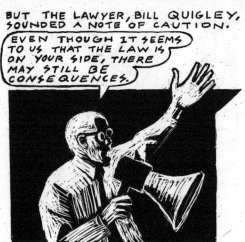

BUT THE LAWYER, BILL QUIGLEY, SOUNDED A NOTE OF CAUTION.

EVEN THOUGH IT SEEMS TO US THAT THE LAW IS ON YOUR SIDE, THERE MAY STILL BE CONSEQUENCES.

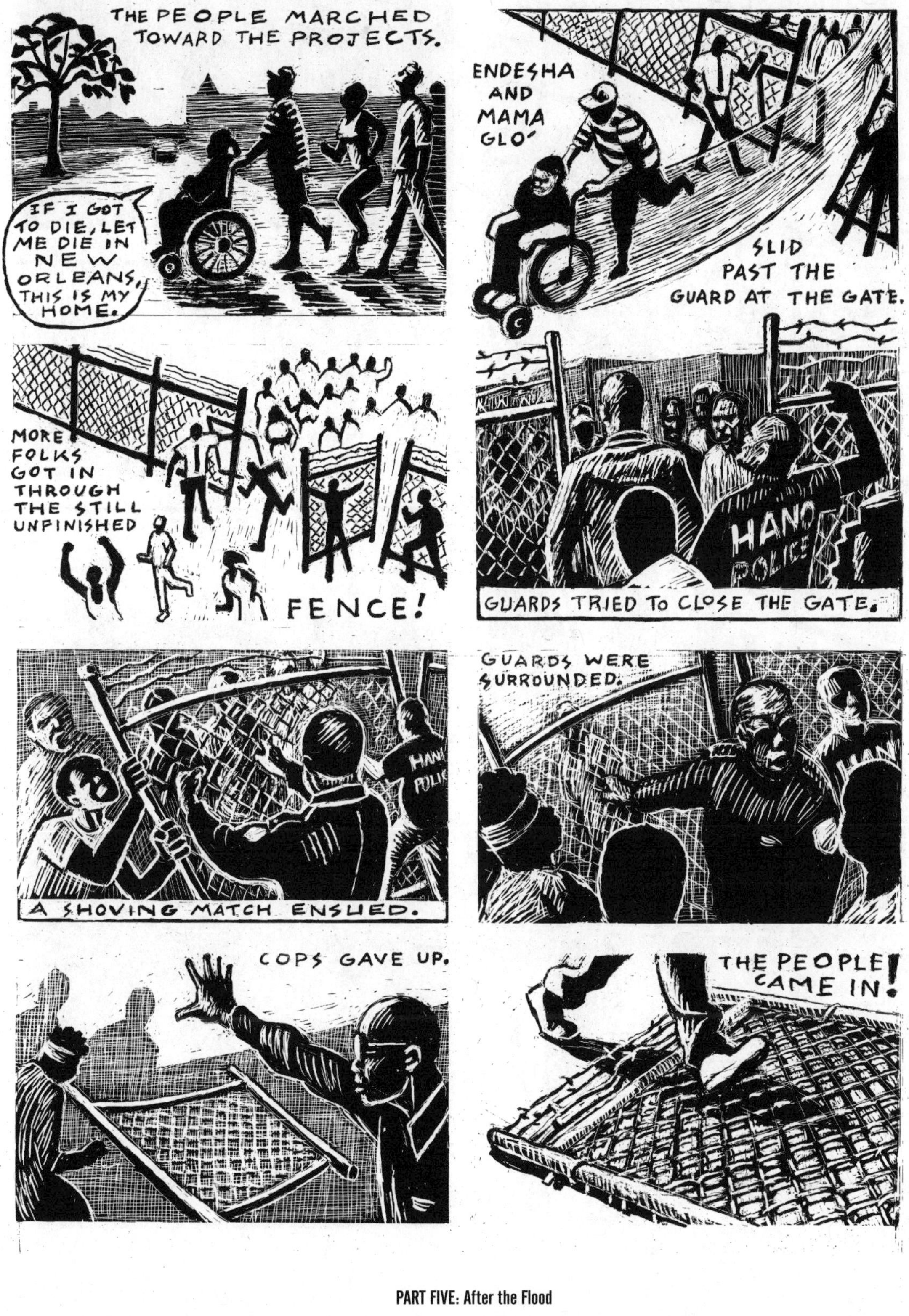
THE PEOPLE MARCHED TOWARD THE PROJECTS.
IF I GOT TO DIE, LET ME DIE IN NEW ORLEANS, THIS IS MY HOME.
ENDESHA AND MAMA GLO'
SLID PAST THE GUARD AT THE GATE.
MORE FOLKS GOT IN THROUGH THE STILL UNFINISHED
FENCE!
HANO POLICE
GUARDS TRIED TO CLOSE THE GATE.
A SHOVING MATCH ENSUED.
GUARDS WERE SURROUNDED.
COPS GAVE UP.
THE PEOPLE CAME IN!

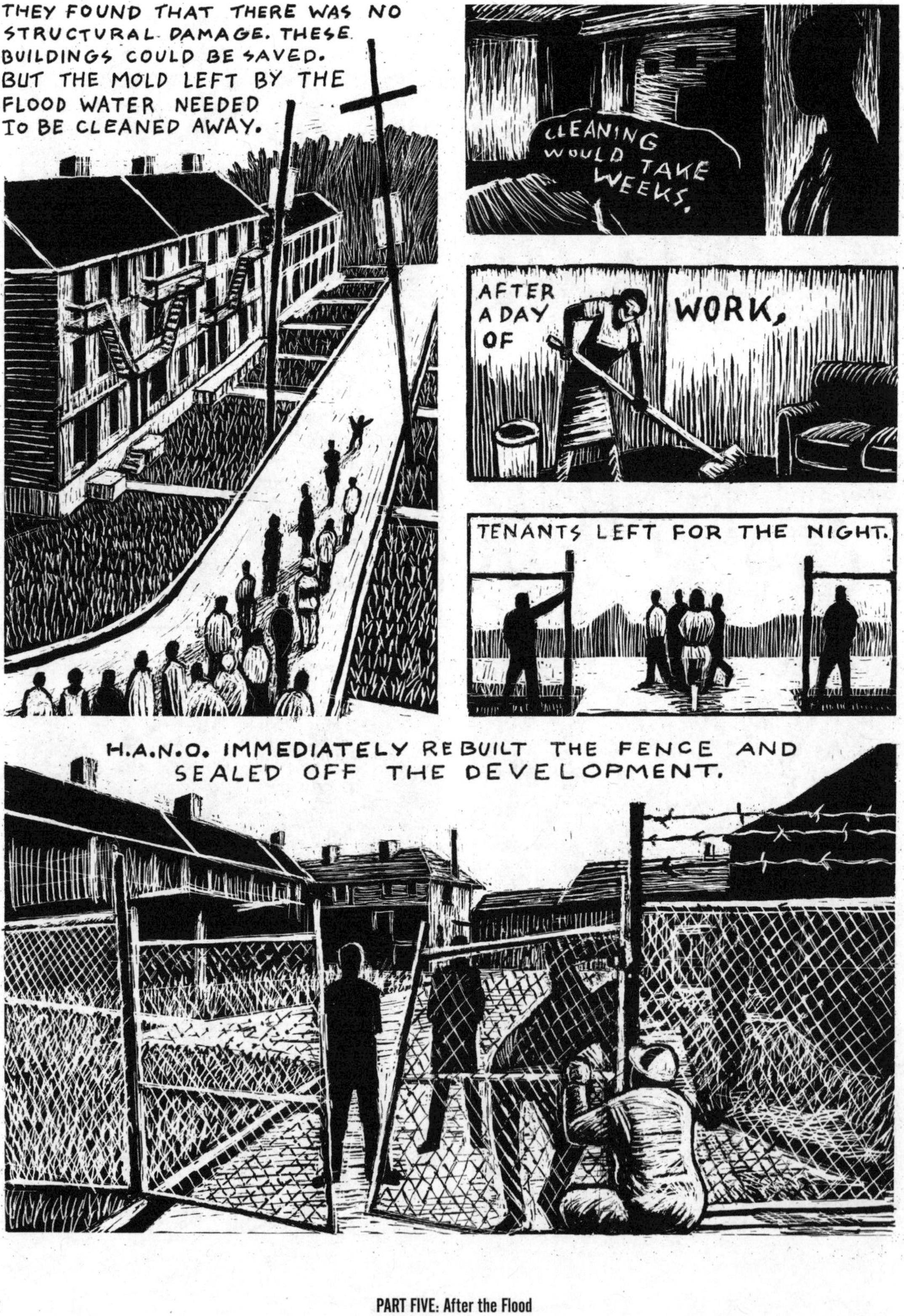
THEY FOUND THAT THERE WAS NO STRUCTURAL DAMAGE. THESE BUILDINGS COULD BE SAVED. BUT THE MOLD LEFT BY THE FLOOD WATER NEEDED TO BE CLEANED AWAY.
CLEANING WOULD TAKE WEEKS.
AFTER A DAY OF
WORK,
TENANTS LEFT FOR THE NIGHT.
H.A.N.O. IMMEDIATELY REBUILT THE FENCE AND SEALED OFF THE DEVELOPMENT.

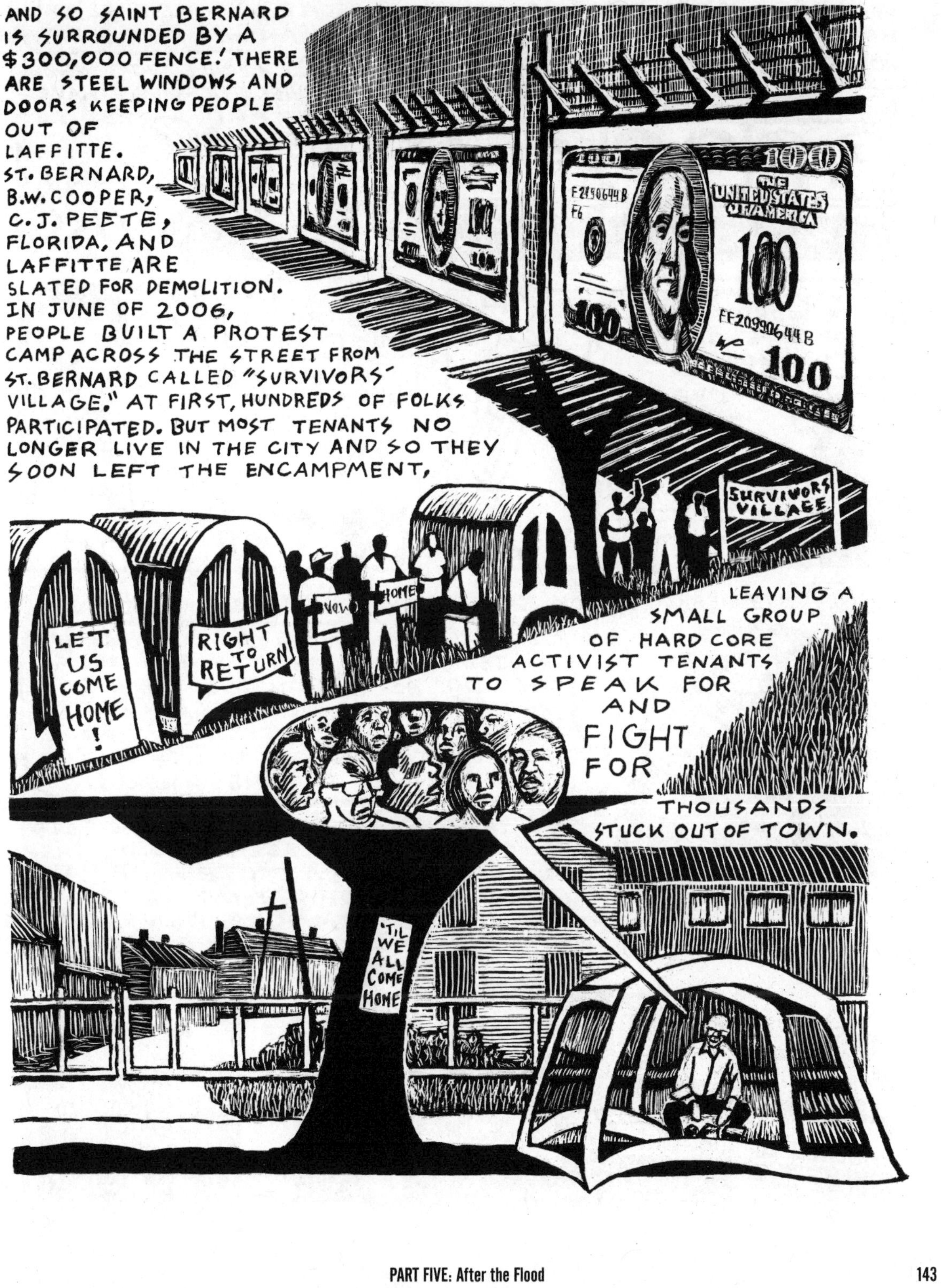
AND SO SAINT BERNARD IS SURROUNDED BY A $300,000 FENCE! THERE ARE STEEL WINDOWS AND DOORS KEEPING PEOPLE OUT OF LAFFITTE.
ST. BERNARD, B.W. COOPER, C.J. PEETE, FLORIDA, AND LAFFITTE ARE SLATED FOR DEMOLITION.
IN JUNE OF 2006, PEOPLE BUILT A PROTEST CAMP ACROSS THE STREET FROM ST. BERNARD CALLED "SURVIVORS' VILLAGE." AT FIRST, HUNDREDS OF FOLKS PARTICIPATED. BUT MOST TENANTS NO LONGER LIVE IN THE CITY AND SO THEY SOON LEFT THE ENCAMPMENT,
SURVIVORS VILLAGE
LET US COME HOME !
RIGHT TO RETURN
NOW
HOME
LEAVING A SMALL GROUP OF HARD CORE ACTIVIST TENANTS TO SPEAK FOR AND FIGHT FOR THOUSANDS STUCK OUT OF TOWN.
'TIL WE ALL COME HOME

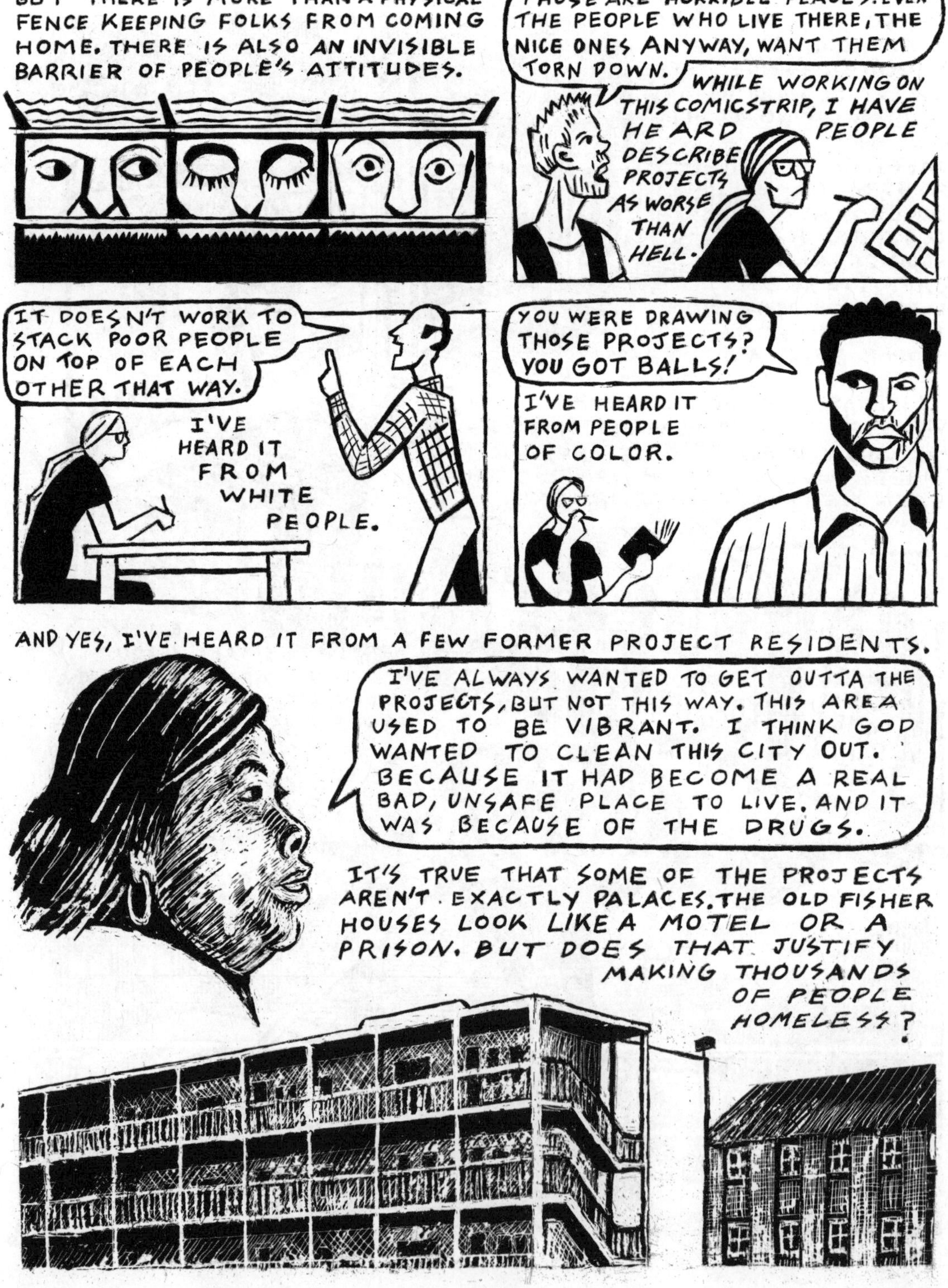
BUT THERE IS MORE THAN A PHYSICAL FENCE KEEPING FOLKS FROM COMING HOME. THERE IS ALSO AN INVISIBLE BARRIER OF PEOPLE'S ATTITUDES.
THOSE ARE HORRIBLE PLACES. EVEN THE PEOPLE WHO LIVE THERE, THE NICE ONES ANYWAY, WANT THEM TORN DOWN.
WHILE WORKING ON THIS COMICSTRIP, I HAVE HEARD PEOPLE DESCRIBE PROJECTS AS WORSE THAN HELL.
IT DOESN'T WORK TO STACK POOR PEOPLE ON TOP OF EACH OTHER THAT WAY.
I'VE HEARD IT FROM WHITE PEOPLE.
YOU WERE DRAWING THOSE PROJECTS? YOU GOT BALLS!
I'VE HEARD IT FROM PEOPLE OF COLOR.
AND YES, I'VE HEARD IT FROM A FEW FORMER PROJECT RESIDENTS.
I'VE ALWAYS WANTED TO GET OUTTA THE PROJECTS, BUT NOT THIS WAY. THIS AREA USED TO BE VIBRANT. I THINK GOD WANTED TO CLEAN THIS CITY OUT. BECAUSE IT HAD BECOME A REAL BAD, UNSAFE PLACE TO LIVE. AND IT WAS BECAUSE OF THE DRUGS.
IT'S TRUE THAT SOME OF THE PROJECTS AREN'T EXACTLY PALACES. THE OLD FISHER HOUSES LOOK LIKE A MOTEL OR A PRISON. BUT DOES THAT JUSTIFY MAKING THOUSANDS OF PEOPLE HOMELESS?

BEFORE KATRINA.

AFTER KATRINA.

IT IS ABSOLUTELY TRUE THAT NEW ORLEANS' PUBLIC HOUSING HAD A SERIOUS CRIME PROBLEM.

BUT MOST OF NEW ORLEANS' HOUSING PROJECTS HAVE BEEN CLOSED FOR ALMOST 2 YEARS AND THE MURDER RATE IS AS HIGH AS IT WAS PRE-KATRINA. WE CAN NO LONGER BLAME CRIME ON PROJECTS AND POOR PEOPLE. ILLEGAL BUSINESS IS PART OF THE ECONOMY OF NEW ORLEANS.

YOUR HOME IS AWFUL SO WE ARE MAKING YOU HOMELESS FOR YOUR OWN GOOD!

IT'S AN ABSURD THING TO TELL A PERSON! IT'S NOT SURPRISING THAT MANY PUBLIC HOUSING RESIDENTS ARE NOT GRATEFUL FOR SUCH TREATMENT. MAYBE IT'S TIME TO STOP TALKING DOWN TO THESE PEOPLE AND START LISTENING TO WHAT THEY HAVE TO SAY.

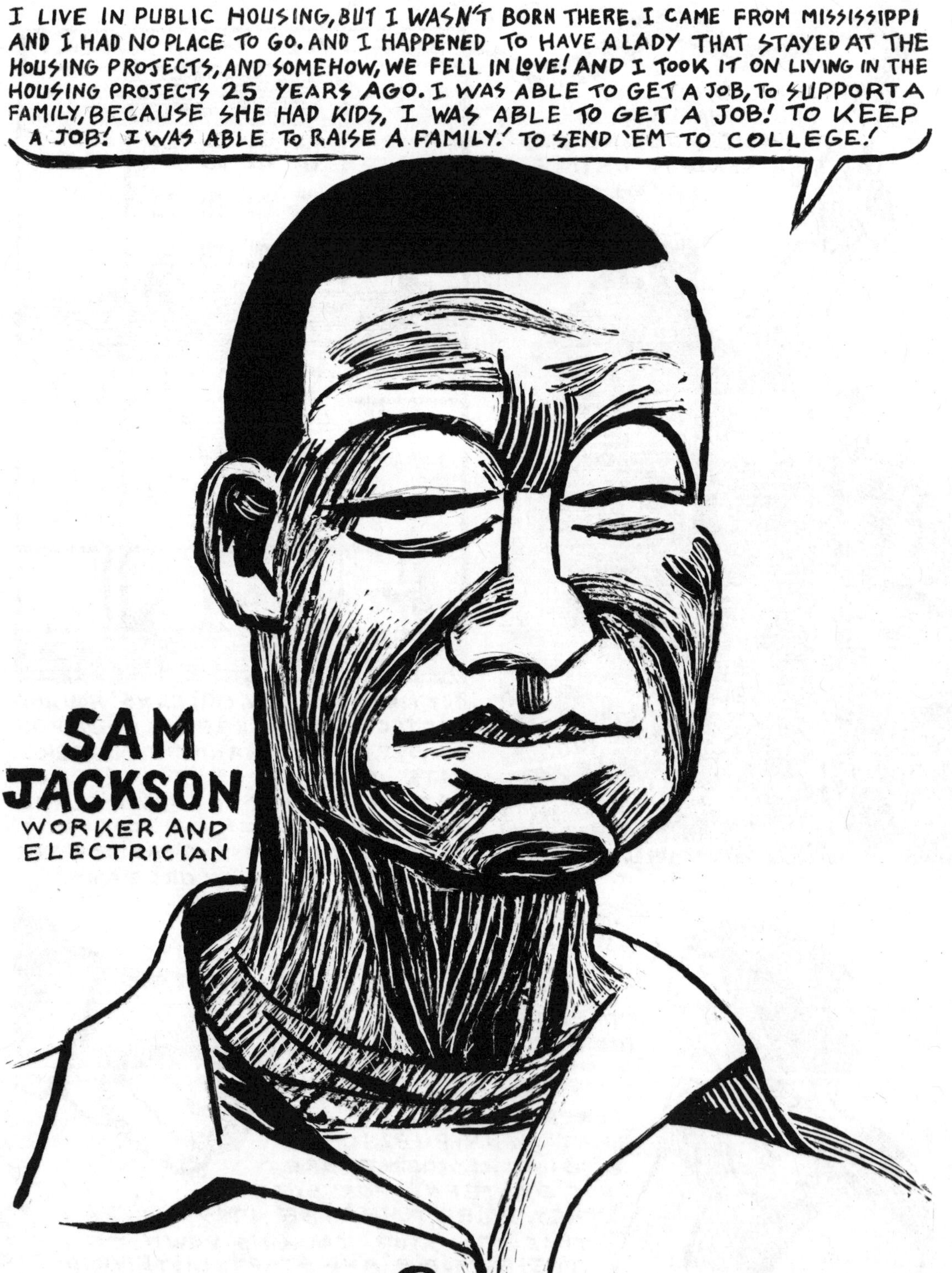
I LIVE IN PUBLIC HOUSING, BUT I WASN'T BORN THERE. I CAME FROM MISSISSIPPI AND I HAD NO PLACE TO GO. AND I HAPPENED TO HAVE A LADY THAT STAYED AT THE HOUSING PROJECTS, AND SOMEHOW, WE FELL IN LOVE! AND I TOOK IT ON LIVING IN THE HOUSING PROJECTS 25 YEARS AGO. I WAS ABLE TO GET A JOB, TO SUPPORT A FAMILY, BECAUSE SHE HAD KIDS, I WAS ABLE TO GET A JOB! TO KEEP A JOB! I WAS ABLE TO RAISE A FAMILY! TO SEND 'EM TO COLLEGE!
SAM JACKSON
WORKER AND ELECTRICIAN

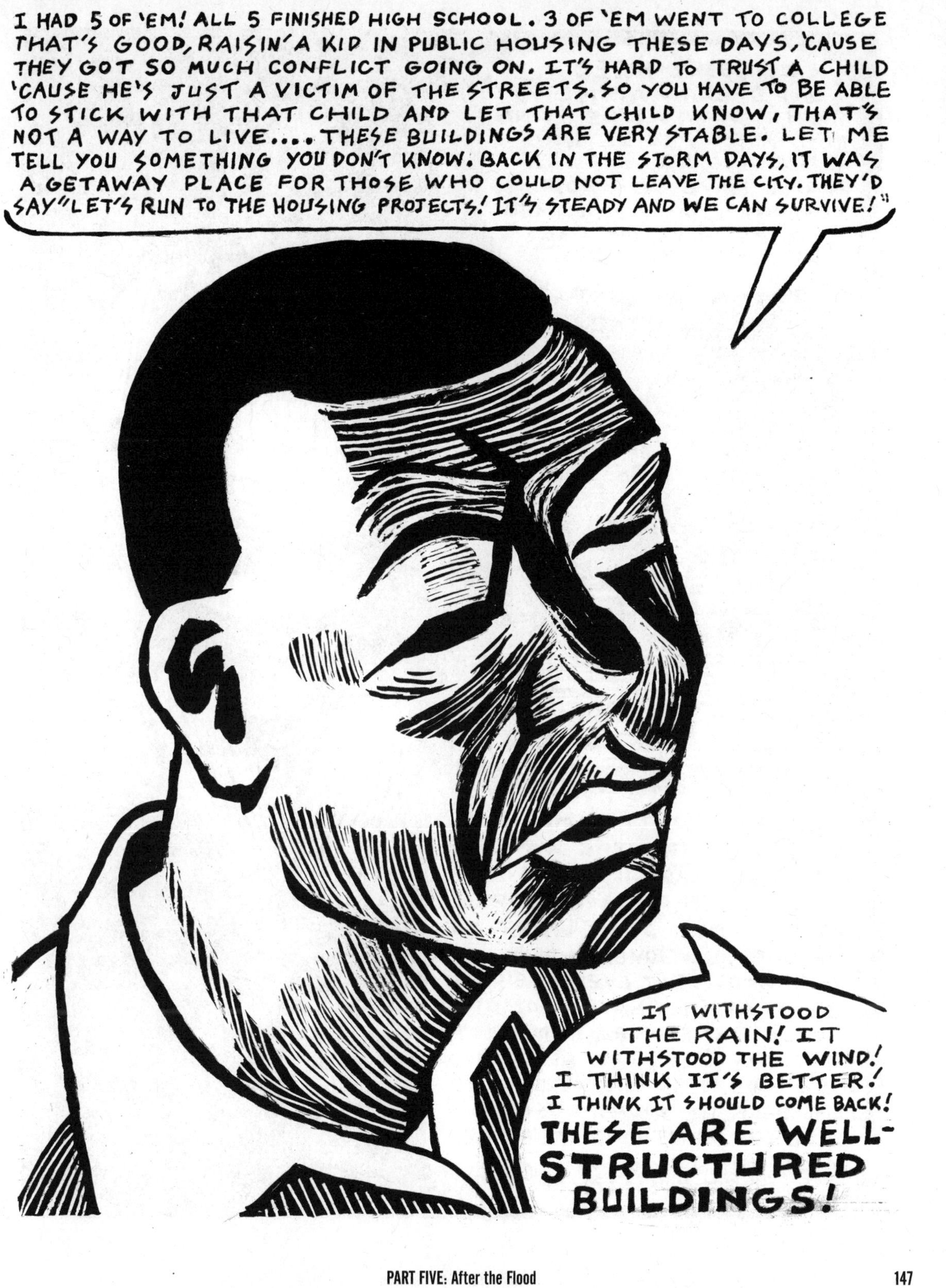
I HAD 5 OF 'EM! ALL 5 FINISHED HIGH SCHOOL. 3 OF 'EM WENT TO COLLEGE THAT'S GOOD, RAISIN' A KID IN PUBLIC HOUSING THESE DAYS, 'CAUSE THEY GOT SO MUCH CONFLICT GOING ON. IT'S HARD TO TRUST A CHILD 'CAUSE HE'S JUST A VICTIM OF THE STREETS. SO YOU HAVE TO BE ABLE TO STICK WITH THAT CHILD AND LET THAT CHILD KNOW, THAT'S NOT A WAY TO LIVE.... THESE BUILDINGS ARE VERY STABLE. LET ME TELL YOU SOMETHING YOU DON'T KNOW. BACK IN THE STORM DAYS, IT WAS A GETAWAY PLACE FOR THOSE WHO COULD NOT LEAVE THE CITY. THEY'D SAY "LET'S RUN TO THE HOUSING PROJECTS! IT'S STEADY AND WE CAN SURVIVE!"
IT WITHSTOOD THE RAIN! IT WITHSTOOD THE WIND! I THINK IT'S BETTER! I THINK IT SHOULD COME BACK! THESE ARE WELL-STRUCTURED BUILDINGS!

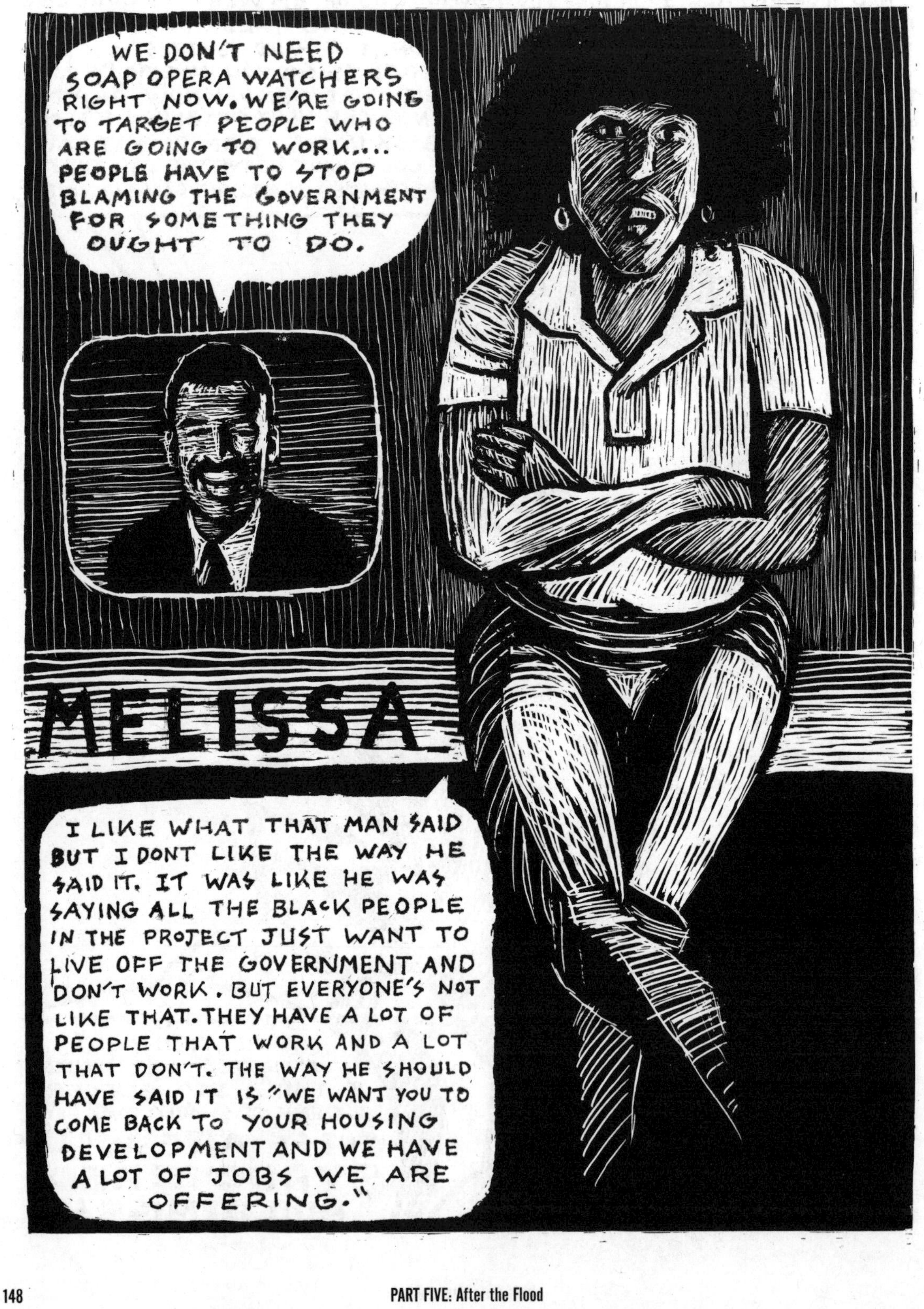
WE DON'T NEED SOAP OPERA WATCHERS RIGHT NOW. WE'RE GOING TO TARGET PEOPLE WHO ARE GOING TO WORK.... PEOPLE HAVE TO STOP BLAMING THE GOVERNMENT FOR SOMETHING THEY OUGHT TO DO.
MELISSA
I LIKE WHAT THAT MAN SAID BUT I DONT LIKE THE WAY HE SAID IT. IT WAS LIKE HE WAS SAYING ALL THE BLACK PEOPLE IN THE PROJECT JUST WANT TO LIVE OFF THE GOVERNMENT AND DON'T WORK. BUT EVERYONE'S NOT LIKE THAT. THEY HAVE A LOT OF PEOPLE THAT WORK AND A LOT THAT DON'T. THE WAY HE SHOULD HAVE SAID IT IS "WE WANT YOU TO COME BACK TO YOUR HOUSING DEVELOPMENT AND WE HAVE A LOT OF JOBS WE ARE OFFERING."

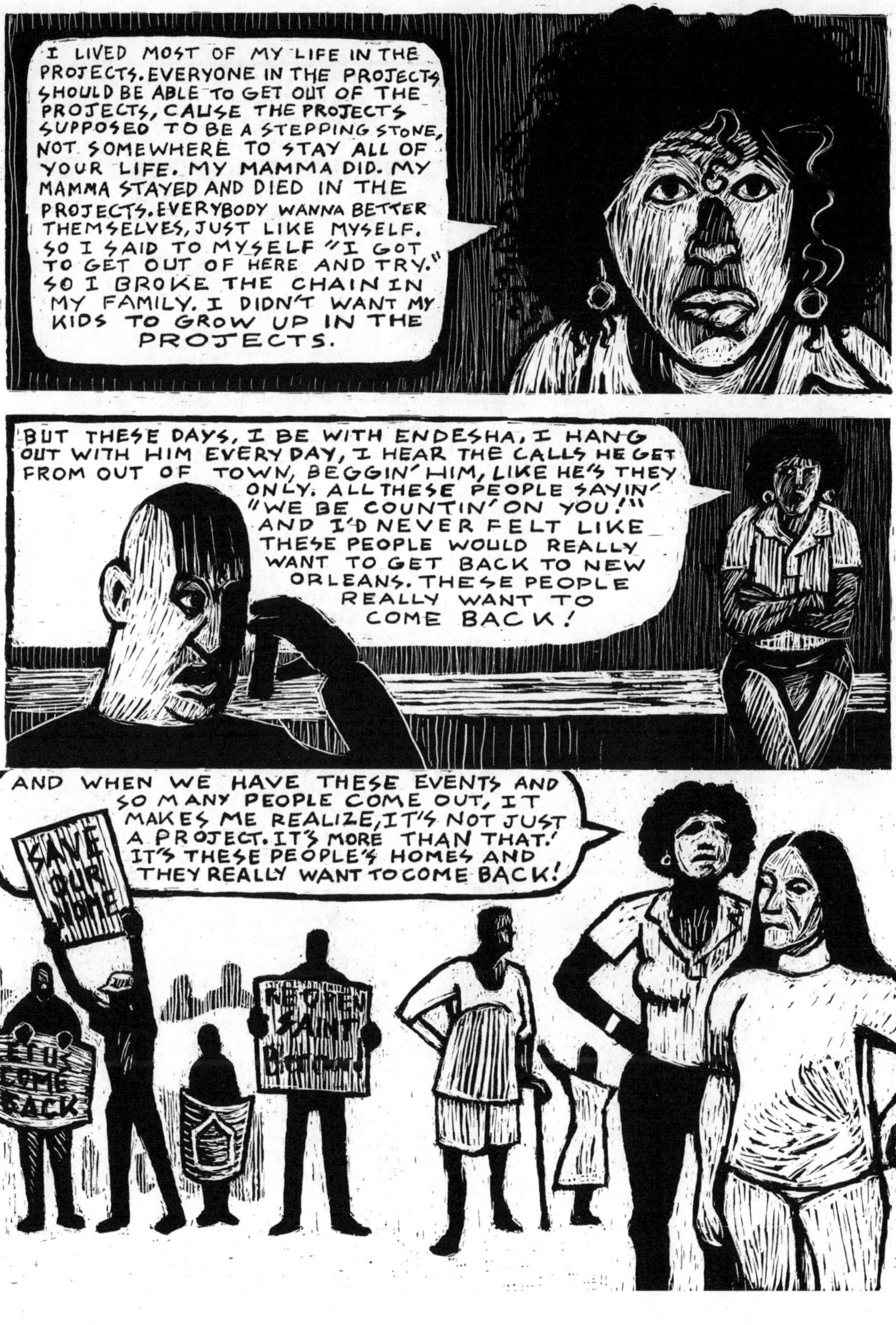
I LIVED MOST OF MY LIFE IN THE PROJECTS. EVERYONE IN THE PROJECTS SHOULD BE ABLE TO GET OUT OF THE PROJECTS, CAUSE THE PROJECTS SUPPOSED TO BE A STEPPING STONE, NOT SOMEWHERE TO STAY ALL OF YOUR LIFE. MY MAMMA DID. MY MAMMA STAYED AND DIED IN THE PROJECTS. EVERYBODY WANNA BETTER THEMSELVES, JUST LIKE MYSELF. SO I SAID TO MYSELF "I GOT TO GET OUT OF HERE AND TRY." SO I BROKE THE CHAIN IN MY FAMILY. I DIDN'T WANT MY KIDS TO GROW UP IN THE PROJECTS.
BUT THESE DAYS, I BE WITH ENDESHA, I HANG OUT WITH HIM EVERY DAY, I HEAR THE CALLS HE GET FROM OUT OF TOWN, BEGGIN' HIM, LIKE HE'S THEY ONLY. ALL THESE PEOPLE SAYIN' "WE BE COUNTIN' ON YOU!" AND I'D NEVER FELT LIKE THESE PEOPLE WOULD REALLY WANT TO GET BACK TO NEW ORLEANS. THESE PEOPLE REALLY WANT TO COME BACK!
AND WHEN WE HAVE THESE EVENTS AND SO MANY PEOPLE COME OUT, IT MAKES ME REALIZE, IT'S NOT JUST A PROJECT. IT'S MORE THAN THAT! IT'S THESE PEOPLE'S HOMES AND THEY REALLY WANT TO COME BACK!
SAVE OUR HOME
LET US COME BACK

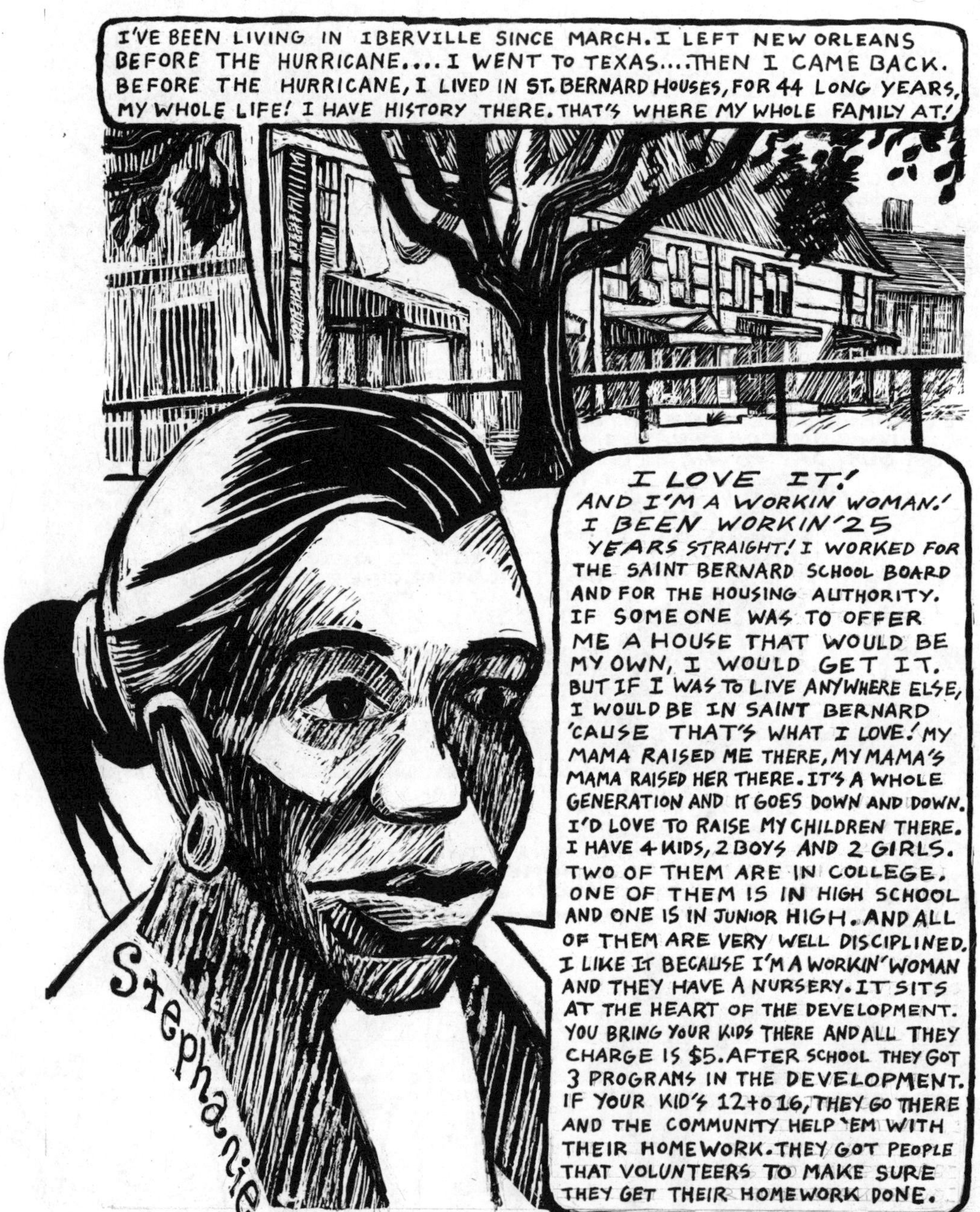
I'VE BEEN LIVING IN IBERVILLE SINCE MARCH. I LEFT NEW ORLEANS BEFORE THE HURRICANE.... I WENT TO TEXAS.... THEN I CAME BACK. BEFORE THE HURRICANE, I LIVED IN ST. BERNARD HOUSES, FOR 44 LONG YEARS, MY WHOLE LIFE! I HAVE HISTORY THERE. THAT'S WHERE MY WHOLE FAMILY AT!
I LOVE IT! AND I'M A WORKIN WOMAN! I BEEN WORKIN' 25 YEARS STRAIGHT! I WORKED FOR THE SAINT BERNARD SCHOOL BOARD AND FOR THE HOUSING AUTHORITY. IF SOME ONE WAS TO OFFER ME A HOUSE THAT WOULD BE MY OWN, I WOULD GET IT. BUT IF I WAS TO LIVE ANYWHERE ELSE, I WOULD BE IN SAINT BERNARD 'CAUSE THAT'S WHAT I LOVE! MY MAMA RAISED ME THERE, MY MAMA'S MAMA RAISED HER THERE. IT'S A WHOLE GENERATION AND IT GOES DOWN AND DOWN. I'D LOVE TO RAISE MY CHILDREN THERE. I HAVE 4 KIDS, 2 BOYS AND 2 GIRLS. TWO OF THEM ARE IN COLLEGE, ONE OF THEM IS IN HIGH SCHOOL AND ONE IS IN JUNIOR HIGH. AND ALL OF THEM ARE VERY WELL DISCIPLINED. I LIKE IT BECAUSE I'M A WORKIN' WOMAN AND THEY HAVE A NURSERY. IT SITS AT THE HEART OF THE DEVELOPMENT. YOU BRING YOUR KIDS THERE AND ALL THEY CHARGE IS $5. AFTER SCHOOL THEY GOT 3 PROGRAMS IN THE DEVELOPMENT. IF YOUR KID'S 12 to 16, THEY GO THERE AND THE COMMUNITY HELP 'EM WITH THEIR HOMEWORK. THEY GOT PEOPLE THAT VOLUNTEERS TO MAKE SURE THEY GET THEIR HOMEWORK DONE.
Stephanie

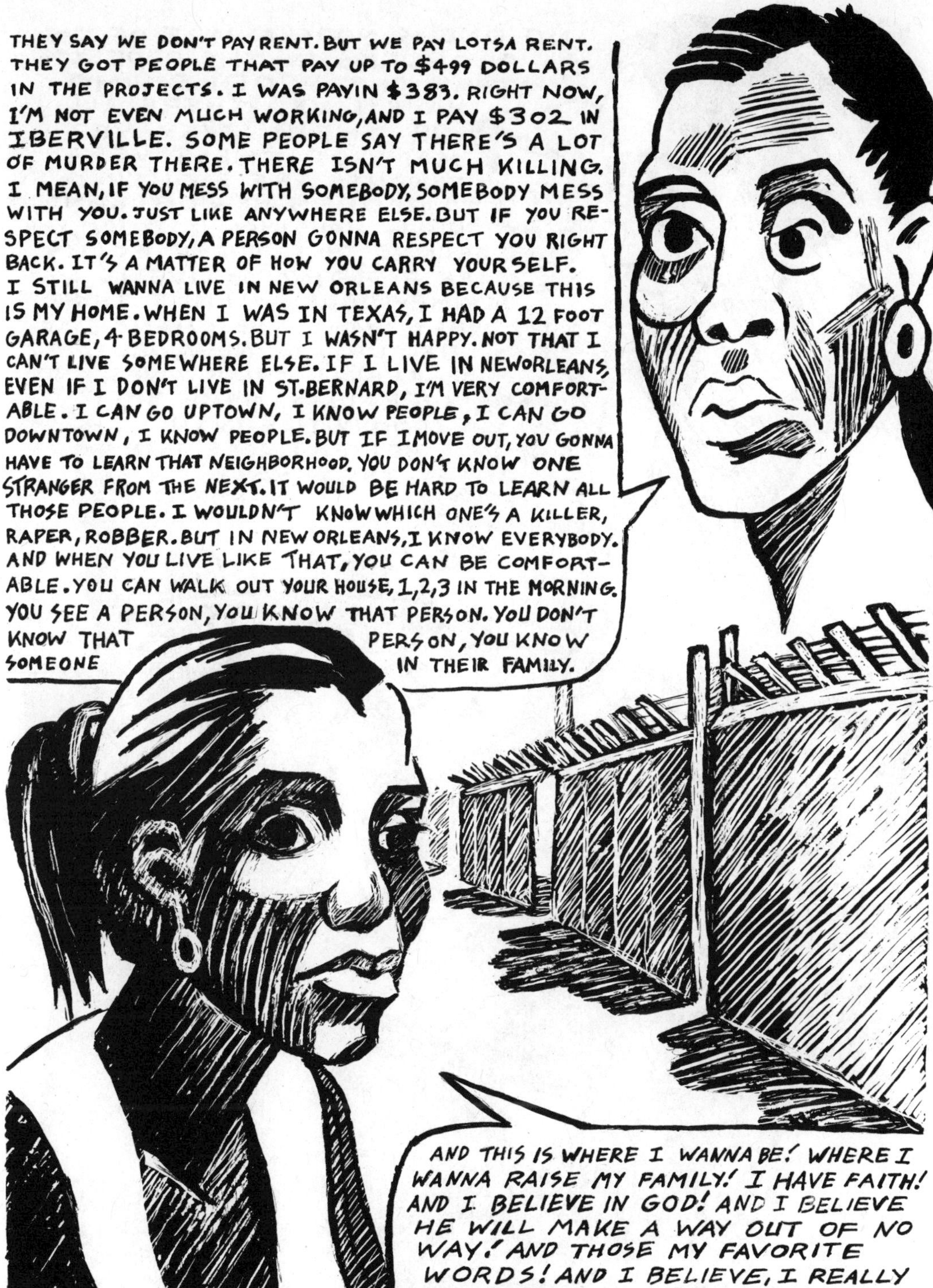
THEY SAY WE DON'T PAY RENT. BUT WE PAY LOTSA RENT. THEY GOT PEOPLE THAT PAY UP TO $499 DOLLARS IN THE PROJECTS. I WAS PAYIN $383. RIGHT NOW, I'M NOT EVEN MUCH WORKING, AND I PAY $302 IN IBERVILLE. SOME PEOPLE SAY THERE'S A LOT OF MURDER THERE. THERE ISN'T MUCH KILLING. I MEAN, IF YOU MESS WITH SOMEBODY, SOMEBODY MESS WITH YOU. JUST LIKE ANYWHERE ELSE. BUT IF YOU RESPECT SOMEBODY, A PERSON GONNA RESPECT YOU RIGHT BACK. IT'S A MATTER OF HOW YOU CARRY YOURSELF. I STILL WANNA LIVE IN NEW ORLEANS BECAUSE THIS IS MY HOME. WHEN I WAS IN TEXAS, I HAD A 12 FOOT GARAGE, 4 BEDROOMS. BUT I WASN'T HAPPY. NOT THAT I CAN'T LIVE SOMEWHERE ELSE. IF I LIVE IN NEW ORLEANS, EVEN IF I DON'T LIVE IN ST. BERNARD, I'M VERY COMFORTABLE. I CAN GO UPTOWN, I KNOW PEOPLE, I CAN GO DOWNTOWN, I KNOW PEOPLE. BUT IF I MOVE OUT, YOU GONNA HAVE TO LEARN THAT NEIGHBORHOOD. YOU DON'T KNOW ONE STRANGER FROM THE NEXT. IT WOULD BE HARD TO LEARN ALL THOSE PEOPLE. I WOULDN'T KNOW WHICH ONE'S A KILLER, RAPER, ROBBER. BUT IN NEW ORLEANS, I KNOW EVERYBODY. AND WHEN YOU LIVE LIKE THAT, YOU CAN BE COMFORTABLE. YOU CAN WALK OUT YOUR HOUSE, 1,2,3 IN THE MORNING. YOU SEE A PERSON, YOU KNOW THAT PERSON. YOU DON'T KNOW THAT PERSON, YOU KNOW SOMEONE IN THEIR FAMILY.
AND THIS IS WHERE I WANNA BE! WHERE I WANNA RAISE MY FAMILY! I HAVE FAITH! AND I BELIEVE IN GOD! AND I BELIEVE HE WILL MAKE A WAY OUT OF NO WAY! AND THOSE MY FAVORITE WORDS! AND I BELIEVE, I REALLY BELIEVE, THEY GONNA BE OPEN!

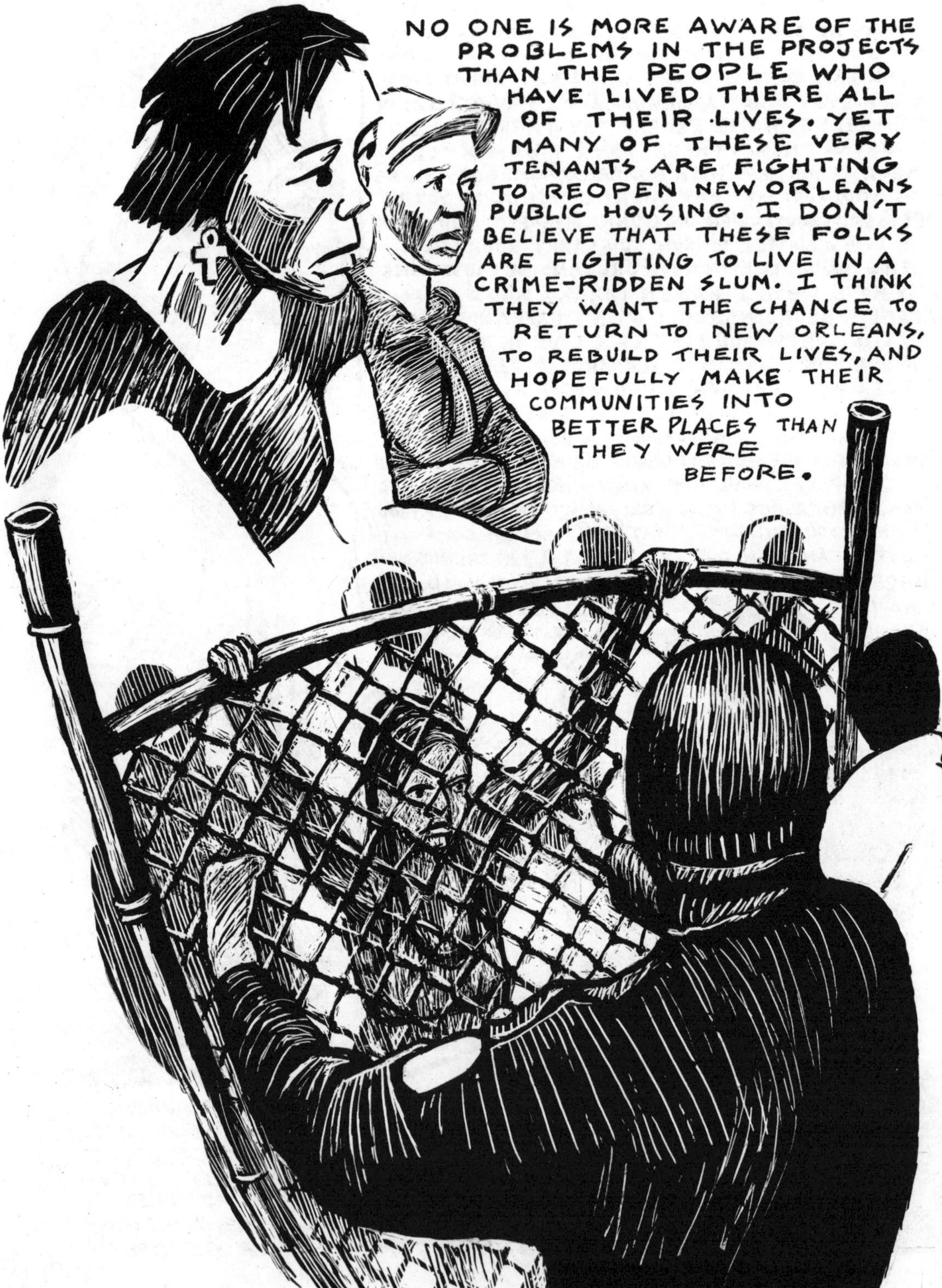
NO ONE IS MORE AWARE OF THE PROBLEMS IN THE PROJECTS THAN THE PEOPLE WHO HAVE LIVED THERE ALL OF THEIR LIVES. YET MANY OF THESE VERY TENANTS ARE FIGHTING TO REOPEN NEW ORLEANS PUBLIC HOUSING. I DON'T BELIEVE THAT THESE FOLKS ARE FIGHTING TO LIVE IN A CRIME-RIDDEN SLUM. I THINK THEY WANT THE CHANCE TO RETURN TO NEW ORLEANS, TO REBUILD THEIR LIVES, AND HOPEFULLY MAKE THEIR COMMUNITIES INTO BETTER PLACES THAN THEY WERE BEFORE.

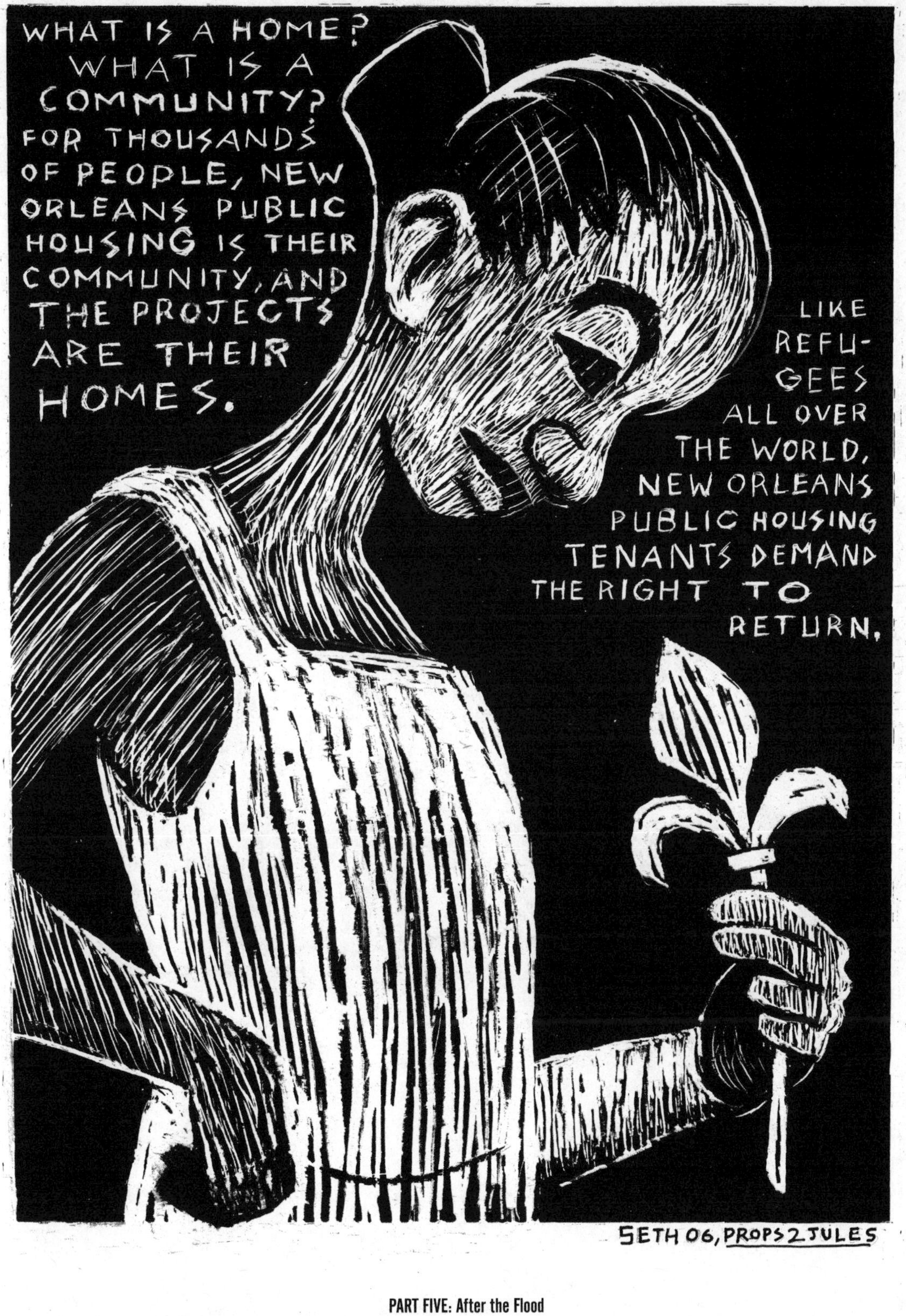
WHAT IS A HOME? WHAT IS A COMMUNITY? FOR THOUSANDS OF PEOPLE, NEW ORLEANS PUBLIC HOUSING IS THEIR COMMUNITY, AND THE PROJECTS ARE THEIR HOMES.
LIKE REFUGEES ALL OVER THE WORLD, NEW ORLEANS PUBLIC HOUSING TENANTS DEMAND THE RIGHT TO RETURN.
SETH 06, PROPS 2 JULES

LOUISIANA IS NOT NIGERIA

I went out to the Bayou country with a sketch pad, a tape recorder, and a digital camera, because an activist had told me wild anecdotes about abusive actions on the part of oil companies during Hurricane Katrina. It sounded a lot like the comicstrip we did about Nigeria. What I found was a lot more complex. People were very hesitant to criticize the oil companies providing employment— and ecological devastation. Louisiana isn't Nigeria. It is America. People there seemed desperate in a way that many Americans are. Caught between living and making a living.

Top right: A dangerous alligator.
Above: A more dangerous oil facility.

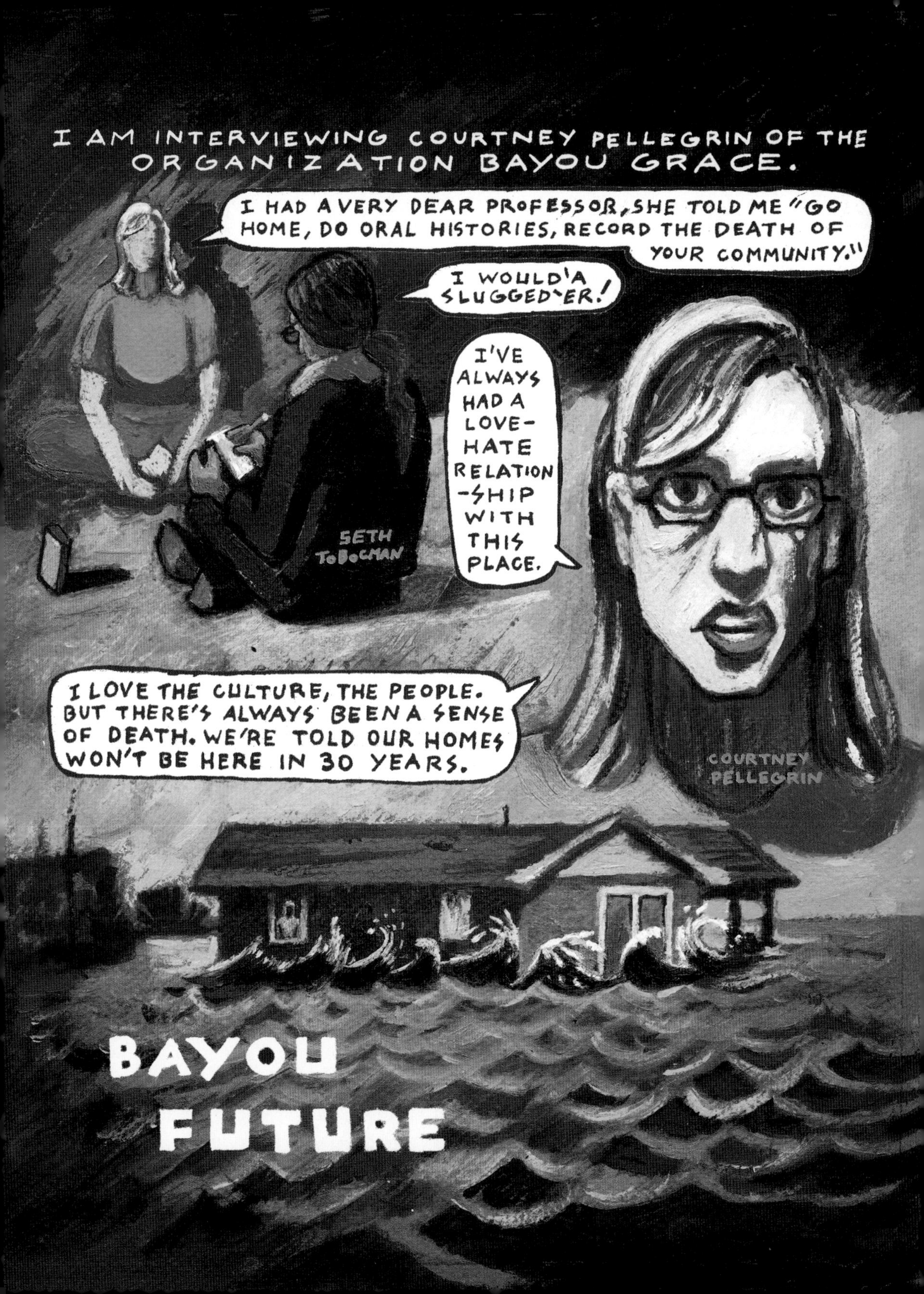
I AM INTERVIEWING COURTNEY PELLEGRIN OF THE ORGANIZATION BAYOU GRACE.
I HAD A VERY DEAR PROFESSOR, SHE TOLD ME "GO HOME, DO ORAL HISTORIES, RECORD THE DEATH OF YOUR COMMUNITY."
I WOULD'A SLUGGED 'ER!
SETH TOBOCMAN
I'VE ALWAYS HAD A LOVE-HATE RELATION-SHIP WITH THIS PLACE.
I LOVE THE CULTURE, THE PEOPLE. BUT THERE'S ALWAYS BEEN A SENSE OF DEATH. WE'RE TOLD OUR HOMES WON'T BE HERE IN 30 YEARS.
COURTNEY PELLEGRIN
BAYOU FUTURE

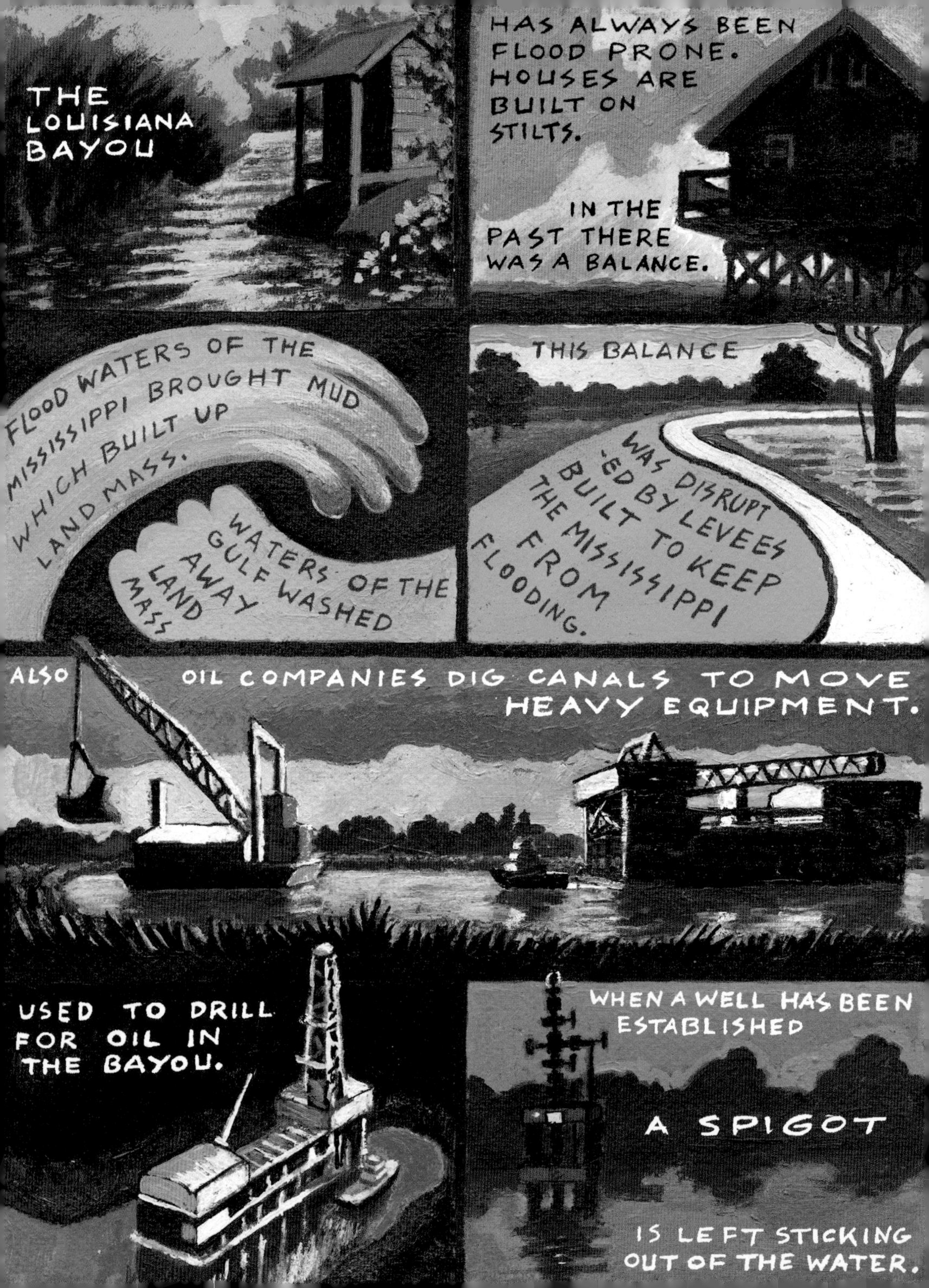
THE LOUISIANA BAYOU
HAS ALWAYS BEEN FLOOD PRONE. HOUSES ARE BUILT ON STILTS.
IN THE PAST THERE WAS A BALANCE.
FLOOD WATERS OF THE MISSISSIPPI BROUGHT MUD WHICH BUILT UP LAND MASS.
WATERS OF THE GULF WASHED AWAY LAND MASS
THIS BALANCE
WAS DISRUPT-ED BY LEVEES BUILT TO KEEP THE MISSISSIPPI FROM FLOODING.
ALSO
OIL COMPANIES DIG CANALS TO MOVE HEAVY EQUIPMENT.
USED TO DRILL FOR OIL IN THE BAYOU.
WHEN A WELL HAS BEEN ESTABLISHED
A SPIGOT
IS LEFT STICKING OUT OF THE WATER.

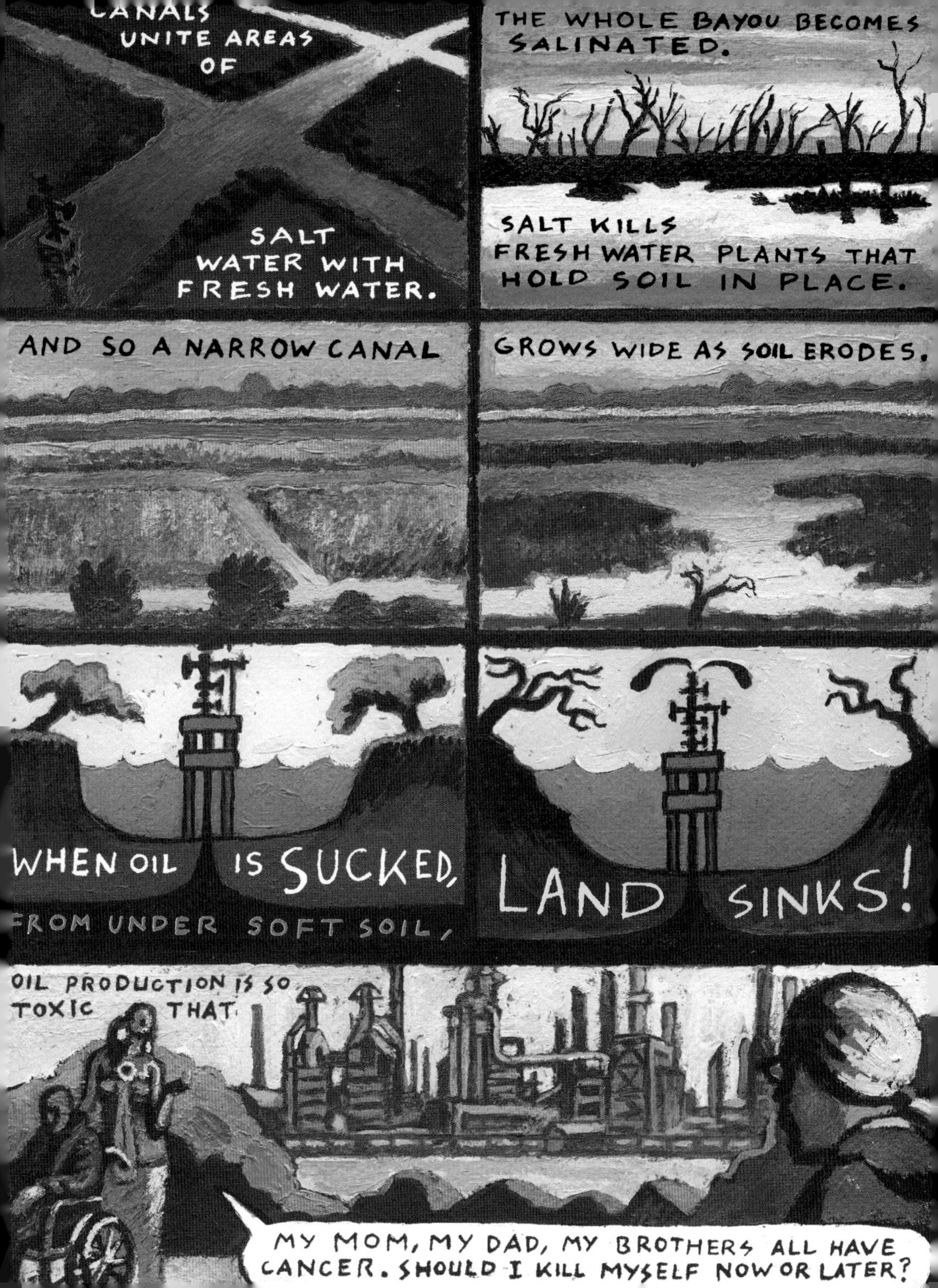
CANALS UNITE AREAS OF
SALT WATER WITH FRESH WATER.
THE WHOLE BAYOU BECOMES SALINATED.
SALT KILLS FRESH WATER PLANTS THAT HOLD SOIL IN PLACE.
AND SO A NARROW CANAL
GROWS WIDE AS SOIL ERODES.
WHEN OIL IS SUCKED,
FROM UNDER SOFT SOIL,
LAND SINKS!
OIL PRODUCTION IS SO TOXIC THAT
MY MOM, MY DAD, MY BROTHERS ALL HAVE CANCER. SHOULD I KILL MYSELF NOW OR LATER?

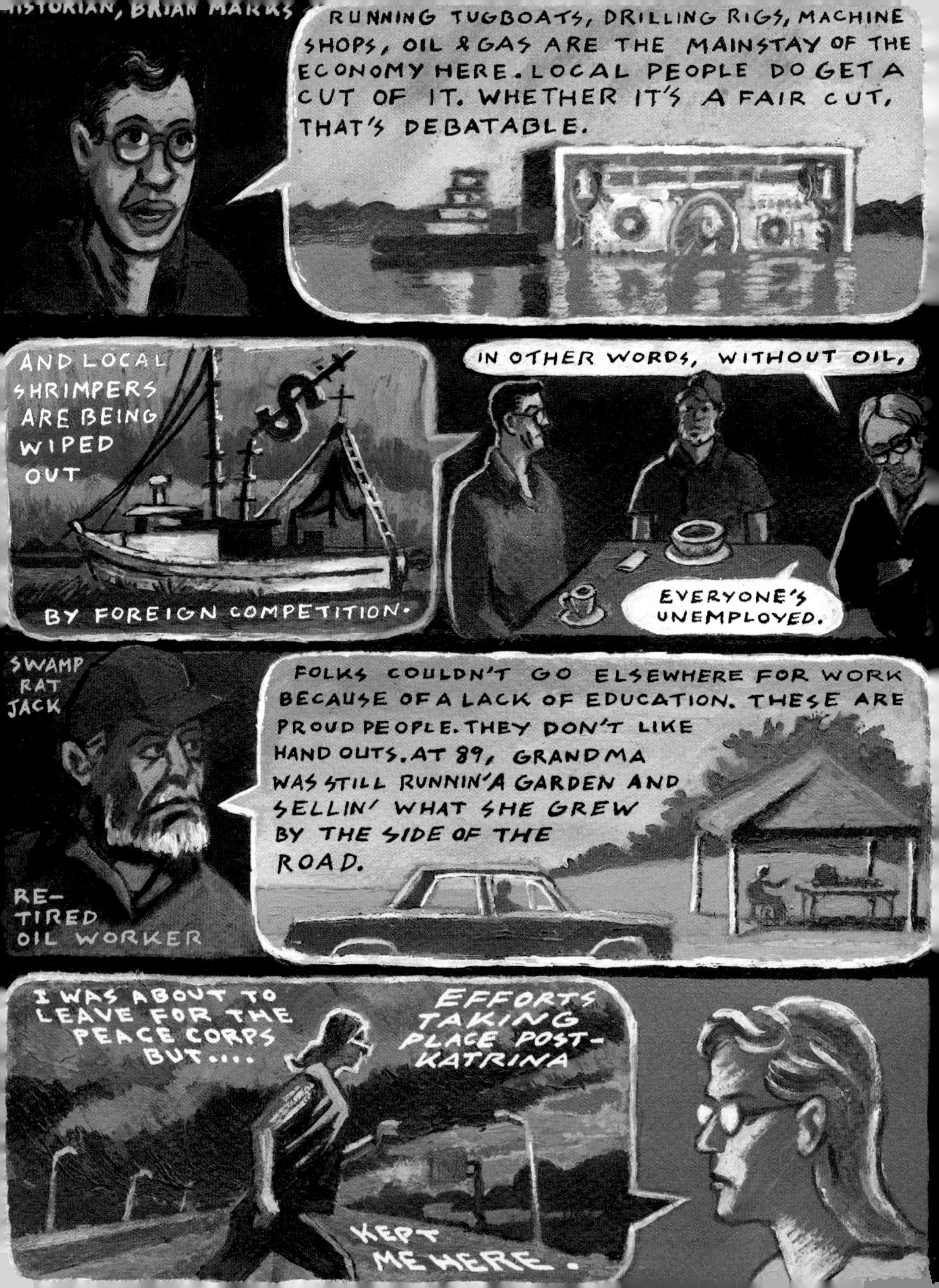
HISTORIAN, BRIAN MARKS
RUNNING TUGBOATS, DRILLING RIGS, MACHINE SHOPS, OIL & GAS ARE THE MAINSTAY OF THE ECONOMY HERE. LOCAL PEOPLE DO GET A CUT OF IT. WHETHER IT'S A FAIR CUT, THAT'S DEBATABLE.
AND LOCAL SHRIMPERS ARE BEING WIPED OUT
BY FOREIGN COMPETITION.
IN OTHER WORDS, WITHOUT OIL,
EVERYONE'S UNEMPLOYED.
SWAMP RAT JACK
RE-TIRED OIL WORKER
FOLKS COULDN'T GO ELSEWHERE FOR WORK BECAUSE OF A LACK OF EDUCATION. THESE ARE PROUD PEOPLE. THEY DON'T LIKE HAND OUTS. AT 89, GRANDMA WAS STILL RUNNIN' A GARDEN AND SELLIN' WHAT SHE GREW BY THE SIDE OF THE ROAD.
I WAS ABOUT TO LEAVE FOR THE PEACE CORPS BUT....
EFFORTS TAKING PLACE POST-KATRINA
KEPT ME HERE.

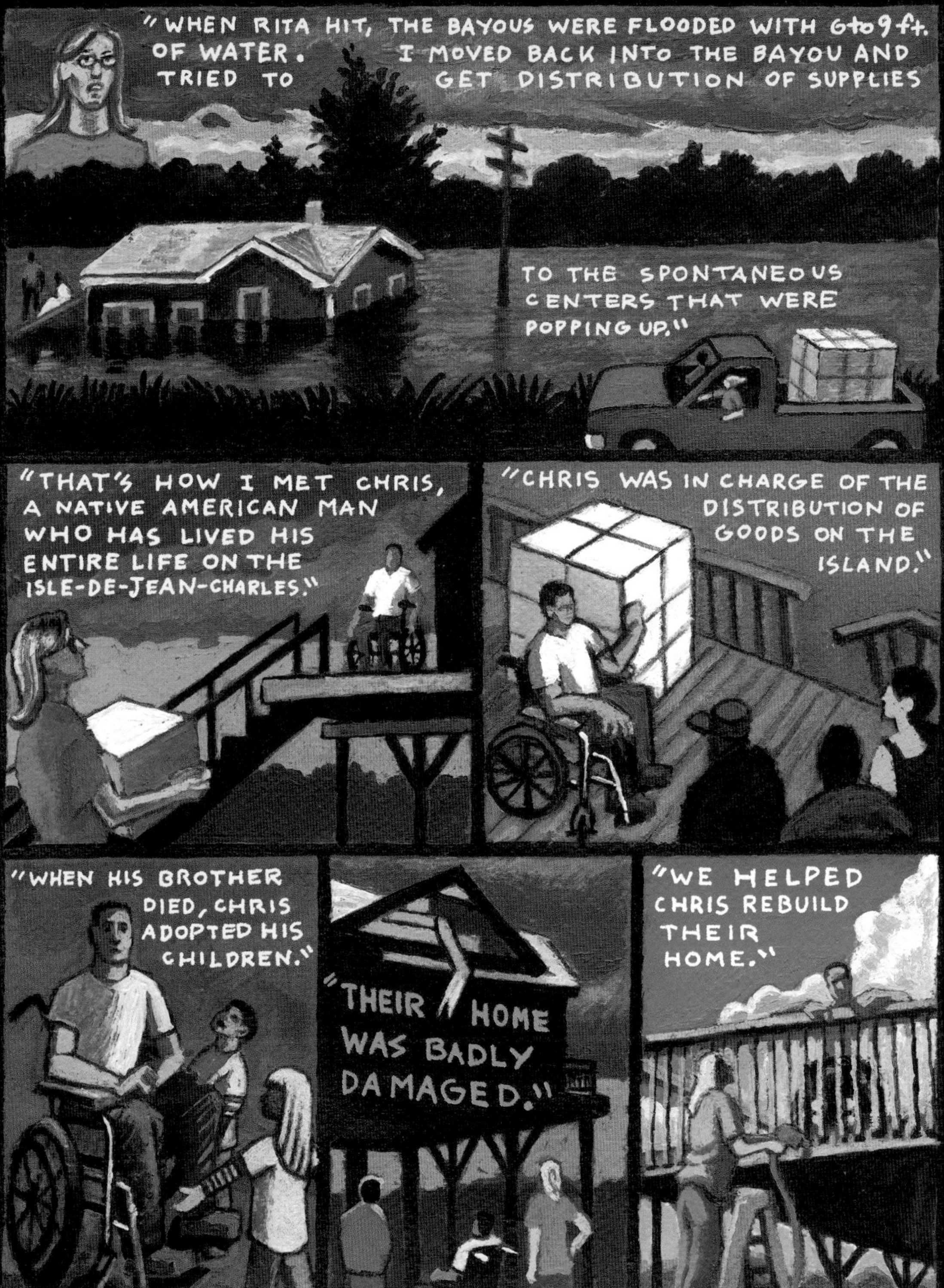
"WHEN RITA HIT, THE BAYOUS WERE FLOODED WITH 6 to 9 ft. OF WATER. I MOVED BACK INTO THE BAYOU AND TRIED TO GET DISTRIBUTION OF SUPPLIES
TO THE SPONTANEOUS CENTERS THAT WERE POPPING UP."
"THAT'S HOW I MET CHRIS, A NATIVE AMERICAN MAN WHO HAS LIVED HIS ENTIRE LIFE ON THE ISLE-DE-JEAN-CHARLES."
"CHRIS WAS IN CHARGE OF THE DISTRIBUTION OF GOODS ON THE ISLAND."
"WHEN HIS BROTHER DIED, CHRIS ADOPTED HIS CHILDREN."
"THEIR HOME WAS BADLY DAMAGED."
"WE HELPED CHRIS REBUILD THEIR HOME."

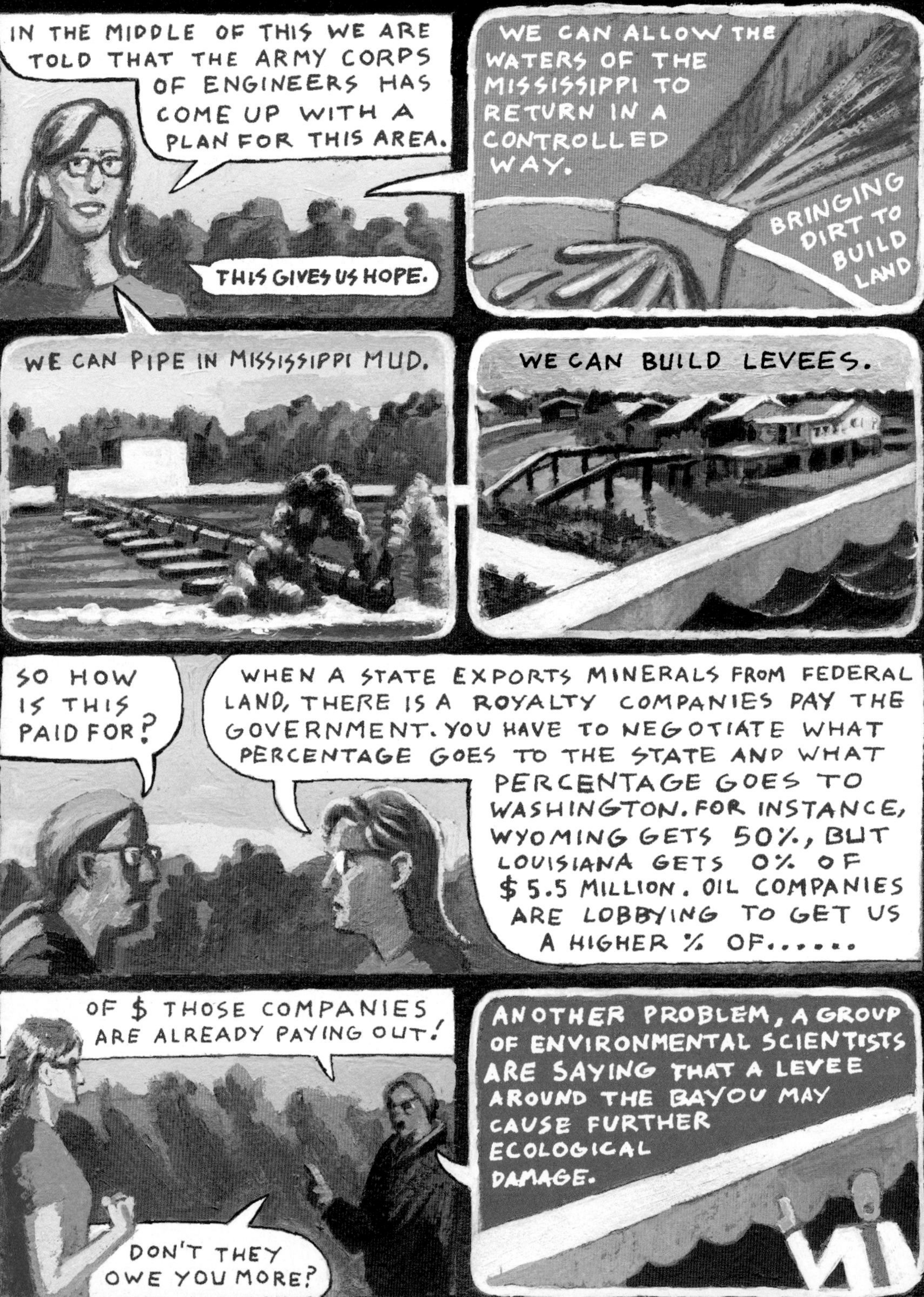
IN THE MIDDLE OF THIS WE ARE TOLD THAT THE ARMY CORPS OF ENGINEERS HAS COME UP WITH A PLAN FOR THIS AREA.
THIS GIVES US HOPE.
WE CAN ALLOW THE WATERS OF THE MISSISSIPPI TO RETURN IN A CONTROLLED WAY.
BRINGING DIRT TO BUILD LAND
WE CAN PIPE IN MISSISSIPPI MUD.
WE CAN BUILD LEVEES.
SO HOW IS THIS PAID FOR?
WHEN A STATE EXPORTS MINERALS FROM FEDERAL LAND, THERE IS A ROYALTY COMPANIES PAY THE GOVERNMENT. YOU HAVE TO NEGOTIATE WHAT PERCENTAGE GOES TO THE STATE AND WHAT PERCENTAGE GOES TO WASHINGTON. FOR INSTANCE, WYOMING GETS 50%, BUT LOUISIANA GETS 0% OF $5.5 MILLION. OIL COMPANIES ARE LOBBYING TO GET US A HIGHER % OF.....
OF $ THOSE COMPANIES ARE ALREADY PAYING OUT!
DON'T THEY OWE YOU MORE?
ANOTHER PROBLEM, A GROUP OF ENVIRONMENTAL SCIENTISTS ARE SAYING THAT A LEVEE AROUND THE BAYOU MAY CAUSE FURTHER ECOLOGICAL DAMAGE.

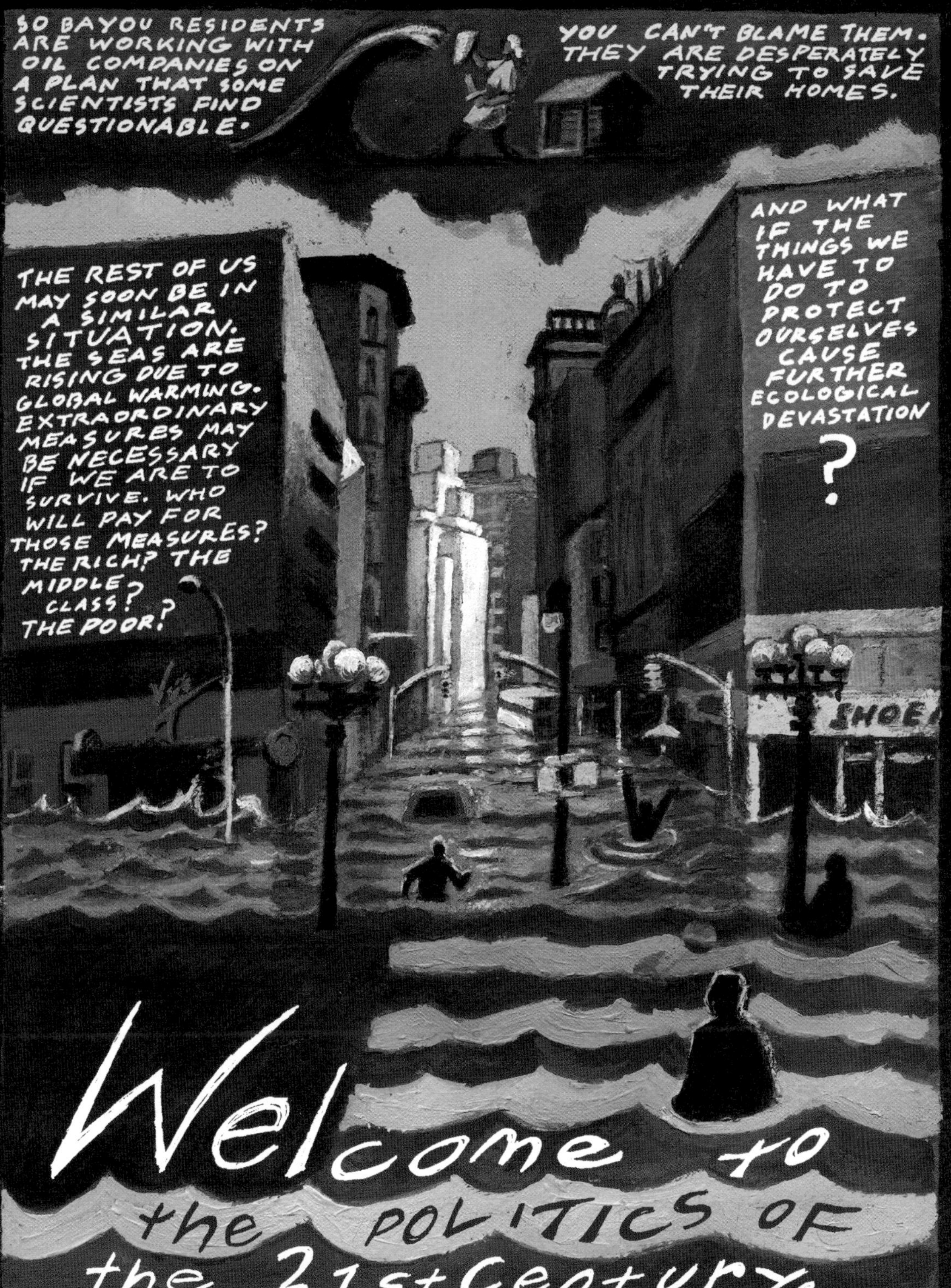
SO BAYOU RESIDENTS ARE WORKING WITH OIL COMPANIES ON A PLAN THAT SOME SCIENTISTS FIND QUESTIONABLE.
YOU CAN'T BLAME THEM. THEY ARE DESPERATELY TRYING TO SAVE THEIR HOMES.
THE REST OF US MAY SOON BE IN A SIMILAR SITUATION. THE SEAS ARE RISING DUE TO GLOBAL WARMING. EXTRAORDINARY MEASURES MAY BE NECESSARY IF WE ARE TO SURVIVE. WHO WILL PAY FOR THOSE MEASURES? THE RICH? THE MIDDLE CLASS? THE POOR?
AND WHAT IF THE THINGS WE HAVE TO DO TO PROTECT OURSELVES CAUSE FURTHER ECOLOGICAL DEVASTATION ?
SHOE
Welcome to the POLITICS OF the 21st Century.

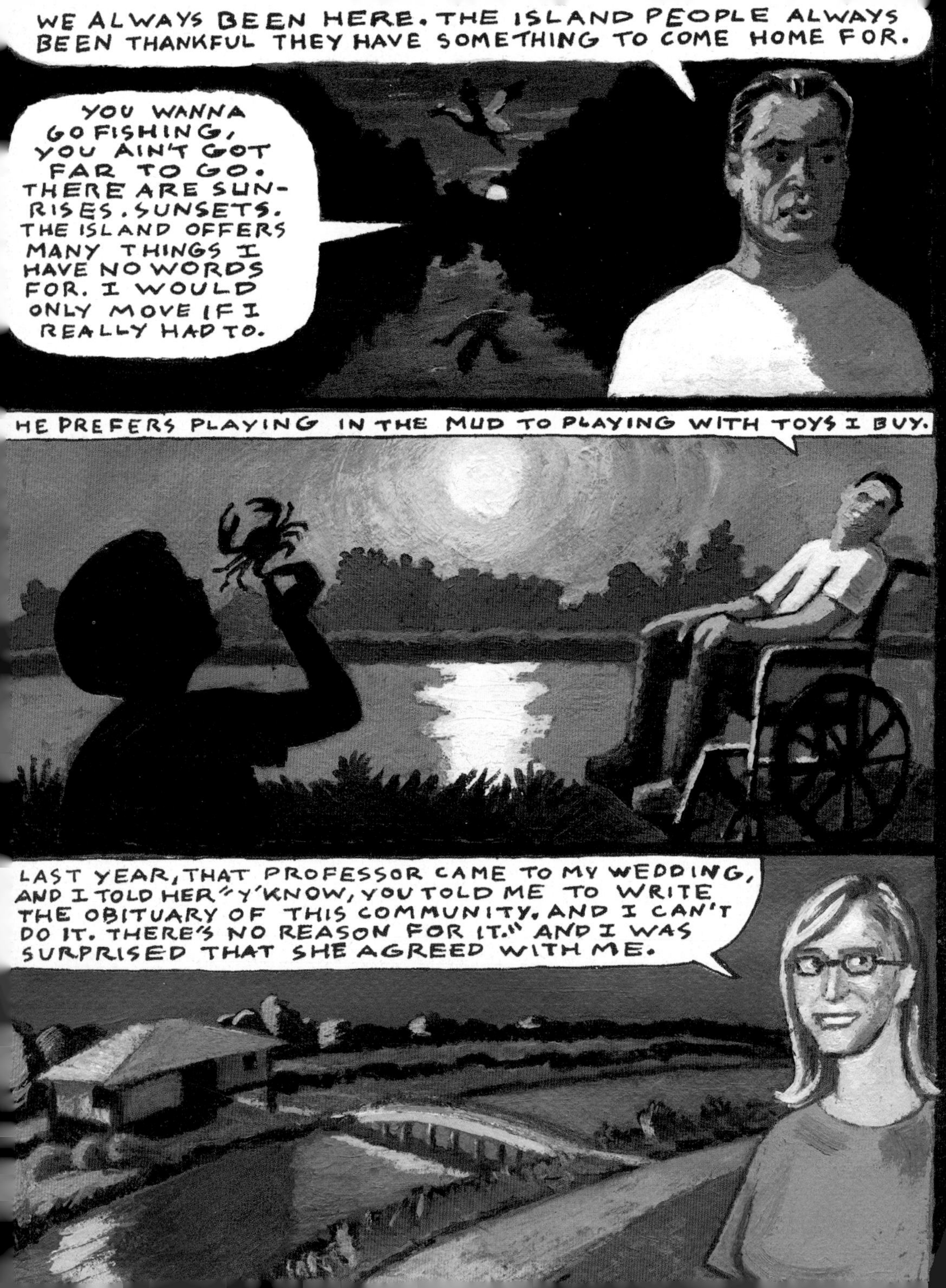
WE ALWAYS BEEN HERE. THE ISLAND PEOPLE ALWAYS BEEN THANKFUL THEY HAVE SOMETHING TO COME HOME FOR.
YOU WANNA GO FISHING, YOU AIN'T GOT FAR TO GO. THERE ARE SUNRISES. SUNSETS. THE ISLAND OFFERS MANY THINGS I HAVE NO WORDS FOR. I WOULD ONLY MOVE IF I REALLY HAD TO.
HE PREFERS PLAYING IN THE MUD TO PLAYING WITH TOYS I BUY.
LAST YEAR, THAT PROFESSOR CAME TO MY WEDDING, AND I TOLD HER "Y'KNOW, YOU TOLD ME TO WRITE THE OBITUARY OF THIS COMMUNITY. AND I CAN'T DO IT. THERE'S NO REASON FOR IT." AND I WAS SURPRISED THAT SHE AGREED WITH ME.